Discover

Florida

PHOTOGRAPHIC EXPOSÉ

IT IS MY POLICY to do most of the photography for these guides, but it's impractical to use photos of all the Florida theme parks: for a start, there are too many. The technical problems are also complex, involving the right vantage point, the correct camera angle, and seizing the action shot first time — regardless of the sun's angle and whether the sky is overcast. Very few parks issue press pictures.

A further problem is that most park managements specify that photos taken on their premises may not be published without written approval, and some demand detailed information before granting that approval.

The Walt Disney Company is happy to supply prints, but is very sensitive about Disney features being used to promote other commercial enterprises — which includes guide books. I may not use Cinderella's Castle or Epcot's Future World dome as cover picture, even though I took the shots, and the most Disney will allow is a montage incorporating features other than its own.

I have decided, therefore, not to use pictures of any theme parks except the miniature of Cinderella's Castle, which in most people's opinion is the essence of Florida.

Cover picture. Downtown Miami looking north along US-1. Photo by Terry Palmer. **Inset: Cinderella's Castle, Walt Disney World. Photo by Terry Palmer; reproduced by courtesy of the Walt Disney Company.**

I lost my entire film of the Kennedy Space Center and so I'm grateful to NASA for the loan of the shuttle launch picture; I certainly wasn't there to see it.

... AND AN INFLATIONARY FOOTNOTE

The USA suffers from inflation, but not as badly as Britain. However, in view of the time that must pass between research and publication of this guide, some prices will rise. Consider all costs quoted to be a close approximation, but erring on the low side.

Discover
Florida

Terry Palmer

HERITAGE
HOUSE

Discover Florida
First published January 1990
ISBN 1.85215.0173
Typesetting extrapolated in 8.5 on 9.5 Rockwell on Linotronic 300 by Anglia Photoset, St Botolph St, Colchester, from in-house computer setting.
Printed by Colorcraft Ltd, Whitfield Rd, Causeway Bay, Hong Kong.
Distributed in the UK and major outlets overseas by Roger Lascelles, 47 York Rd, Brentford, TW8 0QP.
Published by Heritage House (Publishers) Ltd, King's Rd, Clacton-on-Sea, CO15 1BG.

Acknowledgements to Norman and Margaret Arrowsmith, Tolleshunt Knights, Essex, UK, to NASA for the shuttle-launch photograph, to the Walt Disney Company for information, to the Florida Department of Commerce in London and Tallahassee, and to many people throughout Florida who are far too numerous to mention individually.

Also by Terry Palmer: *The Ghost At My Shoulder* (Corgi), *The Ghost Who Loved Me* (Heritage House), *The Cairo Alternative* (Heritage House).

CONTENTS

The author and his wife on the Overseas Highway; that's his money belt around his middle.

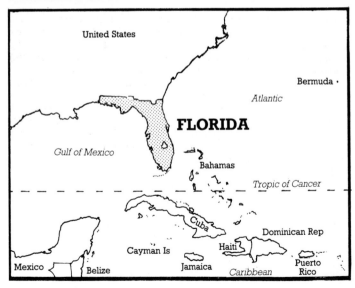

1: WHY FLORIDA?

Not only Mickey Mouse

FLORIDA IS KNOWN AROUND THE WORLD for being the home of
Walt Disney World, the largest and most spectacular theme park on
Earth. The first man to orbit this planet, and the first men on the moon,
left terra firma from the nearby Kennedy Space Center, which now
holds the launch pads for the space shuttles.

Most people who come to this southernmost state of continental
USA (the Hawaiian Islands are further south) make for these two
attractions, but there is infinitely more to see and do in Florida.

US Highway 1, whose northern end is on the Canadian border in
Maine, has its southern end in Key West, almost in the tropics — and
for its last 100 miles becomes the unique Overseas Highway, linking
40 of the Florida Keys with bridges from 37 feet to almost seven miles
(11km) long.

The Everglades is unequalled anywhere else in the world; it's a vast
swamp through which a river 50 miles wide flows from Lake
Okeechobee down to Florida Bay. Here, on the edge of bustling
Miami, you can walk amid the creatures of the wild including
alligators, turtles, and a fascinating world of birds.

Disney's Magic Kingdom and its adjoining Epcot Center have
encouraged a score of other attractions to spring up, ranging from the
massively popular Sea World, home of Shamu the killer whale, to
minor attractions such as the Bok Tower and the Citrus Tower, both of
which claim to stand on peninsular Florida's highest point. In this
central region you also find the city of Frostproof, whose citrus groves
were killed by a sharp frost in 1985.

North lies Daytona Beach, where Henry Ford, Ransom Olds and
Louis Chevrolet set up homes and raced their early motor cars on the
sands, and where even today you can find a traffic jam on the beach,
with the incoming tide swirling around the automobiles.

North, again, you venture into a different Florida altogether, where
winters can be cold and grey and where summer is the tourist season.
Here are Saint Augustine, the oldest city in the United States;
Jacksonville, the USA's largest city in terms of area; and beyond the
Suwannee River, the Panhandle with Florida's state capital of

Tallahassee and oldworld Pensacola.

Where? Florida stretches from 31° N exact, along some of its border with Alabama, to 24° 31' 44" N at the buoy in Key West which claims to be the 'southernmost point' in 'continental USA,' forgetting that it's on an island. The true southernmost point of Florida, and of the USA outside Hawaii, is Ballast Key 10 miles west of Key West and one minute further south. But Key West is indisputably less than one degree outside the tropics, and Miami is on the same latitude as Bahrain.

Palm Beach is the most easterly point at 80° 1' 6" W, the most westerly being a forest at 87° 34' 16" near Mobile, Alabama, beyond the boundary from Eastern Standard Time into Central Standard.

How big? The state covers 58,664 square miles, (151,939 sq km) including 4,510 sq miles of freshwater lakes, which places it slightly larger than England and Wales together, and half the size of Norway. It is 21st among the 50 states in order of size, marginally smaller than neighbouring Georgia, and its highest point is at 345 feet near Lakewood in Walton County, right up near the Alabama state line, the *lowest* highest point of any of the states.

Pascua de Flores. Ponce de Leon, who sailed on Columbus's second voyage to the Americas, was searching for the legendary Fountain of Youth when he landed near the present Saint Augustine between 2nd and 8th April, 1513. The day was known in Spain as *Pascua de Flores,* the 'Feast of Flowers,' which gave the Spanish colony its name, La Florida, the 'flowery one.' The region saw French, English and Seminole occupation before the Americans made it a territory in 1822 and conveniently dropped 'La' from its name. But Amelia Island in the north-east has lived under nine flags and Pensacola in the Panhandle has changed ownership 13 times.

Sunshine State. The Americans love to give their states a touch of individuality. Florida, which achieved statehood on 3 March, 1845, the 27th entrant into the USA, is nicknamed the Sunshine State, with the mockingbird as its emblem, *Swannee River* (with a vowel missing) as its song, the orange blossom as its flower, and "In God we trust" as its motto. Better to forget that the original slogan was "Let Us Alone."

2: BEFORE YOU GO

Paperwork and planning

PASSPORTS and VISAS

In 1988 the United States abolished for a three-year trial the legal requirement for Europeans and several other nationals to carry an entry visa, but it's still preferable to have one. The application form is complex and designed primarily to eliminate people with no jobs and no roots who might decide to stay on as illegals, but there are 33 grounds for exclusion from the USA, including having a mental handicap, tuberculosis, a criminal record, or past membership of a communist or Nazi organisation. There are obvious problems in taking a party of Downes syndrome sufferers to the Magic Kingdom, but it can be done.

Six months. Provided you satisfy the authorities you're a good citizen, you'll be granted a visa valid 'indefinitely' for 'multiple' entries by every adult mentioned in the passport. You don't need a return or onward ticket and you may stay in the USA for six months.

The visa is good for the remainder of your days, even though the passport holding it may have expired years ago: bring it along with your new passport to satisfy the law.

Return ticket. No visa? Then on your transatlantic flight you'll need to complete the Visa Waiver Pilot Program which asks you to "waive your rights to a hearing before an Immigration Judge to determine your admissibility or deportability." In other words, you can be turned back at the port of entry, and this may happen if you look young and dirty, or have no means of financial support. Theoretically you can also be excluded for any of those 33 other reasons, *and you must also have a return or onward ticket.*

The chances of a genuine tourist being refused entry are very slim, but your stay in the USA will be limited to 90 days.

Choose your airline. *It is the airline's responsibility to issue the Visa Waiver forms, but* **some airlines flying to the States do not carry them.** *If you have no visa and no Visa Waiver form* **you will not be allowed into the USA.**

INDEPENDENT or PACKAGE?

The United States is an easy country to travel in, provided you have access to a car and spend a little time in learning the road signs and classification. America is the home of the automobile, the land of vast distances where the open road stretches to infinity, and with your own set of wheels you are master of your destiny.

But without independent transport you are virtually immobile. The Americans have taken their love affair with the motor car to such extremes that some states no longer have a passenger railway, and the Greyhound bus network has holes hundreds of miles across.

Package. If you can't drive you have no option but to take a package holiday, no matter whether it's stay-put or mobile. Economics may also dictate the solo traveller takes a package deal: automobile renting costs much less when three or four people share the bill, and motel rates are per bungalow, not per person.

Stories of rape and murder may understandably dissuade women from travelling solo, but there's no reason why two women couldn't rent a car and take to the open road.

Fly-drive. You may be tempted by the fly-drive compromise, buying ready-made independence; this is certainly the way to get the cheapest car-hire deal, sometimes reduced to a tempting £1-a-week, but check whether you're paying for it in the air fare, and when you arrive make certain your insurance offers adequate cover. And look for any age restriction: some rental companies won't take your business if you're under 25 and none will accept a male under 21.

HEALTH CARE and INSURANCE

At last the Americans are beginning to realise the advantages of Britain's National Health Service and Sweden's comprehensive social systems, but until Congress relents, half the population will go in daily dread of needing hospital treatment; the breadline American qualifies for Welfare and only the wealthy can afford the heavy insurance premiums.

Don't risk it. Take full medical and hospital insurance to cover your stay, and make certain it includes provision for an air ambulance home.

There are no health risks in the United States, and Florida is well clear of the malaria and yellow fever belts. But take a simple first aid kit with plenty of insect repellent if you're visiting south Florida between Easter and Christmas; that covers most of the year.

The state's television and radio stations, and some newspapers, give the pollen count the year round, indicating that hay fever has no closed season. Here's a tip worth knowing: if you suffer from hay fever and similar breathing allergies, give up *cow's* milk *completely* in *all* its forms — and that includes butter, cheese, and milk used in cooking, and means you must check the contents of all prepared foods. It works for me and for many other people; I had hay fever very badly until an American dietician gave me this tip years ago, and I'm now totally clear as long as I keep to the strict diet. Note the italics: goat's milk is acceptable, and your misery is in direct proportion to the amount of cow's milk you take.

MONEY MATTERS

The United States works on a credit-card economy, with Visa and Mastercard (abbreviated to MC) by far the most popular. Next come the charge cards, American Express (Amex or AE) and Diners Club (DC), followed by Discovery, a credit card breaking into the market, and rounded up by an assortment of cards such as Carte Blanche (CB), Cirrus, Choice, and others which are valid only in the stores that issue them.

Access. The Access credit card is accepted wherever you see the Mastercard sign.

You can use your card to buy petrol, groceries, airline tickets, to rent a motel room, to get into the Magic Kingdom, to get cash from an all-night dispenser at a number of banks, occasionally to make a phone call — and you'll find it very inconvenient to rent a car if you *don't* have a card.

There are exceptions. A few small motels and hotels aren't equipped to take cards, or the management isn't happy with the 4½% discount charged; some petrol stations (sorry, gas stations) offer you 4% discount for cash; and a lot of places won't accept cards for purchases worth less than $10.

Currency. All the world must know that the US currency is the dollar, divided into 100 cents, but you may not realise until too late that the one-dollar bill looks very much like the 100-dollar note. Apart from the two zeros the notes show different presidents, Washington and Franklin respectively. There's equal confusion between the other notes: 5, 10, 20 and 50 dollars.

The coinage is fairly simple: a copper one-cent coin called a 'penny' (it was worth a pre-decimal British penny years ago), the larger five-cent coin known as the 'nickel,' down again in size for the 10-cent 'dime' which has *one dime* embossed on it, and the 25-cent coin suitably called the 'quarter.'

Susan B. Anthony. Foreigners should avoid the $2 bill and the Susan B. Anthony one-dollar bills and coins, all withdrawn for lack of public support despite the fact that Susan was the campaigner who won the vote for women. The Disney Dollar is valid only within Walt Disney World, but the number kept as souvenirs must boost Mickey's income.

How to take money. Travellers cheques, preferably in *dollars,* are the safest form in which to take your money as they're cashable at all banks, at most hotels and at many large stores. If you're bringing cash be prepared for a 1% commission and in some banks a $500 limit per transaction — or pay the commission at home and bring dollars.

Currency. You may meet the occasional adult who thinks the dollar is the world's only currency, but the banks know different. They'll change travellers cheques or currency in Aussie and Hong Kong dollars; in Belgian, French and Swiss francs; in sterling; in Scandinavian krone and krona; in Deutschmarks, Italian lira, Dutch guilders, pesetas, and yen.

Cheques. Forget Eurocheques. Forget cheques on your bank account back home: in Florida, as throughout the USA, the dollar reigns supreme.

Plastic money. The other option is to use your credit card to buy dollars at a bank; after you prove your identity you can draw out your remaining credit balance at one transaction, subject to a computer check. Outside of banking hours your Visa card, backed up with your Personal Identification Number, can provide cash at bank dispensing machines; Barnett Bank's SuperTeller is the most common. There are less access points for Access cards.

Warning. Make certain that you are given every throw-away carbon paper from your credit card transaction, as this copy of your signature can be forged to obtain further funds from your account. The credit card companies are changing their system to remove this loophole.

Banks. Barnett's, which calls itself Florida's bank, has more than 500 branches in the state, but there is no shortage of competition. Barnett's main rivals are the Atlantic National Bank of Florida, the Southeast Bank and the Sun Bank, but there are others. You can find banks almost anywhere: in the downtown area, in the shopping malls, in airports (of course), in the smallest village (which Floridians will insist on calling a 'city'), and in Walt Disney World, where the Sun is the official bank.

Banking hours. Basic business hours for banks are 0900-1700 Mon-Thurs, 0900-1800 Fri, closed at weekends and public holidays, but some branches stay open later, some open on Saturday mornings, and those with drive-thru counters may open at 0800.

DRESS SENSE

Dress as casually and as colourfully as you like; you won't be out of place. But avoid too much sexuality such as plunging necklines and skin-tight jeans. Most large stores insist on shirts and shoes being worn, but true formal wear will be needed only if you're dining at the smartest restaurants.

Swimwear follows the latest fashions, currently exposing the hips and half the cheeks of the backside, but bosoms are covered. Men's trunks are getting rather tight and skimpy. *See also: What to Take.*

DISABLED &

Physically disabled people in wheelchairs are almost guests of honour in the USA, though see *Passports and Visas* for possible restrictions on the mentally disabled. The & symbol used in this book indicates where wheelchair travellers may expect to enjoy the majority of the amenities, but in most cases this is the management's opinion, not mine.

There are more steps and ramps at Gatwick or Heathrow than at Orlando or Miami airports. Once you've arrived in Florida you'll find that most car parks with a capacity of more than 50 vehicles have space reserved by law for the wheelchair-bound, that Walt Disney World makes a point of hiring out wheelchairs and strollers, and that from 1989 all new buses are fitted with wheelchair lifts and clamps. This latter point is little consolation as few tourists use the buses, but if you can manage to get into a car you'll have no problems in seeing Florida.

Among the many activities open to you *without leaving your wheelchair* are: a tour of Walt Disney World and some of its attractions; entry to almost all the other theme and amusement parks, though you won't see everything that's happening; a visit to all the short nature trails in The Everglades National Park; exploration of the Keys and Key West; a ride to the top of the Citrus Tower.

If you are *partly mobile* you can see more of Walt Disney World and go on some of the state's glass-bottomed boats and airboats at the management's discretion.

You need to be *fully mobile* to take a coach tour of the Kennedy Space Center and in my opinion you need to be superhuman to face Space Mountain!

WHAT TO TAKE

As I assume you'll be hiring a car your main requirements are your charge or credit card with a considerable credit balance (you'll spend more than you planned) and your driving licence (driver's license).

If you plan to drive independently and stay at motels without forward reservation, you should be prepared for a night or two in the car, which means a cushion and sleeping-bag or blankets; don't go for lightweight equipment in winter as the temperature can drop below freezing as far south as Miami.

Some of the cheaper motels don't supply washbasin plugs so a inch (3cm) spare is useful. And take a simple heating element for making your morning tea or coffee; you'll need an adapter (see 'Electricity').

Clothing. See 'Climate' in Chapter 3 and for winter travel take clothes suitable for a wide range of temperatures; in summer pack a lightweight raincoat – although Walt Disney World and some other entertainment parks loan plastic coats free for the occasion.

Insects. You'll also need insect repellent from June to late November, particularly in the Everglades where the mosquitoes are otherwise near intolerable. A combined hat and veil as worn by beekeepers is a good investment.

WHEN AND WHERE TO GO

In winter, concentrate your efforts no further north than Orlando; in summer, the whole state is yours for the asking.

Seasons: south Florida. Everywhere south of Lake Okeechobee has its high season in winter, when motel prices are at their highest. Summer here is the wet season, when insects plague the Everglades, and palmetto bugs, similar to giant cockroaches, swarm in Miami and the Keys; while everywhere else in the USA is enjoying the summer, south Florida slumps into low season. South Floridians have a smart name for Americans who come to the deep south for the winter: they're snowbirds.

Seasons: central Florida. Walt Disney World and its spinoff attractions, plus the Kennedy Space Center, make the central belt a year-round vacationland, with little concession to low-season rates at any time. Watch for major motor racing events at Daytona, Miami, St Petersburg and Sebring which can double the price of rooms.

May is the sunniest month, and June to October the must humid. Most rain falls in summer as storms, but as you mark the transition to temperate north Florida you find more winter rain than in the south.

Seasons: north Florida. Jacksonville and the Panhandle have their high season in summer. People who have driven from Canada and New England, or perhaps only from Kansas City, to escape the winter's snows, are not going to linger in north Florida when the coconut palms and the white beaches of the south are only a short drive away. In any event, the northern part of the state often catches hard frosts and snow. North Florida has less to offer, but offers it better from May until September's Labor Day.

3: FLORIDA FACTFILE

Facts and figures

BUSINESS HOURS

Banks. As already noted, basic business hours are 0900- 1700 Mon-Thurs, 0900-1800 Fri, closed at weekends and public holidays. Some branches stay open later, some open on Saturday mornings, and those with drive-thru counters may open at 0800. Banks at airports are open whenever the airport is in operation.

Sunday opening. Sunday is the great American day of rest — but not for people in the retail, catering or tourist businesses. Banks and government offices close on Sunday but almost everything else is open for business, and many traders find it their most important day.

Car hire companies. Competition is so keen that rental companies keep very long hours, opening early and closing very late, seven days a week. Actual hours vary according to local conditions, and agencies at the major airports, not just Orlando and Miami, are open as long as there's a chance of business.

Post Offices. The US Mail's counters open at 0830 or 0930 and stay open until 1700, Mon-Fri; Saturday 0930-1200, closed on Sun and public holidays. All but the smallest offices have stamp vending machines and scales for weighing your parcels, accessible round the clock.

Government Offices. 0900-1700 Mon-Fri, closed on public holidays. Most Chambers of Commerce follow these hours, but many Visitor Centers (see 'Tourist Information' for definition of terms) are open 0800-1700, every day, and when the chamber and the visitor centre are in one office, the longer hours apply.

Shops. Most major supermarkets open at 0800 every day and close at 2100 or 2200 Mon-Sat and 1900 on Sun, but some small privately-owned supermarkets and drugstores are open around the clock. Almost everything stops for Christmas Day but many stores are open for Independence and Thanksgiving, some of their peak trading days. Specialist shops such as hardware stores close around 1700, and are not open on Saturday afternoon or Sunday.

Travel Agents. Normally 0900-1700 Mon-Fri, 0900-1300 Sat.

Petrol Stations. Gas stations are open around the clock unless night-time business doesn't warrant it.

Theme parks and tourist attractions. Opening hours range from 0900 to 1000 but closing times vary; museums usually close at 1700, some theme parks stay open until sunset, others much later: see the appropriate entry.

CLIMATE

In **winter,** North America is covered by a mass of very cold air while the Caribbean has a mass of warm air. The interplay between these systems governs Florida's weather which can have enormous temperature ranges; in 1989, Atlanta (Georgia) recorded its highest February reading of 80°F (27°C), yet a few days later the city had snow. Night temperatures in the Florida Panhandle can dip down into the teens F (down to −10°C), but the daytime average is 64°F (18°C).

Central Florida usually has one or two minor frosts each winter, and snow falls about once in 15 years, but severe frosts struck in 1985 and ruined much of the citrus orchards.

South Florida is normally frost free and enjoys a winter temperature from the upper 50sF to the high 70sF (15°C to 25°C), but I've known it range from 83°F to 30°F in winter.

The **summer** temperatures are much more stable everywhere in the state, with a normal range from the 70s into the low 90s (around 23°C to 33°C), the sea moderating the excesses.

Rain. But summer is the wet season, when most of the south's 60 inches (1,500mm) of rain falls, usually in the form of tropical storms that send down monsoonal rain, followed by cloudless skies half an hour later. Humidity is high, making you feel clammy with sweat.

Hurricanes. As the rainy season comes to a close, some of the tropical storms in the Caribbean islands intensify and become hurricanes, the dread of everybody living around the Gulf of Mexico and up the Atlantic seaboard. Hurricane alerts are now so precise that the course and intensity of these monsters can be predicted with fair accuracy, and ample warning given for evacuation; you'll see the evacuation routes marked on the road signs.

Hurricanes are rare, with bad ones coming perhaps once in a generation, but there are several tropical storms each season, another point to watch if you holiday between August and November.

These are the *average maximum daytime* temperatures in °F and °C, and the average rainfall in inches and millimetres.

	JANUARY	JULY	RAINFALL
Jacksonville	55 − 13	81 − 27	54 − 1,350
Tampa	61 − 16	81 − 27	51 − 1,285
Miami	67 − 19	82 − 28	60 − 1,500
Key West	70 − 21	83 − 28	39 − 970

ECONOMY

The name of Orange County, which holds Orlando and the Magic Kingdom, gives a clue to the state's interest in the mighty citrus: Florida produces half the world's grapefruit and a quarter of its oranges, and has the world's largest concentration of citrus groves despite the hazards of the weather.

In 1984 there were 665,400 acres of citrus, and then came the big freeze of 1985 which killed large areas of trees, particularly around Clermont, though the little city of Frostproof further south also proved its name was a bit too optimistic, despite the heaters in the groves. Clermont has replanted most of its orange trees but at Lake Ridge to the north they planted vines instead and made their first wine in the fall of 1989.

Here are the leaders in the Florida citrus league, and they're oranges unless otherwise stated:

Hamlin: Oct–Dec, usually seedless with thin peel, grown for juice.

Pink Seedless grapefruit: Oct–May, amber-pink flesh, juicy.

Duncan grapefruit: Oct–July, large, round and yellow, thin peel with seeds in the centre of the fruit.

White Seedless grapefruit: Oct–July, medium-large, whiteish flesh in thin skin. Easy to segment, and juicy.

Navel: Nov–Jan. Extra large with thickish peel. Seedless; easy to segment.

Pineapple: Dec–Feb, Medium to large, noted for sweetness and juice.

Indian River: Dec-Mar, pink juicy grapefruit.

Robinson tangerine: Oct-Nov, medium-large and peels easily.

Dancy tangerine: Nov-Feb, small-medium with loose peel; called the 'zipperskin fruit.' Sweet.

Honey tangerine: Feb–mid Apr, also known as Murcott or blood orange. Small-medium, flattish, easy to peel. Red flesh.

Temple: Jan–Mar, a popular eating orange.

Honeybell: Jan–Feb, a 5-week season. Smooth or rough skins but very juicy; also known as Minneola tangelo, a tangerine-grapefruit hybrid.

Valencia: Mar–July, the traditional orange of Spanish origin. Thin peel, juicy.

Orlando tangelo: Nov–Jan, oval, medium-large. Juicy tangerine-grapefruit hybrid.

Tomatoes. Homestead, south of Miami, is the centre of a large tomato-growing district from September to May. Look for the 'U Pick' (pick-your-own) signs and have them straight from the plant at 25¢ a pound.

Sugar. South of Lake Okeechobee, cane sugar is the dominant crop, while the state's farmers also grow small amounts of soya bean,

Sugar! Miles and miles of it grows in the Clewiston area.

tobacco and peanuts. And there are vast tracts of wild woodland, covering more than a million acres.

Brahmin bulls. Florida has more than 2,000,000 cattle, and is second only to Texas in beef and dairy production. The Spanish brought the first cattle for their settlement near St Augustine, but modern livestock didn't flourish until crossbred with Indian Brahmin bulls to give them some tolerance to summer's heat.

Phosphates. Florida produces around 38,000,000 tons of phosphates a year, almost the entire USA yield, resulting in vast open mines and spoil tips in Polk County, east of Tampa. The stuff is worth around $1,275,000,000 a year.

Retirement. Florida is understandably the USA's most popular retirement home, which brings in considerable funds, but tourism is now a major earner with around 39,000,000 visitors to the state each year, the great majority from elsewhere in North America.

ELECTRICITY

The USA has 110v alternating current with two- or three-pin sockets. The two main pins are each 16mm long by 6mm wide and 1.5mm thick, with an 11mm gap between them; the third pin is usually optional.

The plugs are small, vulnerable to being hit, and a child can easily pull one from its socket and get a shock. And the people that use these things can send men to the moon and back!

FESTIVALS

There are festivals of some sort almost every day of the year somewhere in the state. The Florida Division of Tourism in London or Tallahassee (see addresses at the start of Chapter 4) issues an events calendar every three months listing what's coming, from lighting the Christmas tree in Gainesville to celebrating Hemingway's birthday in Key West, and the Florida Department of Natural Resources lists its own festivals at six-month inervals; information is available from each park (see further in this chapter) or ✆ (904).488.7326.

There are far too many to list, so here are a select few:

Collier-Seminole State Park: Amerind arts festival, March.

Daytona Beach: Birthplace of Speed antique car rally at Thanksgiving.

Dunedin: Highland games, with bagpipes, in March.

Fort Walton and Destin: Billy Bowlegs Festival at the end of May; a treasure hunt for cash prizes reliving the story of the man who called himself 'King of Florida.'

Gasparilla Island: go sea-shell hunting with a park ranger every month.

Key West: Ft Zachary Taylor holds Massing of the Colours to honour the dead of two world wars, February; Hemingway's Birthday, 21 July.

Naples: swamp buggy races, last Sunday in February and October; a mudmobile bonanza with the crowning (or drowning?) of the Mud Duchess.

Panama City: Indian Summer Seafood Festival in early October (the 'Indian summer'), with parades and pageant.

St Augustine: Easter 'Parada de los Caballos y Coches,' (Horse and Carriage Parade); Spanish Night Watch, 3rd Saturday in June; locking up the town for the night, old-style; August carnival marks the town's birthday; Christmas Carnival. Springtime festival in Mardi Gras style, recalling the city's history.

Tampa: Gasparilla Festival; pegleg pirates in a galleon relive the invasion by the pirate José Gaspar.

FLORIDA FOR FREE

The Florida timeshare explosion is over; nowadays its 'interval ownership' and next year it'll be something else. Meanwhile, timeshare salesmen on the street are very courteous — and they offer a wide range of gifts to tempt you to a presentation where the really hard sell comes. A free room at a smart hotel? Two free tickets to the Magic Kingdom? These are among the offers, so why not grab them? But be careful of the sales talk.

(To be fair, timeshare has come clean; it's even on offer at the Marriott Hotel by Walt Disney World.)

There's a wide range of attractions that don't have an entry fee, including: **Jacksonville,** Mayport Naval Station; **Lake Wales,** Citrus World orange-juice canning factory; **Orlando,** Tupperware museum; **Pensacola,** Naval Aviation Museum.

Discounts. Keep a look out for discount offers in tourist newspapers, in chambers of commerce, and sometimes in motel reception offices. You can save from 10% to 50% on hotel bills and entrance fees, but few motels are in these schemes. Membership of the American Autombile Association brings its own discount at many hotels and motels...and they seldom want to see proof of membership. And you can always ask for a discount at a motel if trade appears to be bad. You might get it.

LANGUAGE

It's no surprise that English is the official language of Florida, yet there was a recent statewide referendum on whether it should be replaced by Spanish.

Spanish runs English very close in Miami where large chunks of the city speak nothing but *español,* and you can easily imagine yourself in Mexico as consonants are slurred, lacking the crispness of the Castillano spoken in central Spain. In addition to Mexicans there are immigrants – some of them illegal – from Cuba, Nicaragua, and elsewhere in Central America, while refugees from Papa Doc's régime in Haiti have brought in French and Creole as minor languages.

LAUNDROMATS

Coin-operated do-it-yourself laundries are widely available, normally open through the night. Expect to pay $2.50 to use a large washing machine, and 25¢ for a dryer.

MAPS

It's so very useful to have a good map of Florida when you plan your holiday. The Gousha Chek-Chart at 16 miles to the inch is distributed in the UK by Roger Lascelles (address, page 4) through booksellers for £1.50, and Lascelles also supplies town plans of Miami, St Petersburg-Tampa, and Jacksonville. Further maps are available at Stanford's Map Centre, 12 Long Acre, London WC2.

Once you're in Florida you'll have no difficulty in collecting other maps. Chambers of Commerce and Visitor Centers hand out free state maps on a scale of 17 miles to the inch and sell, for $2 upwards, street maps of their own cities: so don't, for example, ask for a West Palm Beach map when you're in Palm Beach.

Rand McNally produces good maps of every state, available at a price in touristy shops, and when you're on the Keys look for Teall's two large-scale maps of those islands. They're financed by advertising and should be free but some gift shops charge $2 each.

Florida, an excellent road atlas from DeLorme Mapping Co, PO Box 298, Freeport, Maine, 04032, ISBN 0-89933-209-9, at $12.95, marks every road and street in the state at a scale of 1:150,000 (1 inch = 2.3 miles). Maps spread across 103 pages, each about 9½ by 14½ inches, making it cumbersome for car navigation. It is available in Britain after some persistence.

NEWSPAPERS

Florida, like most of the USA, is inundated with newspapers. Every major city has at least one daily, and most small cities − towns, by European standard − manage a weekly.

The state's leading papers are the *Diario las Americas* (Miami), *Florida Times-Union* (Jacksonville), *Miami Herald, Miami News, Orlando Sentinel, Palm Beach Post, Pensacola News Journal, Sarasota Herald Tribune, St Petersburg Times,* the *Sun-Sentinel* and the *Fort Lauderdale News* from the same publisher, and the *Tampa Tribune.*

Due to the problems of distribution, the USA has few national papers but the middle-market *USA Today* is the most popular. Foreign newspapers are not normally available.

Florida's gutter press is as bad as Britain's, carrying headlines such as *Pregnant bride has twins at altar while 150 guests watch: minister delivers baby.*

Race you down to Key West?

POLICE

As any television viewer will know, the United States has several kinds of police. The **Highway Patrol** is organised on a statewide basis with its officers enforcing traffic rules and investigating motor accidents *outside city limits*.

Within the city limits, well-defined by signs at the roadside, the **City Police** has jurisdiction over traffic and criminal offences, but is not concerned with civil processes such as repossessing vehicles for finance companies, or divorce. The chief of the City Police is usually nominated by the mayor, who is an elected officer, but some cities in Florida have different arrangements.

The **Sheriff** is the chief law enforcement officer for the *county,* responsible for criminal offences outside city limits, and civil offences anywhere in the country. The Sheriff, who is elected for a four-year term, is also in charge of the county jail and for some aspects of traffic enforcement, overlapping the role of the Highway Patrol. In Duval county, which is mainly occupied by Jacksonville, the city and the county forces are combined.

But that's not all. There is the statewide **Department of Law Enforcement** which investigates major crime and operates a sophisticated laboratory at Sanford, near Orlando, and the Florida Marine Patrol. And then there is the federal **Drug Enforcement Agency** which works with the DLE, as Miami is the United States' major importer of smuggled drugs, and the **Federal Bureau of Investigation,** the famed FBI, which tackles headline-grabbing crimes. In case you're wondering, Florida doesn't have the death penalty.

Finally, there's the **Secret Police,** but I don't know anything about it.

POPULATION

Florida had 11,675,000 people in 1986 and one of the fastest population growths in the USA, with a nett increase of 900 people a day throughout the 1980s. Newcomers are mostly the wealthy retired from the north and the poorer immigrant from the Caribbean, the latter usually settling in Miami, now the 41st largest city in the country. But Jacksonville, 22nd in the national league, is Florida's biggest conurbation.

POST OFFICE

The US Mail operates the postal service and has no connection whatever with the telephone companies. As already stated, its business hours are 0830 or 0930 until 1700, Mon-Fri; Saturday 0930-1200; closed on Sun and public holidays. All but the smallest offices have stamp vending machines and scales for weighing your parcels, accessible round the clock.

You can also buy stamps where you buy your postcards — but don't rely on anybody else to post them.

Mailboxes for posting your letters look similar to large blue rubbish bins on legs and often carry details of collection times in the pull-down posting flap.

Zip code. The string of two letters and five digits after an address is the zip code — the postcode — which allows mechanical sorting of mail from the city of posting; it doesn't help sort the mail at the receiving end.

PUBLIC HOLIDAYS
January: 1, New Year's Day; 3rd Monday, Martin Luther King Day.
February: 3rd Monday, Presidents' Day.
May: last Monday, Memorial Day.
July: 4, Independence Day.
September: 1st Monday, Labor Day.
October: 2nd Monday, Columbus Day.
November: 11, Veterans' Day; 4th Thursday, Thanksgiving.
December: 25, Christmas Day.

When New Year's Day, Independence Day and Christmas Day fall at a weekend, they are celebrated on the nearer weekday, but November's holidays are fixed.

PUBLIC TOILETS
In the USA the word 'toilet' refers to the lavatory pan, hence 'public toilets' do not exist. Instead, look for the sign *Restroom* in every large building, from a supermarket to a public library; sometimes you'll find

These Naples condos are too vulnerable to hurricane damage.

PRIVATE

one on each floor. There are virtually no restrooms on the street, although a few beaches have them.

The restroom provides the lavatory and washbasin, occasionally a drinking fountain as well, but is not a 'rest room' in the British sense. And only in such places as airports will you see the male and female silhouette used instead of this polite euphemism.

While some restrooms are miniature palaces in marble, at the bottom end of the scale they are meeting places for drug pushers, homosexuals and muggers; if the approaches to a restroom look dubious, don't go any further.

RADIO and TELEVISION

The USA, land of superlatives, had 9,158 radio stations and 50 radio networks in 1986, and in 1987 there were 46 national cable television networks and 1,315 commercial and educational TV stations, so it's not surprising that the average TV set can cope with around 80 channels.

Radio. Although your contact with radio is likely to be confined to the set in your rented car and your hotel console, it will soon become apparent that quality has given way to quantity, though the music on offer is seldom pop.

With each large city having several stations it's pointless quoting wavebands, but the Public Service Broadcasting stations are the best for general news and weather reports.

Television. The weekly *TV Guide* on sale at supermarkets for 75¢ lists all programmes available on all channels and is far more complex than the state's Amtrak and Greyhound timetables together.

The keen viewer in Miami, to take just one example, has access to 12 broadcast channels, and 27 others available by subscription, cable, and satellite, and again quality has given way to quantity.

The broadcasters, comparable with ITV (Independent Television) and Channel Four in Britain, are dominated by NBC (National Broadcasting Company), CBS (Columbia Broadcasting System) and ABC, and financed by advertising. The PSB (Public Service Broadcasting) network is remotely akin to the BBC in that it's financed by its viewers and doesn't carry direct advertising. These giants network their material across the States with local stations — WTVJ, WPLG, and many other acronyms — adding local news and colour and collecting the advertising revenue.

If you want serious state and world news, plus a morning weather forecast, try channels 7 or 10 — but if you want *Popeye* at 0630 Monday thru Friday, tune to channel 9 coming from New York.

The subscription, cable, and satellite channels offer everything from serious documentaries as on the Discovery Channel, through feature films old and new on Home Box Office (you'll see 'HBO' advertised outside many motels), to the Financial News Network and

Black Entertainment TV, unlikely partners who share their channel, FNN by day and BET by night.

And then there's the Disney Channel, the Playboy Channel, Sports Network, The Weather Channel and, in our Miami example, the Dade County Education Channels 1 and 2.

There's probably not a motel in Florida which doesn't have television in every bungalow, though few sets offer more than six channels. Hotels are more discerning, some with no television at all and, at the top of the price range, some with everything available.

STATE versus FEDERAL

The federal government, based in Washington, DC, is responsible for matters of national interest, such as printing the currency, setting interest rates and levying federal taxes; for the armed forces and diplomatic relations abroad; and for the US Mail, the interstate road system, and immigration policy.

Each state sends two senators to Congress and a varying number of members to the House of Representatives; Florida's quota is 19, a figure beaten by only six other states.

The state government, in Florida based in the capital, Tallahassee, is responsible for virtually everything else — and Florida has decided, for example, not to levy an income tax on private citizens.

Local taxes. That doesn't mean there are no more taxes to pay, because each county decides its own level of taxation which may vary year by year. For example, in Dade County, which contains Miami, all businesses must charge a 6% sales-and-use tax. In addition some businesses (but not food shops) must charge a 3% convention development tax to pay for the new county hall, and businesses directly involved with tourism, such as Coral Castle, motels and hotels, bear a 2% tourist tax. And on top of it all there is property tax.

When buying food at a supermarket or a fast-food diner, and petrol, postage stamps, airline and bus tickets and, of course, when paying road tolls and admission fees to the many attractions, the price includes all local taxes.

But when you buy a book, restaurant meal, souvenir, motel or hotel room, roll of film, or a 'pre-owned' car, sales tax will be added, the rate depending on what you buy and where you buy it.

STATE PARKS

Florida has 105 officially-designated parks, preserves, reserves, recreation areas, museums, ornamental gardens, and sites of archaeological, botanical, geological or historical interest. Further details are available at the Department of Natural Resources, address in Chapter 4, but here's a list of the *parks* with what they offer: campsites, **▲**; picnic sites, **✗**; swimming, **≈**; fishing, **F**; boating or canoeing, **⅄**.

Blackwater River, off US—90 15m NE of Milton, nr Pensacola, ✆(904).957.4111; hilly pine forest with sandy-bottom rivers; 🛖 ✖ ⌂ **F**

Blue Spring, off I—4 and US—17 2m W of Orange City, N of Orlando, ✆(904)775.3663; a winter refuge for manatee, with good canoeing; 🛖 ✖ ⌂ **F** ↵

Bulow Creek, N of Ormond Beach; just a hiking trail.

Caladesi Island, W of Dunedin, near Clearwater, ✆(813).443.5903; a sandy island accessible only by boat; ✖ ⌂ **F**

Cayo Costa, a 4-mile-long island accessible only by boat and S of Gasparilla I, ✖ ⌂

Collier—Seminole, off US—41 17m SE of Naples, ✆(813).394.3397; mangrove swamp and marsh; 🛖 ✖ ⌂ **F** ↵

Faver-Dykes, off US—1 15m S of St Augustine, ✆(904).794.0997; dense forest; ✖ **F** ↵

Florida Caverns, off SR—167 3m N of Marianna west of the time zone boundary, ✆(904)482.3632; caves, and a natural bridge over the tiny Chipola River; 🛖 ✖ ⌂ **F**

Fort Clinch, off SR—A1A at Fernandina Beach N of Jacksonville, ✆(904).261.4212; forested dunes and a sandy beach; 🛖 ✖ ⌂ **F**

Fort Cooper, Inverness, SW of Ocala, ✆(904).726.0315; hardwood forest on the edge of town, closed at dusk; ✖ ⌂ **F**

Gold Head Branch, off SR—21 6m NE of Keystone Heights, NE of Gainesville, ✆(904).473.4701; sandhills, a deep ravine, and a small lake; 🛖 ✖ ⌂ **F** ↵

Highlands Hammock, on SR—634 off US—27—98 6m W of Sebring, ✆(813).385.0011; 3,800 acres (15 sq km) of virgin forest with plenty of wildlife, camping reservations needed in winter; 🛖 ✖

Hillsborough River, off US—301 6m SW of Zephyrhills, NE of Tampa, ✆(813).986.1020; encloses part of river and small man-made lake; 🛖 ✖ ⌂ **F**

Hontoon Island, on St John's River, off SR—44 6m SW of De Land, SW of Daytona Beach; access only by boat; virgin wilderness;✆((04).734.7158; 🛖 ✖

Ichetucknee Springs, on SR—238 off SR—47 4m NW of Fort White, NW of Gainesville, ✆(904).497.2511; very popular snorkelling spot, limited to 3,000 visitors per day; ✖ ⌂

John D MacArthur Beach, by SR—A1A N of West Palm Beach, ✆(305).627.6097; unspoilt barrier island; ⌂ **F**

John Pennekamp Coral Reef, Key Largo, Chapter 13; 🛖 ✖ ⌂ **F** ↵

Jonathan Dickinson, off US—1 13m S of Stuart, N of West Palm Beach, ✆(305).546.2771; 11,000 acres (44 sq km) of natural forest beside the Loxahatchee River; 🛖 ✖ ⌂ **F** ↵

Lake Kissimmee, on Camp Mack Rd, 15m E of Lake Wales, ✆(813).696.1112; pinewoods on floodplain, with plenty of birdlife; 🛖 ✖ **F**

Lake Louisa, off Lake Nellie Rd, 7m SW of Clermont, W of Orlando, ✆(904).394.2280; picnic spot for day use only; ✕ ⌒ **F**

Little Talbot Island, off SR–A1A 17m NE of Jacksonville, ✆(904).251.3231; virgin barrier island 5m long; **A** ✕ ⌒ **F** ⅄

Manatee Springs, by Suwannee River off SR–320 6m W of Chiefland, ✆(904).493.4288; mixed forest; **A** ✕ ⌒ **F** ⅄

Myakka River, off SR–72 17m E of Sarasota, ✆(813).966.3154; plenty of wildlife; **A** ✕ **F** ⅄

Ochlockonee River, off US–319 4m S of Sopchoppy, near coast S of Tallahassee, ✆(904).962.2771; part-open pinewoods; **A** ✕ ⌒ **F**

O'Leno, off US–41 20m S of Lake City, ✆(904).454.1853; hardwood forest with natural arch over Santa Fe River; **A** ✕ ⌒ **F**

St George Island, access by causeway from Eastpoint on US–98–319 E of Apalachicola, ✆(904).670.2111; undeveloped sandy island 9m long, ideal for escapist camping; **A** ✕ ⌒ **F**

St Joseph Peninsula, ✆(904).227.1327; long sandspit off Port St Joe E of Apalachicola; **A** ✕ ⌒ **F**

Suwannee River, on US–90 W of Live Oak, ✆(904).362.2746; isolation; limestone cliffs to river; **A** ✕ **F**

Tomoka, off North Beach St, 3m N of Ormond Beach, ✆(904).677.3931; forest with picnic spots; **A** ✕ **F**

Torreya, on Apalachicola River off SR–271 off SR–12, S of I–10 but not accessible from it, ✆(904).643.2674; hilly forest country with several rare plants; **A** ✕ **F**

Wakulla Springs, off SR–267 S of Tallahassee, ✕ ⌒

Wekiwa Springs, off minor roads NW of Orlando, ✆(305).889.3140; forest with popular swimming hole; **A** ✕ ⌒ **F** ⅄

TELEPHONES

In my humble opinion, shared with a number of European visitors, the American telephone system has become overloaded with technology, innovation, and choice.

For a start, Florida's telephone system is split between Southern Bell, US Sprint, MCI, ITT, AT&T and the People's Telephone Company. Southern Bell has the majority of the local traffic and most of the public phones, but doesn't route overseas calls; ITT and AT&T are big in that market.

Calling home. The easiest way to call home is to reverse the charges — 'call collect.' Regardless of who owns the box, dial **1.800.4455667** and you should get a direct line to British Telecom in London. Place your collect call or give your BT credit card number, and you're through.

Or dial 0 and ask the operator to place a collect or a telephone credit card call (any country's card is acceptable) with your home number. You may need to dial 00 and repeat the message, but you pay nothing...yet. Allow for the time difference, then hope you haven't left your answering machine connected: it won't be programmed to accept your call.

In airport terminals you can use your telephone credit card or your Visa, MC, Access, or Amex card to pay for the call. This is where the fun starts, as there are virtually no instructions. Dial the international access code (01 in the USA), your country code (see below), then your home number which must not exceed nine digits, so Britons omit the 0 from their area code.

Insert your card as shown then, on instruction, choose one of the telephone companies listed by pressing the appropriate button: try ITT or AT&T on your first half-dozen attempts to get a connection.

Cash. But if you want to pay cash, heaven help you! Arm yourself with at least $5 worth of quarters − 20 coins − and dial away: 01 + country code + area code + local number. As in Britain, there are no telephone offices in which you can use the operator's services and pay cash over the counter.

Or use your hotel phone and pay the premium.

Several subscribers list their numbers not as digits but as four-letter words, still feasible as the dials and pushbuttons have letters as well as figures. Maybe Britain lost out by abandoning that idea?

Some International Dialling Codes:

Australia	43	Belgium	32
Denmark	45	Finland	358
France	33	Germany (W)	49
Hong Kong	852	Iceland	354
Ireland	353	Luxembourg	352
Malta	356	Netherlands	31
New Zealand	64	Norway	47
South Africa	27	Sweden	46
Switzerland	41	United Kingdom	44

Local calls. For local calls dial 1 + area code + local number, and a synthesised voice will tell you how much money to push in the slot; you may use nickels, dimes or quarters. For directory inquiries dial 0 + your area code + 555 + 1212 − or dial 0 and explain your quandary.

Toll-free. In the USA, as in Britain and elsewhere, phone numbers prefixed 800 are toll-free: somebody else pays the bill. Always dial 1 before the 800.

Danger points. Phone boxes are everywhere, so don't choose one on a busy street corner where traffic noises drown your conversation. And avoid those boxes which have a private individual's name and address stuck over the company's logo: this individual owns the box and keeps all the money you lose by your inexperience.

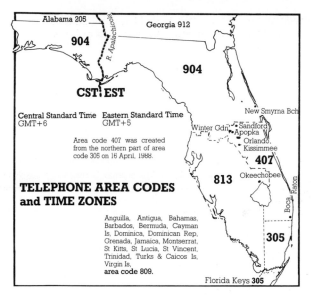

Alabama 205

Georgia 912

904

R. Apalachicola

904

CST EST

Central Standard Time   Eastern Standard Time
GMT+6   GMT+5

Area code 407 was created
from the northern part of area
code 305 on 16 April, 1988.

New Smyrna Bch

Winter Gdn · Sandford
· Apopka
Orlando
· Kissimmee

407

**TELEPHONE AREA CODES
and TIME ZONES**

813   Okeechobee

Boca Raton

Anguilla, Antigua, Bahamas,
Barbados, Bermuda, Cayman
Is, Dominica, Dominican Rep,
Grenada, Jamaica, Montserrat,
St Kitts, St Lucia, St Vincent,
Trinidad, Turks & Caicos Is,
Virgin Is,
area code 809.

305

Florida Keys **305**

Telephone directories. Directories are not easy to find. If your hotel or motel can't oblige, try the public library — and major libraries are open on Sundays. As a point of interest, the Miami classified directory (yellow pages) alone fills 2,401 pages and two volumes, but some counties have combined classified and alpha directories of a hundred pages.

Soap operas. The phone will also give you the latest news on the television soap operas, the stock market, the weather forecast, or tell you your horoscope.

TIME

Most of Florida is on Eastern Time, GMT−5, but that part of the Panhandle west of the Apalachicola River is on Central Time, GMT−6.

Between the first Sunday in April and the last Saturday in October, the United States adopts Daylight Saving Time by advancing all clocks one hour. Except for Arizona and Eastern zone Indiana, which don't bother.

TIPPING

The customary tip in a bar or restaurant is 15%. Tip taxi-drivers at your discretion up to 15%, but don't tip anybody else — certainly not in the fast-food diners.

TRANSPORT

Florida has around 94,000 miles of roads, maintained either at federal, state or county expense, and in 1983 it issued 11,400,000 vehicle license (licence) plates, almost one vehicle for every person in the state. New rear plates, date-stamped, are supplied each year as proof of payment of the road tax, which ranges from $25 to $80 depending on the age and size of the vehicle. There are no front license plates.

The state had 3,421 miles of railroad (railway) at the start of the decade, but much of it was for carrying sugar cane and phosphates to the processing plant.

And in 1984 Florida had 591 airports! Sixteen were of international status, including three commercial seaplane bases.

WATER

Tap water is perfectly safe to drink everywhere, but in most of the state it is slightly chlorinated. Genuine French Perrier water is available at a price but several stores sell local demineralised (and dechlorinated) water by the gallon plastic container. But why not try the delicious real fresh orange juice? Floridians have strange tastes — they seem to prefer Pepsi, Coke, 7up and similar drinks.

Although Florida has 30,000 lakes, its lack of altitude gives problems in building reservoirs and gravity-fed aqueducts, and sometimes in winter water is rationed. Until recently the people of the Keys relied on collecting rainwater but they now drink the chlorinated stuff pumped down from Miami.

WEIGHTS and MEASURES

The USA uses imperial weights and measures — 16 ounces to the pound (1lb = 453.59gm); the mile (1.6093km), though road distances are occasionally given in km; petrol is sold exclusively by the gallon, *but note that the US gallon equals 3.79 litres while the Imperial gallon, used in Britain, equals 4.55 litres.*

The US bushel is also slightly smaller than the Imperial bushel, at 0.0353 cubic metre. Pre-decimalisation Britons may recall that the Imperial bushel is 8 Imperial gallons, but who cares that the US bushel is 9.9 US gallons? You might, when you're buying a bag of fruit at the roadside: it's sold by the ¼ and ½ bushel.

WHAT YOU WON'T LIKE ABOUT FLORIDA

If you like the bread that grandma used to make, you'll hate Florida's sliced sponge-rubber offerings. Apart from this your main dislike will be coming home at the end of your holiday.

4: TOURIST INFORMATION

Chambers of Commerce and other contacts

FLORIDA IS BIG ENOUGH TO HANDLE ITS OWN TOURIST INQUIRIES. The state's main tourist office is at the **Florida Department of Commerce, Division of Tourism, 126 West Van Buren St, Tallahassee, FL 32301,** with its European office, the **Florida Div. of Tourism, 18-22 Westbourne Grove, London W2 5RH, ✆01.(071).27.1661.** There is no other office in Europe.

Welcome Center. Each city or county chamber of commerce is responsible for promoting the community's tourism which, in small places, merely means having a photocopied list of the local motels. The larger cities and those with a heavy tourist trade produce elaborate brochures, free newspapers and, for a fee, detailed street maps. As the chambers operate standard government office hours, some of them have developed separate Welcome Centers or Visitor Centers, usually situated on the main road into the city and opening at weekends and public holidays.

The chambers act as booking agents for hotels and motels, and if you're planning a stay-put holiday or want guaranteed rooms on your travels, it's a good idea to write or phone the relevant chambers before you leave home to reserve the accommodation you want.

Given plenty of time to spare, contact the Florida Division of Tourism in London for phone numbers and PO box addresses of all the chambers of commerce in the state. Or write to the Florida Chamber of Commerce, 136 S. Bronough St, Tallahassee, FL 32303 enclosing $8 — or eight one-dollar bills which you can buy at your bank — for the street addresses which are more useful.

For convenience, here's an *abridged* file of those addresses you're most likely to need, either in the planning stage or when you're on holiday.

Abbreviations: Boulevard, **Blv**; Chamber of Commerce, **CC**; Causeway, **Cswy**; Highway, **Hwy**; Mile marker, **MM**; State Road, **SR**; Tourist Development Council, **TDC**; Welcome Center, **WC**; street names with compass bearings are abbreviated to **N, E, S, W.**

Daytona Beach area

Daytona Beach Area CC, PO Box 2775, Daytona Beach FL 32015, ✆255.0981.

Daytona Beach Shores CC, Suite A, 3616 S Atlantic Blv, Daytona Beach Shores FL 32019, ✆761.7163.

(Daytona Beach:) Volusia County TDC, PO Box 2775, Daytona Beach FL 32015.

New Smyrna–Edgewater CC, PO Box 129, New Smyrna Beach FL 32069, ✆428.2449.

Ormond Beach CC, 165 W Granada Ave, PO Box 874, Ormond Beach FL 32074 ✆671.3454, ✆677.3454.

Port Orange–South Daytona CC, 1018 Ridgewood Ave, Port Orange FL 32019, ✆761.1601.

Everglades

Everglades Area CC, PO Box E, Everglades City FL 33929 ✆695.3941.

There is also an excellent Visitor Center at the entrance to the Everglades National Park on SR 9336 from Homestead, Miami. Open 0800-1700 every day.

Florida Keys

Florida Keys WC, 103400 Overseas Hwy, Key Largo, FL 33037 (MM 103.4) [Mon-Sat 0900-1700].

Islamorada CC, PO Box 915, Islamorada, FL 33036 (MM 82.5; (look for the red caboose (railway wagon)) [Mon-Fri 0900- 1700, closed lunch], ✆664.4503.

Lower Keys CC, PO Box 511, Big Pine Key, FL 33043 (MM 31.9) [Mon-Sat 1000-1500], ✆872.2411.

Key West: Greater Key West CC, PO Box 984, Key West, FL 33041 (402 Wall St, nr N end Duval St) [Mon-Fri 0830-1700, Sat-Sun 0900-1700], ✆294.2587.

Marathon: Greater Marathon CC, 3330 Overseas Hwy, Marathon, FL 33050 (MM 48.5) [Mon-Fri 0900-1700] ✆743.5417.

Fort Lauderdale area (Broward County)

Coconut Grove CC, 3437 Main Hwy, Coconut Grove FL 33133, ✆444.7270.

Fort Lauderdale (Broward County) CC, PO Box 14516 SE 3rd Ave, Ft Lauderdale FL 33302, ✆462.6000.

Fort Myers area

Cape Coral CC, 2051 Cape Coral Parkway, Cape Coral FL 33904, ✆542.3721.

Fort Myers Beach CC, PO Box 6109 (1661 Estero Blv), Fort Myers FL 33931, ✆463.6451.

The complex emblem from the centre of the state flag honours the American Indian ancestry.

Greater Pine Island CC, PO Box 525, Matlacha, FL 33909, ✆283.0888.

Marco Island CC, PO Box 913,(1102 N Collier Blv), Marco I, FL 33937, ✆394.7549.

Metropolitan Fort Myers CC, PO Box CC, (1365 Hendry St), Fort Myers, FL 33902, ✆334.1133.

Naples Area CC, 1700 N Tamiami Trail, Naples FL 33940, ✆262.6141.

Sanibel–Captiva Islands CC, Causeway Rd, Sanibel Island FL 33957 (at entry to island), ✆472.1080.

Fort Pierce area

St Lucie County CC, 2200 Virginia Ave, Fort Pierce FL 33450, ✆461.2700.

Jacksonville area

Amelia Island–Fernandina Beach CC, PO Box 472, Fernandina Beach FL 32034, ✆261.3248.

Jacksonville Area CC, PO Box 329, Jacksonville FL 32201, ✆353.0300.

Jacksonville Beaches Area CC, PO Box 50427, Jacksonville Beach FL 32250, ✆249.3868.

Jacksonville Visitors' Bureau, 206 Hogan St, Jacksonville FL 32202, ✆353.9736.

St Augustine & St John's County CC, PO Box 0, St Augustine FL 32085, ✆829.5681.

The alligator blends nicely with the vegetation.

Miami area (Dade County)

Coral Gables CC, 50 Aragon Ave, Coral Gables FL 33134, ✆446.1657.

Greater Miami CC, Omni Complex, 7th Floor, 1601 Biscayne Blv, Miami FL 33132, ✆350.7700.

Greater Miami Visitor & Convention Bureau (administrative head of tourism, not for casual inquiries or bookings), Barnett Tower, 701 Brickell Ave, Miami. (Mon-Fri, 0900-1700); Splendid view of downtown Miami from the 27th floor; see cover photo.

Hialeah–Miami Springs CC, 59 W 5th St, Hialeah FL 33010, ✆887.1515.

Homestead–Florida City 650 US Hwy 1, Homestead FL 33030, ✆247.2332.

Key Biscayne CC, 95 W McIntyre St, Key Biscayne FL 33149, ✆361.5207.

Miami Beach CC, 1920 Meridian Ave, Miami Beach FL 33139, ✆672.1270.

Miami–Dade CC, 6255 NW 7th Ave, Miami FL 33150, ✆751.8648.

Miami Shores CC, 9523 NE 2nd Ave, Miami Shores FL 33138, ✆754.5466.

North Miami CC, 13100 W Dixie Hwy, North Miami FL 33161, ✆891.7811.

North Miami Beach CC, 39 NE 167th St, North Miami Beach FL 33162, ✆653.1200.

Okeechobee area

Belle Glade CC, 540 S Main St, Belle Glade FL 33430, ✆996.2745.
Clewiston CC, PO Box 275, Clewiston FL 33440, ✆983.7979.
Okeechobee County CC, 55 S Parrott Ave, Okeechobee FL 33472,
✆763.6464.

Orlando area (Counties of Lake, Orange, Osceola, Polk, Seminole, Sumter, within 50 miles of Walt Disney World; see also Titusville area)

(Altamonte Springs:) Greater Seminole County CC, PO Box 784,
Altamonte Springs FL 32701, ✆834.4404.
Apopka Area CC, 180 E Main St, Apopka FL 32703, ✆886.1441.
Auburndale CC, 11 E Park St, Auburndale FL 33823, ✆967.3400.
Avon Park CC, PO Box 1330, Avon Park FL 33825, ✆453.3350.
Greater Bartow CC, PO Box 956, Bartow FL 33830, ✆533.7125.
(Bushell:) Sumter County CC, PO Box 158, Bushell FL 33513,
✆793.3099.
Clermont CC, PO Box 417, Clermont FL 32711, ✆394.4191.
(Eustis:) Lake County CC, PO Drawer AZ, Eustis FL 32726,
✆728.4955.
Fort Meade CC, PO Box 91, Fort Meade FL 33841, ✆285.8253.
Frostproof, PO Box 968, Frostproof FL 33843, ✆635.4066.
Groveland–Mascotte CC, PO Box 115, Groveland FL 32736,
✆429.3678.
Haines CC, PO Box 986, Haines City FL 33844, ✆422.3751.
Kissimmee–Osceola County CC, PO Box 1982, Kissimmee 32741,
Kissimmee–St Cloud Visitors' Bureau PO Box 2007, Kissimmee FL
32742, ✆847.5000.
Lake Alfred CC, PO Box 966, Lake Alfred FL 33850, ✆956.1334.
Lake Wales CC, PO Box 191, Lake Wales FL 33853, ✆676.3445.
Lakeland Area CC, PO Box 3538, Lakeland FL 33802, ✆688.8551.
Leesburg Area CC, PO Box 269, Leesburg FL 32748, ✆787.2131.
Longwood–Winter Springs CC, PO Box 963, Longwood FL 32750,
✆831.9991.
Maitland–South Seminole CC, 110 N Maitland Ave, Maitland FL
32751, ✆644.0741.
(Orlando:) Orange County TDC, 7600 Dr Phillips Blv, Orlando FL
32819; personal callers try the Visitor Information Center, Mercado
Festival Center, 8445 International Dr, FL 32819, ✆363.5871; see
Orlando map.
Orlando Area CC, PO Box 1234, Orlando FL 32802, ✆425.1234.
(Union Park:) East Orange CC, PO Box 9080, Union Park FL 32817,
✆277.5951.
(Winter Garden:) West Orange CC, PO Box 522, Winter Garden FL
32787, ✆656.1304.

Palm Beach County

Greater West Palm Beach CC, (mainland city) 501 N Flagler Drive, West Palm Beach, FL 33401, ✆833.3711.

Lake Worth CC, 1702 Lake Worth Rd, Lake Worth FL 33460, ✆582.4401.

Palm Beach CC, (covers the island only) 45 Cocoanut Row, Palm Beach FL 33480, ✆655.3282.

Tri-City CC, 6130 W Atlantic Blv, Margate FL 33063, ✆972.0818.

Panhandle (Tallahassee and Pensacola cities; a small selection only)

Emerald Coast TDC, PO Box 4204, Fort Walton Beach FL 32549.

Pensacola Area CC, PO Box 550, 117 W Garden St, Pensacola FL 32593, ✆438.4081.

Tallahassee CC, PO Box 1639, Tallahassee FL 32302, ✆224.8116.

Suwannee River Valley

Dixie County CC, PO Box 547, Cross City, FL 32628, ✆498.5181.

Suwannee County CC, PO Box C, Live Oak FL 32060.

Tampa area (Counties of Citrus, Hernando, Hillsborough, Manatee, Pasco, Pinellas, Sarasota.)

Anna Maria Island CC, PO Box 336, Bradenton Beach FL 33510, ✆778.1003.

(Clearwater:) Pinellas County TDC, 109A Newport Sq, 2333 East Bay Drive, Clearwater FL 33546, ✆544.4777.

(Clearwater:) Pinellas Suncoast CC, Suite 239, St Petersburg–Clearwater Airport, Clearwater FL 33520, ✆531.4657.

Greater Clearwater CC, PO Box 2457, Clearwater FL 33517 (Visitor Center at west end of Campbell Cswy, SR 60), ✆461.0011.

Holiday Isles CC, PO Box 273, Indian Rocks Beach FL 33535 (covers the keys off Clearwater and St Petersburg, though Treasure Island has its own CC), ✆595.4575.

Homosassa Springa Area CC, PO Box 1098, Homosassa Springs FL 32647, ✆628.2666.

Longboat Key CC, 510 Bay Isles Rd, Longboat Key FL 33548 (offshore from Sarasota), ✆383.1212.

Manatee CC, PO Box 321, Bradenton FL 33506, ✆748.3411.

St Petersburg Area CC, PO Box 1371 (100 2nd Ave, North St), St Petersburg FL 33731, ✆821.4069.

St Petersburg Beach CC, PO Box 66375, St Petersburg Beach FL 33736, ✆360.6957.

Sarasota County CC, PO Box 308, 1551 2nd St, Sarasota FL 33578, ✆955.8187.

(Tampa:) **Greater Tampa CC,** PO Box 420, Tampa FL 33601, ℀228.7777.

Tampa Convention & Visitors' Bureau, 100 S Ashley Drive, Tampa FL 33601 (Mon-Fri 0900-1630), ℀228.7777.

Venice Area CC, 257 N Tamiami Trail, Venice FL 33595, ℀488.2236.

Titusville area (for Cape Canaveral and Walt Disney World)

Cocoa Beach Area CC, 431 Riveredge Blv, Cocoa FL 32922, ℀636.4262.

(Melbourne:) South Brevard CC, 1005 E Strawbridge Ave, Melbourne FL 32901, ℀724.5400.

Titusville Area CC, 2000 S Washington, Titusville FL 32780, ℀267.3036.

OTHER USEFUL CONTACTS.

Florida Attractions Assoc, PO Box 833, Silver Springs, FL 32688.

Florida Boaters Assoc, 1900 79th St Causeway, North Bay Village, FL 33141.

Florida Campground Assoc, PO Box 13355, Tallahassee, FL 32317.

Florida Department of Natural Resources, Marjory Stoneman Bldg, 3900 Commonwealth Blv, Tallahassee, FL 32399, ℀(904).488.7326.

Florida Hotel & Motel Assoc, Inc, 117 West College Ave, Tallahassee, FL 32301.

Florida State Golf Assoc, PO Box 21177, Sarasota, FL 33583.

Florida Tennis Assoc, 9620 N.E. 2nd Ave, Miami Shores, FL 33138.

Florida Trail Assoc, PO Box 13708, Gainesville, FL 32604.

Miami Dolphins (American Football), Suite 1440, 4770 Biscayne Boul, Miami, FL 33137.

National Parks Service, US Dept of Interior, Washington, DC, 20025.

US Travel & Tourism Administration, 22 Sackville St, London W1 2EA.

Walt Disney Co Ltd, (The), 31-32 Soho Square, London W1V 6AP, ℀01(071).734.8111.

Walt Disney Productions is also at: 41 Blv Bischoffsheim, 1000 **Bruxelles** ℀218.5297; Savignystrasse 76, D-6000 **Frankfurt am Main** ℀4969.747774; Ostergate 24BIII, **Købnhavn K** ℀451.123332; 52 Ave Champs-Elyséees, 75008 **Paris** ℀225.1766.

TOUR OPERATORS

This list of British tour operators offering package holidays in Florida is compiled from the *ABC Holiday Guide* and other sources, those marked with 🍴 offering self-catering and those with 🚐 offering RV rental:

Acorn Travel 🍴 🚐, Airtours, Albany Travel 🍴 🚐, American Airplan 🍴 🚐, American Connection 🍴, American Dream, American Express Holidays 🍴 🚐, American Travel Centre, Barclay USA, Bricar Overseas 🚐, Caravan Abroad 🚐, Caribbean Connection 🍴, Caribtours, Chalfont Travel 🍴, Club 18−30, Cosmos Holidays, Cruise America Motorhomes 🚐, Custom Tours 🚐.

Destination Marketing 🍴, Destination USA, Dream Islands of the World, Eady Travel Consultancy 🚐, Elegant Resorts, Falcon Holidays, Fantasy World Club Villasa 🍴, Florida Accommodations Bureau 🍴, Florida Connection, Florida Homeowners Assoc 🍴, Greyhound Lines 🍴, Harlequin Holidays, Hickie Borman 🚐, Intasun.

Jetlife Holidays, Jetsave🍴, Jetways, Jetwing Florida🍴, Key to America 🍴, Kuoni, Martin Rooks 🍴, Meon, Nar UK 🍴 🚐, North American Travel Service 🍴 🚐, Palmer & Parker 🍴, PanAm Holidays 🍴, Pan Am Thriftway, Pegasus, Peregor Travel 🍴 🚐, Portfolio Holidays, Poundstretcher 🍴, Premier Travel 🍴.

Renown Holidays 🍴, 🚐 Holiday America 🚐, 🚐I Travel Services 🍴 🚐, Select Holidays, Sovereign Travel, Speedbird 🍴 🚐, Stirling Holidays 🍴, Thomson, Tradewinds Faraway Holidays, Transamerica Holidays 🍴, Transolar Holidays, Travel Force, Travellers Jetways 🚐, Treasure Island Holidays 🍴, Unijet, Valley USA 🍴, Virgin Holidays 🚐.

5: SPORTS FOR ALL

By land, sea, and air

WHAT'S THE MAIN ATTRACTION IN FLORIDA? Walt Disney World? The splendid beaches? Or the vast array of sports? When you look at sport in its widest sense, including fishing, flying, golf, greyhound racing, horse racing, jai-alai, motor racing, tennis, and the vast assortment of watersports, it's probably a photo-finish. We'll take them in alphabetical order, starting with:

BASEBALL

The unkind European might look at baseball as an adult version of rounders, but if you want to spot the difference you can study some of the USA's best players as 18 teams start their spring training in the Florida Grapefruit exhibition league. Here's where to find them from March 1:

Bradenton: McKecknie Field, Pittsburg Pirates.

Clearwater: Jack Russell Stadium, Philadelphia Phillies.

Dunedin: Grand Field, Toronto Blue Jays.

Ft Lauderdale: Yankee Stadium; New York Yankees.

Ft Myers: Kansas City Royals.

Kissimmee: Osceola Stadium, Houston Astros.

Lakeland: Marchant Stadium, Detroit Tigers.

Miami: Stadium on NW 10th Ave, Baltimore Orioles.

Orlando: Tinker Field, Minnesota Twins.

Pompano Beach: Texas Rangers.

St Petersburg: Al Lang Stadium, St Louis Cardinals; New York Mets.

Sarasota: Payne Park, Sarasota.

Tampa: Al Lopez Field, Cincinnati Reds.

Vero Beach: Holman Stadium, Los Angeles Dodgers.

West Palm Beach: Municipal Stadium, Atlanta Braves; Montreal Expos.

Winter Haven: Chain o'Lakes Park, Boston Red Sox.

CYCLING

America's main roads are built for the automobile, not for the pedal cyclist, but if you get onto the state and the county roads you can cycle for miles and meet scarcely any other traffic. For all you know, the Magic Kingdom could have been whisked away to Fairyland. And there are few hills to hinder you.

There are seven designated cycle routes in the state, designed to take the cyclist to places of interest while avoiding the crowds, and with campsites at convenient stages. Your choice is from 'Canopy Roads' from Tallahassee, 100 miles; 'Crystal Springs,' 100 miles and 'Healing Waters,'300 miles, both from Gainesville; 'Land o'Lakes' from Kissimmee for 150 miles; 'Lakes 'n Hills' from Eustis in Lake County, 100 miles; 'Sugar Beaches' from Pensacola, 90 miles; and the 120-mile 'Withlacoochee Meander' from Crystal River.

As few foreign tourists take cycles, and they're not readily available for hire, if you want to know more contact the chambers of commerce in the relevant areas or find the routes in DeLorme's road atlas of Florida.

FISHING

Freshwater angling. There's no closed season for freshwater fishing in Florida's thousands of lakes, but you need a licence — you get it at the county tax collector's office or its sub-agent's, costing $26.50 for an annual licence, valid from 1 July, or $11.50 for a 10-day licence. There are wide restrictions on the method of catching (no electricity, poisons, use of airboats, etc), the general bag limit and the special bag limits in designated areas: ask for the latest information when you get the licence. In many areas anglers may not take alcoholic drinks with them.

In spring and summer your catch will be bass (perch) with some bream or catfish; in autumn it's bass again, and in winter it's more bass with some crappie. No wonder Florida is known as the Bass Capital of the world.

Bass, however, come in several varieties: largemouth, striped, and sunshine. Bream, called 'brim,' include the bizarrely-named bluegill, crappie (speckled perch), shell-cracker, and stumpknocker. The catfish, named from its sensitive whisker-like feelers, is also common — so common, in fact, that they've been known to come ashore and appear to walk on those whiskers: this was the legendary invasion of the walking catfish.

Where to fish. Try these rivers: the lower Apalachicola; and the Chassahowitzka, Homosassa and Crystal rivers, and the Withlacoochee upstream of Dunnellon, all north of Tampa.

Or these lakes, chosen for their nearness to other places you may be visiting: Ocean Pond and Palestine Lake, east of Lake City; lakes Sampson, Rowell, Santa Fe, Newnans, Lochloosa and Ocklawaha between Gainesville and Palatka; and Lake George by Ocala National Forest.

Palm Beach — but where's the sand? Much of it was swept away in a hurricane.

Around Orlando, lakes Harris, Griffin, Yale, Jessup, Monroe, Harney, Louisa, Butler, Tohopekaliga and East Tohopekaliga, and in the city itself, Lake Conway. And to the south, lakes Kissimmee, Istokpoga, and the big one, Lake Okeechobee itself.

The **Game and Freshwater Fish Commission** is at Farris Bryant Bldg, Tallahassee, FL 32301, with regional offices in Lake City, Lakeland, Ocala, Panama City and West Palm Beach.

SEA FISHING. You have several ways of going sea fishing. You can do it from a beach or pier; join a boat fishing party and go for something you can eat; or charter a boat and go sportfishing.

There are dozens of piers; you can find them for yourself. There are hundreds, maybe thousands, of boats for hire or charter, in every port in the state and particularly along the Keys. Contact the appropriate Chamber of Commerce in advance if you want a firm booking, or just take your chance.

FLYING.
Hot-air ballooning. How would you like to join **Phineas Phogg** in his hot air balloon rising into the early morning skies over Orlando? Have $135 handy and call ✆422.2434 for a seat in the basket, and collection from your hotel (There's more about Church Street Station in Chapter 19).

Balloon Fantasy is in the same line of business, including a champagne brunch when you land; ✆352.6198 for details. **Orange Blossom Balloons** flies every morning, wind permitting, from Kissimmee; contact the company at 5770 W Irlo Bronson Mem Hwy (Space Coast Pkwy, US-192), or ✆239.7677.

Rise & Float Balloon Tours operates from a site opposite Wet 'n' Wild, ✆352.8191, and you can have a tethered balloon flight in Old Town, on US-192 near Walt Disney World.

Gliding. Sail Plane Rides will take you up in a glider for a passenger's view of central Florida's lake district; ✆(813).299.8689 for a reservation. The Kendall Glider Port at 16800 SW 237th Ave, Miami, ✆232.2700, is a glider base where you can buy 30 minutes for $30; contact Thorpe Aviation, PO Box 970594, Miami, FL 33197.

Light aircraft. Flying *as a passenger* aboard light aircraft is possible from a number of airfields, but foremost among them is Marathon in the Keys. And if you don't fancy chartering a plane you can go scheduled with Eastern Airlines to Miami or Naples several times a day in a Beechcraft, over the Ten Thousand Islands or Florida Bay — and that's flying!

Key West has more than 130 flights a week to Miami International in light aircraft for fascinating views of the 'Glades and the Lower Keys.

Seaplane. Or, for the ultimate, fly from Key West by seaplane to the

Dry Tortugas for $95 round trip. Key West Seaplane Service is based at Murray Marina on Stock Island: the address is 5603 W Junior College Rd, FL 33040, ✆294.6978.

Helicopter. There's no shortage of helicopter rides on the market. Bulldog Airlines will carry you over Epcot and Sea World for 10 minutes and $28, or over central Florida for half an hour and $85; the helipad is at Sonesta Village Hotel off I-4; ✆240.3440.

JC Helicopters offers eight tours of varying duration over the Magic Kingdom, Epcot Centre, and other Orlando locations from the Hyatt Heliport near the Ramada Inn on I-4 and US-192; ✆847.7222. And don't forget the Dade Helicopter Jet Service, near Chalk's International Airline, on Miami's Wilson Island...if they've not both been evicted by the time we go to press.

GOLF

Golf is big business in the Sunshine State, so it's little surprise to see the name 'A. Palmer' listed among the local champions. Florida has more than 800 courses, with six of them in the USA's top 100. You will find more golf holes per person in this state than in any of the other 49, and more courses per given area in south Florida than anywhere else east of the Mississippi.

Of those 800 or so, *Golfweek* magazine lists 485; of those 485, 136 are public; and of those 136, four have been listed in the state's top 50 in 1985-1988. Here they are:

Golden Ocala G&CC 7300 Hwy 27 NW, Ocala FL 32675, ✆629.6229.

Hunter's Creek CG 14401 Sports Club Way, Orlando FL 32821, ✆851.0400.

Key Biscayne GC 6700 Crandon Blv, Key Biscayne FL 33149, ✆361.9129.

Orange Lake CC 8505 W Space Coast Pkwy, Kissimmee FL 32741, ✆239.1050.

And here are some others, chosen not for the quality of the course but purely for their convenience to the main tourist areas:

Alhambra Golf & Tennis Club, 4700 S Texas Ave, Orlando FL 32809, ✆851.6250.

American Golfers' Club, 3850 N Federal Hwy, Ft Lauderdale FL 33308, ✆564.8760.

Apollo Beach Golf & Sea Club, 801 Golf & Sea Blv, Apollo Beach FL 33570, ✆645.6212 (near Tampa).

Bayshore GC, 2301 Alton Rd, Miami Beach FL 33140, ✆532.3350.

Cocoa Beach Municipal GC, Tom Warrinder Blv, Cocoa Beach FL 32931, ✆783.5351.

Daytona Beach Par 3, 2500 Volusia Ave, Daytona Beach FL 32014, ✆252.3983.

Ft Myers CC, 1445 Hill Ave, Ft Myers FL 33901, ✆ 936.2457.

Green Meadows Par 3, 2500 W Michigan, Pensacola FL 32506, ∅453.3541.

Green Valley GC, SR-50 West, Clermont FL 32711, ∅394.2133 (Lake County).

Miami Springs GC, 650 Curtiss Pkwy, Miami Springs FL 33166, ∅ 888.2377.

Ocean Palm GC, 3600 Central Ave S, Flagler Beach FL 32036, ∅439.2477.

Plantation GC, 7050 W Broward Blv, Plantation FL 33317, ∅583.5341 (west of Ft Lauderdale).

Pine Ridge GC, 1005 Elkcam Blv, Beverley Hills FL 32665, ∅746.6177 (Citrus County).

Spring Lake G&CC, 10350 Duane Palmer Blv, Sebring FL 33870, ∅655.1276.

Turtle Creek GC, 1278 Admiralty Blv, Rockledge FL 32955, ∅632.2520.

Several golf courses form part of special resorts, such as the **Walt Disney World Inn,** 1 Magnolia Palm Dr, Lake Buena Vista FL 32830, ∅824.2250, and others are central points in retirement estates to allow the ex-executive to become a workaholic on the greens. For more information contact the Florida Division of Tourism.

Part of Flagler's Folly, the 'Railway that went to sea.' It was later part of the first motor road to Key West.

GREYHOUND RACING

Greyhound racing is as localised a sport in the USA as it is in Britain, but Floridians, who love to 'go to the dogs,' have a choice of 18 tracks and a season that lasts all year. This alphabetic selection covers the main tourist areas of the state:

Bonita Springs — Fort Myers: The track is at 10601 Bonita Beach Rd, Bonita Springs, with race meetings from December to May.

Jacksonville: The Jacksonville Kennel Club at 1440 N McDuff Ave, ✆(904).388.2623, shares its base with the Orange Park Kennel Club and the Bayard Raceway for year-round events.

Key West: Berenson's Key West Kennel Club is at 350 5th Ave, ✆294.9517, and racing is from December to April.

Miami: The Flagler Kennel Club at 401 NW 38th Court ✆649.3000, races from July to December.

Orlando: The Sanford — Orlando Kennel Club's premises are at 301 Dog Track Rd, Longwood, ✆831.1600, with meetings from December to April.

Palm Beach Kennel Club: At 1111 N Congress Ave, ✆683.2222, with racing from October to April.

St Petersburg: Owners of the Derby Lane track claim it's the world's oldest greyhound track in continuous operation. ✆576.1361. January to May.

Tampa Greyhound Track: 8300 N Nebraska Ave; September to January.

HORSE RACING

Horse racing in the USA isn't just a matter of flat racing or steeplechasing; depending on where you are there's trotting and harness racing as well. Florida has five courses, all but one in the Miami area.

Calder track, Tropical Park, 21001 NW 27th Ave (May-Nov); Gulfstream Park, 901 S Federal Hwy (US-1), Hallandale (Nov-May); Hialeah Park, 2200 E 4th Ave (Nov-May); Pompano Park, 1800 SW 3rd St (almost year-round); and Tampa Bay Downs, Oldsmar (between Tampa and Clearwater) (Dec-Mar).

HORSE RIDING

Florida is a long way from the Wild West, but there's still scope for hiring a horse for the hour or the day and just pretending.

For trekking through quiet suburbia, try **Tradewinds Park,** 4400 NW 39th Ave, Pompano Beach FL 33067, ✆973.3220: it's south of the Palmetto Expwy.

Or for a gallop through the breaking surf, promoted as the only stable in the state offering this thrill, contact **Seahorse Stables,** Hwy A1A North, Amelia Island FL 32034, ✆261.4878. Amelia Island is north of Jacksonville, in summer-resort country.

You needn't be a polo player to hire a horse at the **Palm Beach Polo and Country Club,** 13198 Forest Hill Blv, West Palm Beach FL 33414, ✆793.1113, but you can then go trekking through the club's 400-acre (160ha) wildlife refuge.

JAI-ALAI

The Basques of northern Spain have long played the very fast ball game of pelota; the Floridians have now taken it to heart and call it jai-alai, pronouncing it the Spanish way, 'hai-alai.' A player, called a *pelotari,* has a long, banana-shaped basket strapped to his throwing hand and can return a delivery at up to 150 miles an hour.

The game, which is mainly confined to Florida, has become a focal point for locals as well as visitors for an evening out, dining while they watch and betting on their favourite player with the chance of a $100,000 pay-off.

You can sample jai-alai at several places, notably the Jai-alai Fronton at Tampa from January to September; Miami Jai-alai on NW 37th Ave from December to September; and Daytona Beach in any month except October.

MOTOR RACING

Florida's main motor-racing event is the Miami Grand Prix held on public roads — mainly Biscayne Blv — in February. Miami also has the Nissan Indy Challenge around Tamiami Park, in the autumn.

Daytona has its Daytona 500 in February, and the Firecracker 400 and Paul Revere 250 in July, all at the International Stadium. Motor racing began on the sands at Daytona Beach at the turn of the century, but ceased in the 1950s. On the gulf coast, Clearwater has drag races at its Sunshine Speedway, St Petersburg holds its November Grand Prix in the city streets, and tiny Sebring, north-west of Lake Okeechobee, has long been noted for its Twelve Hours of Sebring, held on the potholed runways and taxiways of a disused airport. Boisterous spectators are sometimes as entertaining as the race.

TENNIS

There are thousands of tennis courts. The better-class hotels often have courts on the premises or access to some not far away; or ask at the local chamber of commerce. International-class tennis tournaments are staged at Key Biscayne, Miami.

SALTWATER SPORTS

There's no watersport yet devised that's not available somewhere in Florida, and if you can bring your equipment on the plane you're master of your destiny — but only if you choose your base carefully.

Not all beaches are open to the public: this one is on the keys near St Petersburg.

Beaches and shoreline

Florida has a shoreline of more than 8,000 miles, counting the creeks but not being silly about every indent in the Everglades. Deduct the mangroves and the creeks and you have 780 miles of beach — but only 310 miles of it is open to the public. And of *that*, much is inaccessible or lacks adequate parking space.

The sands at Indian Rock Beach, Madeira Beach, and Treasure Island by St Petersburg, are fronted by hotels, motels, and condos, and if you're not a guest you'll need to be around *very* early to find car parking space. The same comments apply to long stretches of the shore from Miami Beach to Palm Beach, and at Daytona Beach they still park and drive on the sands.

If you're looking for a good beach with nearby parking, and nothing else matters, avoid the big cities. Consider places such as Naples, Sanibel Island, Venice, or Honeymoon Island on the Gulf coast; and on the Atlantic, parts of Miami Beach, Hutchinson Island south of Ft Pierce, and for the summer visitor, Anastasia Island by St Augustine — or go to the Keys.

DIVING

The clear, warm waters and the coral reefs make Florida by far the most interesting of the continental United States for divers. Away from the sea, there are scores of sinkholes in the limestone plateau of Florida, offering an underwater wonderland.

But don't forget: diving can be dangerous. More than 70 divers have died at their sport during the eighties. The **Florida Skindivers' Association** at 4201 13th Lane NE, St Petersburg, FL 33703, ✆522.8885, recommends would-be scuba divers earn a Certified Diver's Card before going solo: in fact, you may find it difficult to get your air tanks refilled if you don't have such a certificate. And before you go into caves, log at least 30 dives in open water, then find yourself a place in a team and plan your cave work scrupulously.

Most divers go down for the thrill of it, and follow the 'look but don't take' policy, but some are spear-fishermen whose activities make things more difficult — and dangerous — for the fishwatcher.

If you're an underwater explorer, these are some of the best places to dive: Amelia and Anastasia islands, for relics from pirate days; Indian River; Fort Pierce, for relics from the Spanish fleet in 1715, when vast amounts of gold, silver, porcelain and jewellery were lost (several million dollars' worth has been found and is on display in Cocoa Beach); Lake Worth, site of several Spanish wrecks; and the Florida Keys — see the item on diving in chapter 13.

Jet skiing
Among the locations where you can hire jet skis are:

Fort Lauderdale: Atlantic Sailing Center, PO Box 22684, Ft Lauderdale FL 33335, ✆454.5281.

Islamorada: Jet Ski on Holiday Isle, PO Box 588, Islamorada FL 33036, ✆664.2321.

Key Largo: Marvin's at Lake Surprise, PO Box 1680, Key Largo FL 33037, ✆451.1353.

Marathon: Adventure Island, 12468 Overseas Highway (MM 54), Marathon FL 33050, ✆289.1500.

St Petersburg: Jet Ski Florida Inc, 3400 Gulf Blv, St Petersburg FL 33706, ✆367.3131.

Sarasota: Don's Ski School, PO Box 2868, Sarasota FL 33578, ✆366.6659.

Parasailing
Try Don's Ski School at **Sarasota,** above, or at the Hilton Hotel Pool Shop, 4060 Galt Ocean Dr, **Ft Lauderdale** FL 33335, ✆454.5281, or Don CeSar Beach Resort, St Petersburg FL 33706, ✆360.1881.

Powerboating
Merc Charter offers statewide powerboat rentals from a range of around 20 models, starting at a 15ft 45hp 4-seater fishing boat and going to a 25ft 260hp 6-seater cruiser with sunbridge. All craft from 18ft upwards have VHF radio, compass, casette players, charts and safety equipment. ✆1.800.448.MERC for details of rates and availability, and to make reservations.

Other charter companies around the state offer everything from sportfishing boats to motor yachts, or you can take a short cruise on a schooner — or go on a longer cruise on an ocean liner. For the latter, see Nightlife, chapter 9; for the smaller craft try Clearwater, Miami and the Florida Keys; see the appropriate chapters.

Sailing
There's limited scope for the European visitor to take the helm of a sailing boat in Florida's waters. Most small boats come down on car roofs or trailers, and almost all the yacht-size sailing boats cater for non-working passengers. You'll find a few possibilities in the Keys and Miami; see chapters 13 and 15.

Water skiing
A selection:
Ft Lauderdale: Bahia Mar Small Boat Rentals, 800 Bahia Mar Yachting Center, PO Box 3457, Ft Lauderdale FL 33316, ✆467.6000; Atlantic Sailing Center (see above).
Miami Beach: Larry's Water Ski School, 185th St, Collins Ave, Miami Beach FL 33160, ✆932.0976.
Pompano Beach: Lyle Lee's Ski College, 3701 NW 9th Ave, Pompano Beach, FL 333064, ✆943.7766.
Sarasota: Don's, above.

Windsurfing
Windsurfing or surfboarding is known as boardsailing in the USA, and there are plenty of locations for hiring the equipment, but bring a wetsuit if possible. Here's a selection:
Clearwater: West Coast Water Sports, 63 Baymont St, Clearwater Beach FL 33515, ✆443.1902.
Ft Lauderdale: Hilton Hotel Pool Shop, see parasailing above.
Key Largo: Windsurfing Key Largo, 4580 Overseas Highway, Key Largo FL 33037, ✆451.3869.
Key West: Windsurfing Key West, 700 Waddell St, Key West FL 33040, ✆296.8897.
Miami: Sailaway, 195 S Dixie Highway, Coral Gables FL 33133, ✆444.8488.
Orlando: Lake Buena Vista Ski Holidays, PO Box 22007, Lake Buena Vista FL 32830, ✆846.4596.
Palm Beach: Sailer's Warehouse, 1748 Australia Ave North, Riviera Beach FL 33404, ✆848.6635.
Pensacola: Surf and Sail, 315, 11-J Via de Luna, Pensacola Beach FL 32561, ✆932.7873.
Sanibel: Windsurfing of Sanibel, 1554 Periwinkle Way, Sanibel Island FL 33957, ✆472.0123.

INLAND WATER SPORTS: Canoeing
Transatlantic visitors' opportunities to go canoeing in Florida are

directly related to the availability of canoes, which are obviously concentrated in the more popular areas.

Be grateful, therefore, for **Canoe Outposts,** which offers half-day, full day or longer canoeing trips, and specialises in the wilderness regions. First-timers and children are welcomed, and you can either bring your own camping gear or hire it from the company. Reservations are essential, so choose your location and contact the appropriate branch of Canoe Outposts:

Suwannee, Alapaha and N Withlacoochee rivers; Rt 1, PO Box 346, Live Oak, FL 32060, ✆(904).842.2129 (between Jacksonville and Tallahassee).

Santa Fé and Ichetucknee rivers; PO Box 592, High Springs, FL 32643, ✆(904).454.2050 (near Gainesville).

Oklawaha River; Rt 1, PO Box 1462, Ft McCoy, FL 32637, ✆(904).236.4606 (near Silver Springs).

S Withlacoochee River; PO Box 118, Nobleton, FL 33554, ✆(904).796.4343 (near Tampa).

Alafia River; 4712 Lithia-Pinecrest, Valrico, FL 33594, ✆(813).681.2666 (near Tampa).

Lt Manattee River; 18001 US-301 S, Wimauma, FL 33598, ✆(813).634.2228 (near Tampa).

Everglades (guided tours, Jan and Feb only) and **Peace River;** Rt 7, PO Box 301, Arcadia, FL 33821, ✆(813).494.1215 (between Sarasota and Okeechobee).

Other canoe rentals. At Chokoloskee, beyond Everglades City, you can rent canoes for $12 a half day and $18 a day; rates are available for longer periods up to a week, which is the length of time you need to cover the **Wilderness Waterway** to Flamingo, following a recognised trail through the Ten Thousand Islands, the mangrove swamps, and Whitewater Bay, with camp sites set up at appropriate intervals.

At Sanford, convenient for Walt Disney World, **Katie's** operates canoe runs from Wekiwa Springs State Park; leave I-4 for SR-434 West. You have the choice of four river routes ranging from six to 12 miles, with the canoe and all your gear dropped off at 0900 and collected at 1600; rates are $12 to $13.50 for adults. Katie's is at 190 Katie's Cove, Sanford, FL 32771, ✆(407).628.1482.

Assorted sports. In the Orlando area, as spinoffs from Walt Disney World, there are these specialist watersports operators: **Airboat Rentals,** along US-192 near Kissimmee, ✆847.3672, for airboats and canoes; **Ski Holidays,** ✆239.4444 for water-ski instruction and practise at all levels on Lake Bryan near Walt Disney World; **Water Sports,** at Orange Lake Country Club near Walt Disney World, ✆239.5199, for jet-skiing, water-skiing, canoeing and rowing; and Katie's, mentioned above.

6: GETTING TO FLORIDA

New World landfall

THE READERS AT WHOM THIS BOOK IS AIMED have but one way to reach Florida: by air. But they have a wide enough choice of airlines and routes.

Cheapest. At the time of writing, the cheapest way to cross the Atlantic to Florida (or to New York) is on a standby flight with Virgin Atlantic from London's Gatwick Airport, with a one-way fare less than £100. But if you haven't a visa you need a return ticket, thus ruling out this option. Other snags are that you cannot book the flight until the day before departure, and acceptance is subject to there being any spare seats.

You can book through your travel agent or phone the airline direct; for the Monday flight you *must* call the airline on Sunday after 0700, ✆0293.38222.

As a visa-holding standby traveller you won't have a return ticket so you must go through the same booking procedure in Florida, where the tollfree (freephone) number is 1.800.862.8621, Mon-Fri from 0730, San-Sun from 0900. *In both cases ticket purchase can be made only by credit card.*

American travel agents are one-up on the British. Book a flight in the USA and you can reserve your seat at the same time. And you can also collect your boarding card, except when booking on the day of the flight.

Fly-drive. Fly-drive deals from Britain operate from Gatwick, Heathrow, Manchester and Stansted, to Miami, Orlando and Tampa, with Intasun, Poundstretcher (British Airways), and Virgin Territory (Virgin Atlantic).

Scheduled flights. Miami has one-stage scheduled connections with Europe via London (Gatwick and Heathrow), Amsterdam, Frankfurt, Madrid, and Paris (Orly and Charles de Gaulle). All other flights involve transfers.

Orlando has one-stage scheduled links with Europe through London (Gatwick and Heathrow), Manchester and Paris (Orly). Again, all other scheduled connections involve transfers.

After experience with standby, scheduled flights and fly-drive to

Florida, and with several airlines, my preference is Virgin Atlantic. While all carriers are efficient, this one manages to put fun into the flight as well.

Inbound to USA. During the journey to the USA, non-Americans are asked to fill in an arrival-departure card. Questions 12 and 13 ask for your address while in the States. Don't put 'travelling;' give a hotel address, and if you don't know one try 'Economy Inn, Biscayne Boulevard.' It exists, so nobody will check your booking. But don't invent a private address as that may be checked.

You'll also fill in a customs declaration which lists prohibited imports. Fruits, vegetables, plants, soil, meats and meat products are rigorously banned, with oranges tabu for fear of disease. And US Customs bans the sale of alcohol during the last 90 minutes of the flight even though you may be 600 miles from land!

AIRPORTS

Florida has 591 airports. I'll write that again, in case you missed it. Florida has 591 airports − not counting military and naval air bases, nor fields which are strictly private. Of that impressive total, 16 are of international status − including the state's most unusual airport, standing on less than an acre of concrete on Wilson Island, between Miami and Miami Beach, and forming the smallest port of entry into the USA.

Chalk's International Airlines. This is the home of just one carrier, Chalk's International Airlines, which flies 17- seat Grumman Mallard seaplanes to Bimini in the Bahamas for a $98 round trip; the aircraft, seen in the title sequences of *Miami Vice,* cruise at 7,500 feet, giving stupendous views. Chalk's claims to be the world's oldest airline in continuous service, having been founded in 1919 by Arthur 'Pappy' Chalk, a First World War flyer, but early in 1989 the company was facing possible eviction from its Wilson Island base.

Bargain fare to the Bahamas? And if you're seriously planning a trip to the Bahamas, Chalk's line can also take you to Nassau Seaplane Base. Combine this with a Virgin Atlantic standby fare Gatwick−Miami and you greatly reduce the cost of the direct flight from London − but you must have a multiple-entry visa.

In fairness I should add the options of flying with Caribbean Express between Nassau and Miami International aboard Brazilian-built 30-seat Bandeirantes, flying Chalk's or Caribbean Express on the Nassau−Ft Lauderdale route, and going with the big boys, including Bahamasair, aboard Boeings and De Havillands.

Dade Helicopters. Five minutes' walk from Chalk's base on Wilson Island is the Dade Helicopter Jet Service, offering tours, charters, and filming flights; there are several other such companies elsewhere in the state which are mentioned in later chapters.

Now back to the main airports. Almost all flights from Europe arrive at Miami, Orlando or Tampa airports.

MIAMI AIRPORT

Miami Airport, MIA on your luggage tags, is large without being enormous. The arrivals terminal is on the ground floor, holding restrooms (toilets), restaurants, and offices for Hertz, Avis, Value, Budget, Dollar and National car hire companies (see Chapter 7 for hiring procedure).

Duty free? The departures terminal is on the first floor, but thanks to an elevated road your car hire courtesy bus has dropped you at the door. Here are elegant shops, simple snack bars, phones that accept Visa cards, and duty-free shops: buy now and collect your purchases as you board the plane. But why bother? Prices are no cheaper than in town.

Inquiries. The airport has a first-floor (second-floor for Americans) inquiry desk near Concourse E, open 0700-2300, with a telephone inquiry service through the night.

Hotel reservations. Two private companies offer to book your hotel room in Miami. Dial 1.800.683.3311 any time for CRS's service, 'the hotel of your choice anywhere in the USA,' or 1.800.356.8392 for Hata USA's service, 'hotels, autos, tours, cruises,' in Miami. Both numbers are toll-free but the hotels will be in the upper price range.

Heliport. A helicopter shuttle operates between Miami International and Opa-locka Airport a few miles to the north, with 12 daily flights between 0945 and 1845. You'll need to take surface transport (or charter a helicopter) to transfer to Chalk's International Airways' base.

Airport buses. The airport terminal is on NW 42nd Ave, also called Le Jeune Rd, and is served by three Dade County bus routes: **route 7** goes to the city centre, 'downtown Miami,' where it connects with the Metrorail (see Chapter 7), but services are up to an hour apart even at peak times. **Route 37** runs north-south, and 1 goes to Kendall.

In 1989 another bus service, the **Tri-Rail Shuttle,** began operations, linking the airport with the Three Counties Rail station, but it's scheduled for commuters rather than airline passengers: again, see Chapter 7.

Taxis. Airport taxis will take you to local hotels or as far as Fort Lauderdale, but choose the right taxi: **red** top for long distance, **blue** top for short runs.

There's short-term car parking opposite the terminal at $1 an hour.

ORLANDO AIRPORT

Orlando Airport, ORL on your baggage labels, is the gateway to central Florida's fun parks and is suitably smart. It's also on two floors, linked by lifts and elevators. Smaller and less busy than Miami it has exactly the same amenities.

Getting to town. The larger car hire companies have offices on the premises, and the smaller firms will come and collect you – so will the smart hotels – but if you're relying on public transport to get into town 10 miles away, you may have delays. Airport Limousine Service runs minibuses and American Sightseeing Tours has full-size buses into town, both at all the major hotels, so you'll have no trouble catching the bus back to the airport.

Taxi. Or there's a Yellow Cab, for which you'll pay $15 fare per person.

TAMPA AIRPORT

Tampa, designated TPA, with its entrance on Boyscout Blv, is a tourist attraction in its own right. Passengers glide around the terminal on moving walkways past exhibits of modern art, as if on the gentlest of fairground rides. Baggage carousels are on the ground floor close to the exit, from where you catch the car hire company's courtesy bus or the public bus into town – unless you're staying at the Marriott Hotel right next to the terminal.

Buses. Bus route 30 takes you from the airport to the town centre, with the options of taking a Yellow Cab or travelling in style with one of the 'limo' services.

7: TRAVELLING IN FLORIDA

The automotive society

CAR HIRE IS CHEAPER IN FLORIDA than anywhere else in the USA. And while Florida's rail network is probably the best of any of the 50 states, it is dreadfully poor compared with European railways: America is too dependent upon the automobile, and Congress may try to slap a 50¢-a-gallon tax on petrol to urge people back onto the public transport that no longer exists.

In the meantime, if you're travelling around this state, or any other, you have little choice but to hire a car — rent an auto as the Americans say. *This book assumes that will be your means of transport.*

AUTOMOBILE RENTAL

The law. The minimum age for holding a 'drivers license' in Florida is 16; the minimum age for hiring a car is 18 for women and 21 for men, but some rental companies insist on 25 years for both sexes for direct bookings. If you're younger than 25, find your rental company before you reach the States, or take a fly-drive package.

Alcohol. It's against Florida state laws to carry an opened container of alcohol in the main body of the car; the half-empty beer can and the uncorked wine must travel in the boot. The minimum age for drinking alcohol in public is 21, by the way.

Any of the police forces may stop you if you're showing signs of being drunk. If an analysis of your breath shows more than 0.5% of alcohol the charge will be DWI, driving while intoxicated; less than 0.5% but traceable, the charge will be DUI, driving under the influence. Blood samples are not taken.

The penalty for a DWI conviction depends upon the circumstances but could reach a year in prison and $1,000 fine. The lesson is obvious: *don't do it.*

Seat belts. As you would expect, driver and front-seat passengers must wear seat belts. Children younger than six must also be strapped in, using special restraints if necessary. And rear-seat passengers must also wear belts if they're fitted to the car.

Speed limits. The nationwide speed limit on ordinary roads is 55mph (88.5kph). Florida allows 65mph (105kph) on certain stretches of its expressways (see later), which also have a *minimum* speed limit of 40mph (64.5kph). Throughout the state, speed limits are adequately posted at the roadside, with slower limits imposed on bends and the occasional hilltop. The official claim is that the speed limit is rigorously enforced but in practise there are countless violations all the time, but speedsters risk a $4 on the spot fine for every mile-per-hour in excess of the limit.

Traffic lights. Florida is one of many states which allow motorists in the right lane to turn right at traffic lights, even when they are at red, provided that the driver has stopped and gives way to all other traffic, including pedestrians on a crossing. The only exception to this manoeuvre is when a sign forbids it.

School buses. Florida law also demands that all traffic in both directions stops when a school bus — that distinctive yellow vehicle seen in so many American films — is loading or unloading.

Hitch-hiking. You're officially advised not to pick up hitch-hikers: do you want to be hi-jacked or sued for negligence?

Petrol. Your hired car will run on unleaded petrol, available in three grades, 'regular unleaded,' RU, 'plus unleaded,' PU, and 'super unleaded,' SU, at prices ranging from around 82¢ to $1.10 a gallon. Prices vary locally, and are highest of all in the Keys. Some gas stations charge more for 'full serve' than 'self-serve,' and some give 4¢ a gallon discount for cash. Don't forget that the US gallon is smaller than the Imperial one.

Renting your auto. Hiring a car is cheap. It's the extras that cost the money, such as Collision Damage Waiver, CDW, which buys you exemption from having to pay for any damage to the car. The rental agreement states 'CDW is not insurance,' and it's certainly not compulsory.

But Personal Accident Insurance, PAI, is compulsory, and is defined in the contract's small print in ponderous tones: *"Lessor shall provide an automobile liability insurance policy"* but *"said insurance DOES NOT provide coverage to Customer for injury to or death of Customer or any guest or passenger of Customer."* In short, PAI is not what its name implies. It doesn't insure you, nor your passenger — nor any litigation-minded hitch-hiker who may break his neck as he accepts the offer of a free lift.

You may be offered something on these lines: hire of small car, $21.95 per day, $84.95 per week (minimum of 5 days). Go for the weekly rate.

Hire of car per week:	$85.00
CDW at $10.95 per day:	$76.65
PAI at $2.95 per day:	$20.65
Total:	$182.30

This is converted to an all-in deal at $139 a week. When you think about it, it's obvious that the rental company is also making a considerable profit on the CDW and PAI.

Finer points. With most agreements, husband and wife may both drive, but almost all contracts stipulate that you may not take the car out of the state as this would invalidate the insurance. Crossing state lines comes as an extra, as does leaving the car in another city — for all but Alamo Rentals. And finally, the agreement starts the moment you sign the contract.

Paying. Use your credit card to guarantee payment, though you don't leave the card itself. No card? Sorry — you'll have to pay the total cost in cash at the outset.

Learning the hard way. All rented automobiles (with a few noteworthy exceptions which will become apparent) are in factory condition, and expect the latest in gadgetry. Before you drive away, ask somebody to show you where the spare wheel and jack are hidden, how to get at the petrol tank, and how the headlights work. Be careful of central door-locking systems as you can lock your keys inside, and surely you don't like automatic seat belts that strap you in as you shut the door? I nearly strangled myself on one!

AUTOMOBILE RENTAL AGENCIES

There are innumerable agencies in Florida, each with something slightly different from all the others. Here is a small selection of those in the Miami and Orlando areas, but if you want others (or want to change your lessor), look in the telephone Yellow Pages, under 'A.'

In Miami: (⌀area code 305)

　Airways Rent-a-Car 3930 NW 25th St. ⌀871.3930.

　Ajax Rent-a-Car: 4121 NW 25th St ⌀871.5050.

　Alamo Rent-a-Car: 3355 NW 22th St ⌀633.6076.

　Alpha II Rent-a-Car: 2390 NW 39th Ave ⌀871.3432 or 1.800.330.2574.

　Avis Rent-a-Car: Office at airport ⌀526.3200.

　Budget Rent-a-Car: Office at airport ⌀871.3053.

　Delta Auto Rental: 4120 NW 26th St ⌀871.4224.

　Dollar Rent-a-Car: Office at airport, depot at 1770 NW Le Jeune Rd ⌀887.6000.

　Express Rent-a-Car: 1250 NW 57th Ave ⌀266.3266.

　General Rent-a-Car: 1640 NW Le Jeune Rd ⌀871.3535.

　Hertz Rent-a-Car: Office at airport ⌀871.0300 or 1.800.654.3131.

　Interamerican Car Rental:: 1790 NW Le Jeune Rd ⌀ 871.3030.

　Miami Rent-a-Car: 4120 NW 25th St ⌀871.8383.

　Pass Rent-a-Car: 3970 NW 25th St ⌀871.6262.

　Thrifty Car Rental:: 2701 NW Le Jeune Rd ⌀ 871.2277.

　Value Rent-a-Car: Office at airport, depot at 2875 NW Le Jeune Rd ⌀871.6760.

The depots are concentrated to the north-east of the airport and you can walk around to get the best bargain. Or try Rent-a- Dent on 871.8383.

In Orlando: (∅area code 407)

Al Rent-a-Car: 5309 McCoy Rd ∅851.6910.

Alamo Rent-a-Car: 8200 McCoy Rd ∅855.0210 or 1.800.327.9633.

Budget Rent-a-Car: Office in airport and 10 offices in town; downtown is 1029 N Orange Ave ∅422.1526 or 1.800.527.0700.

Classy Chassie's Rent-a-Car: 760 W State Rd ∅767.2984 (hourly rental available).

Lindo's Rent-a-Car: 5300 S Orange Blossom Trail ∅ 855.0282.

Superior Rent-a-Car: Sandlake Rd – International Drive ∅857.2023.

Thrifty Rent-a-Car: call from airport ∅859.6990.

Ugly Duckling Rent-a-Car: call from airport (Orlando) ∅423.8626 or 1001 Dyer Blv, Kissimmee 847.5599

The phone book lists another 60 rental companies in Orlando.

UNDERSTANDING ROADS and STREETS

For the uninitiated, the USA's system of marking and classifying its roads is very complex. The photomontage shows, left to right:

US Highway. The US highways form the original road network, crossing state lines. They are designated 'US,' are toll-free and colour-coded. Thus all US Highway 1 signs are red, all US Highway 17 signs are yellow, etc. US 1, by the way, runs from the Canadian border in Maine to Key West, Florida. *Note the shape of the shield, used on maps and road signs.*

Interstate. The interstate roads form the newer network, bypassing towns and, as the name implies, crossing state lines. They are designated 'I' and are toll-free. Signs are on a blue ground with a red top. *Again, note the distinctive shape of the shield, used on maps and road signs.*

Toll roads. All Florida's toll roads have green signs. The photo shows a right turn ahead to get access to **Florida's Turnpike,** southbound.

State roads. All state roads in Florida carry this distinctive silhouette with black figures on a white ground. The designation is 'SR' and maps use a circular or oval symbol.

In addition, there are **county roads** designated 'CR' but carrying only tiny signs such as you see used for street names. Some maps use pentagonal symbols for CRs.

Parkway, expressway. All toll roads are named, and some are also classified as state or interstate roads. A **Parkway** is supposedly closed to heavy lorries, and an **Expressway** has a minimum speed limit, usually 40mph, with its maximum occasionally increased to 65mph.

Florida's road signs explained: see 'Understanding roads and streets.'

Toll roads in the state are the 318-mile **Turnpike;** the 8-mile **Airport,** the **Palmetto,** the **North- South,** the **East-West,** and the 9-mile **Dolphin,** all expressways in Miami; the 22-mile **Sawgrass Expressway** by Boca Raton; **Alligator Alley,** the Everglades Parkway across the Everglades, 78 miles long and which is also classed SR-84 and I-75; the **Sunshine Skyway,** a toll bridge across Tampa Bay; the **South Crosstown Expressway,** 17 miles long in Tampa city; the **Beeline Expressway,** from near Walt Disney World to Cape Canaveral, 53 miles away; the 13-mile **Holland East-West Expressway** in Orlando; and the **Turner Butler Expressway** in Jacksonville.

Tolls range from a few cents to several dollars per vehicle, and on the longer routes you buy a few miles at a time.

Divided highway. We've still not finished with the roads. All interstate and toll roads are dual carriageways – divided highways in American English – throughout, while US and SR routes can range from divided highway almost to country lane standard.

East-West. All east-west routes have even-number classification; all north-south routes therefore have uneven numbers: check the photos.

Streets. It's the same in Miami. All **streets** run east-west, all **avenues** run north-south. Several other cities have the same idea, but in St Petersburg the system is reversed.

BUY YOUR CAR

If you're staying in the USA for more than a month you might consider the option of buying a car. The vast majority of 'pre- owned' cars on the market are scarcely distinguishable from new to the untrained eye, and prices start at $5,000, but if you shop around you'll find the occasional used-car lot with perfectly presentable models from $500. At this sort of price you can afford to dispense with CDW, leaving only PAI as a legal requirement. And you'll get something for the car when you sell it. Obviously, make absolutely certain the auto is mechanically sound and the paperwork is in order.

RENT A CAMPER VAN

Camper vans, now known as recreational vehicles or RVs, are notoriously expensive to hire independently, a Class 'A' RV — a palace in a bus — costing $800 a week and $300 a weekend; but these things cost from $70,000 to $220,000 to buy new. Class 'B' RVs are large vans with walk-through access, and Class 'C' are smaller vans with separate cab.

The B or C class RV is still expensive, but you can consider renting one independently in the Orlando area. Try:

Cruise America RV Rentals: 5301 McCoy Rd ✆857.8282.
Holiday RV Rental: 5001 Sand Lake Rd ✆351.3252.
U-Haul: 4001 E Colonial Drive ✆894.6011.

Or contact one of the **tour operators** offering RVs, *but note that some of them don't make flight arrangements.*

Cruise America (above) also buys used RVs. And that's another option for a large party travelling the States for a long while. Buy a new RV; when you've done with it, sell it to a leasing company who'll rent it out for two years, splitting the profit. But go into the figures very carefully at the outset.

PUBLIC TRANSPORT
In Miami

Miami has by far the best public transport in Florida. From Florida City in the south, to Broward County in the north, the 2,000 square miles of Greater Miami has three overlapping public transport systems.

Its **Metrobuses** run on four networks; north—south along the avenues; east—west along the streets; from downtown to the main suburbs; and serving Miami Beach. For a detailed route map ring Metro—Dade Transit Information on ✆638.6137. Route 7, which serves Miami Airport and the downtown area, is the one that tourists find more useful.

Metrorail is an overhead railway running from Kendall in the south, beside US—1 to the city centre and then zigzagging north—west to Hialeah. Metrorail has a baby brother, the **Metromover,** running on a circular route in the city centre, linking with Metrorail and the main bus terminal.

And finally there is **Tri-Rail,** the Three Counties Rail or TCR line, named from Dade, Broward and Palm Beach counties and which came into service in 1989. TCR runs from Miami Airport station (near, but not at the airport) to West Palm Beach.

Fares and schedules. The system is geared towards the commuter, with Tri-Rail running just nine times a day in each direction, from 0515 to 1910, with nothing from 0915 to 1550. Tri-Rail's one-way fare is $2 to any station; Metrobus and Metrorail cost $1.

Other cities. Other cities have their own Transit Authority buses offering basic commuter services which are of virtually no use to the tourist—which is why you hired a car.

AMTRAK

The United States once had a splendid railroad system. And then came Henry Ford and his fellow car makers. By the 1960s the famous railroads were all going bankrupt, and in 1971 Congress gathered the pieces and created Amtrak, the government-owned passenger network which operates on track still owned by other authorities. It's a ghost of what used to be.

In fact, there is no Amtrak service at all in Wyoming, South Dakota, Oklahoma and Maine, and the national schedule fits into 66 pages. Florida's entire passenger train network is so tiny that I quote it here in full, more for interest than practicality.

	The Silver Star		The Silver Meteor		The Silver Meteor		The Silver Star	
Jackonsville	0455	0455	1008	1008	1710	1710	0058	0055
Palatka	0601	↓	1112	↓	↑	1545	↑	2340
Daytona Beach	0649	↓	1158	↓	↑	1458	↑	2253
Sanford	0711	↓	1219	↓	↑	1438	↑	2233
Winter Park	0733	↓	1245	↓	↑	1415	↑	2209
Orlando	0804	↓	1315	↓	↑	1400	↑	2153
Kissimmee	0825	↓	1335	↓	↑	1324	↑	2122
Lakeland	0909	↓	1443	↓	↑	1214	↑	2040
Tampa	0952	↓	1532	↓	↑	1142	↑	2008
Gainesville	--	0534		↓	↑	2342	--	
Ocala	--	0619	--	↓	↑	--	2255	--
Wildwood	--	0644	--	↓	↑	--	2230	--
Cypress Gdns	--	0808	--	1441	1212	--	2107	--
Sebring	--	0846	--	1519	1133	--	2028	--
Okeechobee	--	↓	--	1554	1056	--	↑	--
West Palm Beach	--	1017	--	1650	1004	--	1905	--
Delray Beach	--	↓	--	1711	0940	--	↑	--
Boca Raton	--	1049	--	1725	0926	--	1836	--
Ft Lauderdale	--	1106	--	1742	0908	--	1820	--
Hollywood	--	1119	--	1755	0854	--	1808	--
Miami	--	1158	--	1843	0834	--	1749	--

Yes, it means that only two trains a day arrive and depart from Miami! Both start at Boston (MA) and go through New York before splitting at Jacksonville for the twin destinations of Tampa and Miami. In addition, The Palmetto from Boston terminates at Jacksonville, and there's an Auto Train (travel by train with your car) between Lorton (VA) and Sanford.

Sample fares? Miami-Jacksonville single, $67; round trip $88. Miami-New York, 1st class sleeper, round trip, $503.

Railpass. Or you can buy a USA Railpass for 14, 21 or 28 days' unlimited travel in the USA. This is available only to foreign visitors through their travel agents or exceptionally at certain Amtrak offices, including Miami.

And the lesson to be learned from a poor rail service? Avoid getting caught in the morning and evening rush hour road traffic around the cities, particularly in the Miami–West Palm Beach conglomerate.

GREYHOUND

The USA's bus network, epitomised by Greyhound, the market leader, is better than its railways. Greyhound began as the Jitney Line in Minnesota in 1914, took its present name in 1926, and now dominates the bus market in the USA, Canada, Australia and New Zealand.

It has an extensive network in Florida, and reaches down to Key West three times a day through a franchise-holder. Routes serve Walt Disney World from Jacksonville and Miami, allowing several hours sightseeing, and there are through routes from Miami to Los Angeles, Detroit and New York. Timetables are too complex to reproduce here but copies are available from Greyhound International, 14-16 Cockspur St, London SW1Y 5BL, ✆01.(071).839.5591.

Ameripass. Contact Greyhound's London office if you want an Ameripass, allowing you unlimited travel on Greyhound routes in the USA for a set time. The 1989 rates are £80 for 7 days, £125 for 15 days and £180 for 30 days. It's worth noting that the company is now in the package holiday business, operated from this London address.

HITCH-HIKING

It bears repeating that hitch-hiking can no longer be considered an acceptable way of travelling in the USA. It is illegal on all toll roads and several freeways, banned in many cities and throughout the Florida Keys, and frowned upon everywhere else. Read Chapter 11 and learn why you shouldn't stop for anybody.

8: EATING, SLEEPING, WINING, DINING

Have a nice day!

PART OF THE ATTRACTION OF A VISIT TO FLORIDA is to experience the American lifestyle, familiar around the world thanks to cinema and television. But what exactly *is* a motel, a deli, or a drugstore? More to the point — what is the cost of living?

EATING

These are sample retail prices (taxes apply only on the last three items) of typical supermarket foods and other commodities, taken in 1989. Bulk buying is common.

All the comforts of home? The Okeechobee Inn even has a Gideon Bible.

Tomato catsup (ketchup), 7lb $3.69
Mustard, 1 gallon (3.79 liter) $3.39
Dill pickles, 1 gallon $4.09
Mozerella cheese, ½lb $1.69
Meat: boiled ham, lb (453gm) $2.59
– beef steak, 1lb $2.49
– chuck steak, 1lb $1.15
– oven-ready chicken, per lb .... 79¢
– Libby's corned beef, 340gm $1.99
Coffee: Nescafé classic (instant), 2oz (57gm) $1.69
– Maxwell House 26oz (not a misprint) $4.95
Evaporated goat milk, 12.5fl.oz (369ml) $1.77
– cow milk, same size .... 55¢
Preserves, etc: pancake and waffle syrup, 24 fl.oz .... 99¢
Kraft brand jams, 10oz (283.5gm) $1.25
– marmalade, 10oz .... 93¢
– guava jelly, 10oz $1.15
Rose's lime marmalade (made USA), 1lb $2.69
grape jelly, 2lb $1.19
Chocolates: Cadbury's Krisp, 5oz $1.19
Nestlé Crunch, 5oz $1.19
Chocolate chip cookies, 9oz (255gm) $1.39
Wrigley's gum, 50 pieces $1.19
Wines, spirits, etc: Grant's whisky, 1 liter $12.29
Gordon's gin, 1.75 liter $16.75
Budweiser beer, 4 x 12fl.oz cans $3.37
Le Domaine, Californian champagne, brut, 750ml $3.99
Portuguese blush, 750ml $3.99
German Schwartze Katze, white, 750ml $4.69
Perrier water (French), 28fl.oz .... 89¢
demineralised drinking water, gallon .... 59¢–85¢
soft drinks: root beer, sodas (in supermarket), 1 liter .... 89¢
Cigarettes, American brands, 100-pack .... $12–$12.49
Fruit: U-pick strawberries, per 1lb $1.50
– tomatoes, U-pick, per 1lb .... 25¢
– – in shop, 1lb .... 50¢–75¢
Miscellaneous: men's Bermuda shorts .... $10–$15
men's training shoes, good .... $5–$7
Kodacolour gold 35mm film, 36 exp $5.50
National minimum rate of pay for adult, per hour *$3.35*
Truck driver, per hour, in Florida only .... *$5.75–$7.00*
Fully qualified aircraft mechanic, per week, in Florida .... *to $1,400.*

Daily bread. Do you remember the bread that grandma used to bake? Crusty, with that mouthwatering flavour? You'll not find its like in Florida. The best bread I know of comes from Croissants de France in Duval St, Key West (closed on Wednesday), where there's always a queue of customers. You'll find tolerable bread at the Publix, Winn-Dixie, and Kash 'n Karry supermarkets, and at Chefs de France in 'France' in the World Showcase at Epcot Center, but after that it's sliced white sponge-rubber masquerading as bread.

SLEEPING

Accommodation in Florida is understandably dearer than in Mediterranean holiday areas and is the major item on the independent traveller's budget. But your choice is vast: for example, there are more than 800 hotels and motels listed by the Greater Miami Chamber of Commerce, and scores of others unlisted. Despite that, motels tend to cluster and it's possible to travel 50 miles without seeing one.

Motels

The independent traveller, European or American, favours the motels, particularly for one-night stops.

Prices. Prices start at $20 *per bungalow* with the high-season south Florida tariff averaging $35 on the mainland and $45 on the islands. There are seldom any discounts for single occupancy in bungalows with sleeping for two, but you may find a slight discount when two people share a double bed in a bungalow with sleeping for four.

There's a wide fluctuation in pricing. In the Panhandle in winter you'll find $20 the average — but this is low season; it rises to around $35 in summer. In central Florida, away from the main attractions, there are the odd $20 high-season bargains, but prices respond very quickly to demand: between Daytona Beach and St Augustine $50 is the asking figure during the Daytona 500 race meeting. The Keys are the most expensive, the priciest motel I know of being in Key West — at $99. This is steep, considering that few motels offer food of any kind, and when they do it's a simple continental snack — and that means *European* continental.

Quality. Price has no bearing on quality. Standards range from tatty, with rags nailed at the windows, to 'squeaky clean' with bedside telephone and multi-channel TV. An example is in south Miami where the Kent Motel, the first one out of town on US-1, is a $40 disaster — but at nearby Homestead on SR-997 the Grove Motel is $25-worth of English-run charm with the feminine touch. The ethnic minorities are taking over the Miami motels and, sadly, prices are rising while quality declines.

One to top the bill? The Okeechobee Inn at South Bay, near the lake.

Efficiency. On the string of islands which fringe Florida, such as Miami Beach, Palm Beach, Daytona Beach, Treasure Island and

Sanibel Island, and to a lesser degree on the Florida Keys, motels have become 'efficiencies,' offering self-catering chalets on weekly rentals ranging from $300 to $500 and upward, and sleeping four. These places are not interested in one-night customers and are usually booked up several weeks ahead in high season.

If this is the type of accommodation that interests you, and at $100 a week per person it's quite a bargain, you *must* make a reservation from home through the appropriate chamber of commerce: refer to the addresses in Chapter 4 or contact the Florida Division of Tourism for a complete list. I am assured that the chambers inspect all the premises they recommend, and you won't find yourself in a disaster area.

Checking times. Under normal circumstances, start looking for a motel by 1700; at 1800 motel managers cancel all no-show bookings but they could already be flashing 'no' in front of the 'vacancies' sign and you may have to pay more than you budget or sleep in the car. Checking-out time is almost always 1100.

Motel hide-and-seek. Motels are like sheep: they gather in flocks. If you can't find any on the Interstate or the US highway, try the next off-the-road city. In St Augustine they're on St Augustine Beach; in Miami, on the Tamiami Trail; in Tampa, on Hillsborough Ave; in the Orlando area, try US-192 between Walt Disney World and Kissimmee but be prepared to pay more, or try the two by Clermont's Citrus Tower and book ahead for as long as you're staying in the district.

Hotels

Hotels are inevitably more expensive than motels, and you won't find any filthy ones, but otherwise my motel comments apply to hotels; some offer efficiencies and some are even into timeshare.

In addition to the chambers of commerce, you could contact the Florida Hotel & Motel Association (address in 'other contacts,' Chapter 4) for a list of its 800 members. A dollar bill would be appreciated for postage.

Stargazing? Hoteliers fix their own rates, responding to market pressure; there is no state authority which dictates prices. Nor is there any system of grading hotels and awarding them star ratings.

And others

Hotels, motels and RVs don't have the market to themselves. For longer-term rentals you could move into a **condominium:** ask the chamber of commerce for likely lessors. The **Bed 'n Breakfast** company and **Grandma Newton** run chains of bed-and-large-breakfast guest houses charging from $35 to $75 a room, and for the filthy rich there are **houseboats.** Sample contacts are Miller's Suwannee Houseboating, PO Box 280, Suwannee, FL 32962 and Flamingo Lodge Outpost Resort, Everglades National Park, PO Box

428, Flamingo, FL 33030.

And finally, there's **camping.** Camping on the roadside is banned (has anybody checked on the RVs that park overnight on the Overseas Highway?), but your Florida state map marks plenty of accredited sites, particularly in the Keys, the Everglades, Ocala National Forest and near the quieter beaches. You can even camp in Walt Disney World! Most sites have toilet blocks and some even have entertainment.

There are several camping organisations but the best-known is KOA, Kampgrounds of America, at PO Box 30558, Billings, Montata 59114.

WINING and DINING

Fast food. America is the land of the fast-food diner, where Grandy's, Wendy's, McDonald's, Kentucky Fried Chicken, Burger King, Denny's, Pizza Hut and many other franchised eateries compete in a vast market.

The 'Oldest House' in Key West looks quite new; it now doubles as the Wreckers' Museum.

Most fast-food firms in Florida pay the legal minimum wage of $3.35 an hour (they can get a $1.50 an hour grant for each black person employed at this wage), and many are open 18 hours out of 24, yet the staff are invariably courteous. "Have a nice day!" has a ring of sincerity.

Choose from drive-thru, dine-in or carry-out. Come at six in the morning or midnight. You'll find prices are low, food is plentiful and coffee is there on tap — but the nutritional value is questionable. Does the fast-food habit explain why so many Americans of all ages have enormous bellies?

Restaurants. You need to go to a restaurant for a meal in which the steak and chicken are recognisable, nothing has been in the freezer, and prices are still comfortably low — but take heed that there are some very expensive restaurants, notably in Palm Beach. These single-portion tasters are taken from several family-priced restaurant menus in the Orlando area:

__Starters__ Bucket of steamed mussels with butter, white wine, garlic $4.95

Langostinos (Chilean lobsters) with butter and garlic $4.95

__Soups__ Clam chowder, by the bowl $2.75

__Main course__ Stuffed chicken (marinated in sesame oil, with garlic and ginger) $11.95

Spaghetti with meat balls $5.50

Filet mignon, king cut $17.95

Pork chops (two 1½ inch chops) $13.95

__Dessert__ Key lime pie $2.75

Black Forest gateau $2.25

To which, of course, you must add the relevant taxes.

Early bird. Many restaurants chase early-evening diners by offering Early Bird meals at up to 50% cheaper, provided you are seated by a given time, usually 1800 or 1830. You're normally offered the standard menu but occasionally you'll find early birders choosing from a slightly different menu.

Key lime pie. You cannot spend long in Florida without realising that key lime pie is the state dish, more popular that blueberry pie. So here's one version of the recipe:

Take 4 eggs, separated, ½ cup lime juice, 14oz (400gm) can of sweet condensed milk, ½ teaspoon cream of tartar, and ⅓ cup sugar.

Beat yolks until thick, blend in lime juice and milk, stirring until thick. Pour into pre-baked pie case. Beat egg-white and cream of tartar until stiff, add sugar slowly, beat until glossy. Spread on previous filling, bake at 350°F until brown. Chill before serving.

If it sounds like lemon meringue, I'm not surprised. But it's delicious!

9: NIGHTLIFE
And luxury mini-cruises

FLORIDA LACKS ONLY ONE FEATURE to make it a rival for top spot on the nightlife circuit of the Atlantic seaboard: it doesn't have a dry-land casino. If it's roulette and vingt-et-un you want, your options are to go to Freeport or Nassau in the Bahamas or to take a cruise — or put the two together and cruise to the Bahamas.

SeaEscape. SeaEscape, Ltd ('Ltd,' not 'Inc,' as the company and its ships are registered in the Bahamas) offers a Frivolous Friday cruise from Port Canaveral and a Saturday Sampler from Fort Lauderdale, sailing with the sunset and docking in the small hours, with a dinner-dance at sea. Or you can go to sea for the day, sailing in late morning and coming back before dusk, from Canaveral, Lauderdale or Tampa; your ticket says 'Destination - nowhere.'

Or you can SeaEscape to the Bahamas for a day from Miami, trying the on-ship and the Bahamian casinos. Fares in 1988 started at $99 per person, all-in, but if this is for you shop around for a discount voucher before you book. ✆1.800.432.4055 when you get to Florida.

Chandris Line. The Chandris Fantasy Cruises from Miami aboard *Britanis* or *Galileo* take you on two-night weekend cruises to Nassau, the Bahamian capital, with a full programme of wining, dining, gambling or whatever else takes your fancy: winter 1988-89 fares ranged from $189 to $340, per person. And from Monday to Friday you can cruise Chandris to Mexico — or back to the Bahamas. ✆ from Dade County only, 984.8954, or ask your travel agent before you leave home.

Land-based nightlife. Nightlife is where you find it — and there's plenty to find in Florida. Stay on in Disney's Magic Kingdom after sunset and the whole place takes on a fairytale atmosphere, even if you're only seeing the lights.

Back in the real world of Orlando and Kissimmee you can easily return to fantasy of another sort at **Medieval Times** or **King Henry's Feast** as knights in armour joust while you dine. Or try the **Arabian Nights** experience at Kissimmee, where Roman chariots and Arab stallions put on a splendid dinner- show: fuller details of these and other spectaculars are given in the appropriate chapters when you 'discover Florida.'

In Miami and Miami Beach there are nightclubs of more conventional appeal, offering scantily-clad dancers in glitzy settings, and in winter the occasional appearance of a star from showbiz, with tickets costing up to $200. Hotel and motel receptions here and throughout the state have handbills with the latest information.

Blast off! Atlantis is launched in 1985;
Enterprise sits beside a Saturn V rocket
* — NASA photo.*

10: MOVING IN?

The Florida room

FLORIDA IS AMERICA'S PLAYGROUND, and there's no reason why it shouldn't be Europe's playground as well. Transatlantic air fares are down to an acceptable level even without Virgin's standby ticket, and with your US tourist visa granting you a six-month stay, Florida could be your winter home.

Surprisingly, you needn't be a millionaire to buy a decent bungalow in the Sunshine State. Although some of the smartest properties in Palm Beach, the most exclusive city, cost $3,000,000 or more - Burt Reynolds is one of the residents - you can buy four walls and a roof in any price range. Look at these examples from realtors' advertising handouts:

South Apopka. 12ft x 60ft mobile home, 2 bedrooms, 1 bath, ready to move in, furnished. Utility shed with washer. $7,000 negotiable - only 10 miles from Orlando. There are thousands of caravans and mobile homes used as permanent dwellings.

Excellent buy! This 3-bedroom home outside city limits. ½ acre lot. New roof in '87. Heat pump installed. Fireplace in family room. Call today! $35,000 – a timber-frame bungalow at Wildwood, 50 miles from Orlando.

Cute! That's the word for this well-kept 3 bedroom home in SE Orlando. Owner has spent the last 2 years renovating this charmer. Central heat and air is only 1 yr old. Access to airport and major highways. Quick sale priced at $54.900 – another smart timber-framed bungalow.

Four-bedroom waterfront plus! Seawall. Florida room, living room, family room and office (or 5th bedroom), all in a blue-water $150K neighborhood. Reduced to $114,500 – an immaculate brick bungalow at Homosassa Springs.

Floridians consider elegant Naples to be one of the smartest and most exclusive cities in the state, yet:

Casa Bonita. Enjoy spectacular sunsets from this 6th floor Gulf-front condo. Tastefully decorated with ceramic tile and mirrored walls. $134,900 furnished.

It's only when you reach the Florida Keys that average prices are really high, and rising the further west you go:

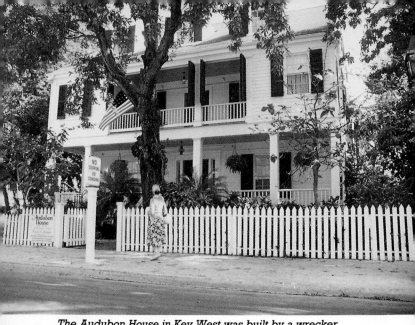

The Audubon House in Key West was built by a wrecker.

Landmark Bahama colonial, built 1866 on large lot, dramatically remodeled with pool, roof decks, cathedral ceilings, indoor fountain and privacy. Recently drastically reduced to $274,900 – one of the beautiful colonial timber-frame houses in Key West.

Tropical secluded estate on approx 3.06 acres. 3 bdrm 3½ bath perched above the lush vegetation with wonderful water view. Shared private road and pier. $639,000 – a new brick-built property in Key West.

Florida is cheap by American as well as European standards, but it is not the cheapest state. For a fairer comparison, early in 1989 the average price of a house in the USA was $135,000, which certainly puts Florida in the bargain basement.

11: MIAMI VICE

But where is it?

MIAMI IS THE WORLD'S LARGEST IMPORTER of illegal drugs, though obviously there are no trade figures available. West Palm Beach has the highest crime rate in the USA of cities of comparable size. The USA has temporarily banned the import of AK47 Kalashnikovs because crooks are outgunning the police.

These facts show that the USA has a very serious level of crime, and Florida has its share: indeed, it has far more than its share of the drugs trade.

You, the visitor, will probably be warned of these points:

● Lock your car doors and windows when driving in cities to avoid a gunman jumping aboard at the traffic lights.

● Don't park in the Miami backstreets, particularly in the Liberty City and Overtown areas. Better still don't visit these areas.

● Don't sound your horn at another motorist in case you anger him and he shoots you with the gun he always carries in his car.

● Make certain you collect the carbons after every credit card purchase, as your signature can be forged.

● Don't linger in seldom-used restrooms, and don't go alone into a restroom that looks small: you could be walking into an ambush.

● Don't pick up hitch-hikers. If anybody waves you down on the road, don't stop under any circumstances.

● Don't resist when you're attacked.

● Don't walk down dark alleys at night. If you're a woman, don't go out at night on your own.

In addition, you may hear stories of motel owners being robbed at gunpoint, of children breaking into a locked car, bypassing the ignition and driving away, within seven seconds. There are the newsworthy crimes such as the audacious theft of a timber- frame house which was lifted onto a trailer and towed away, and poisonous snakes stolen from a zoo — and certainly the television and press will keep you up to date on the latest rape, murder, and kidnapping, as well as the occasional titbit such as "woman's knee joint found in creek."

The warnings are valid and the stories are true, but after a week or so you may begin asking: "If there's all this crime around, why don't I see any of it?"

What you *will* see, instead, is young women driving alone in open sports cars, young men collecting for charity from motorists at traffic lights, men with rolls of dollar bills protruding from their hip pockets, bank tellers (clerks) with thousands of dollars in their tills and not a security screen in sight (true, there's closed-circuit TV), and women walking alone after dark − but *not in the large cities.*

Neighborhood Watch. You'll also see isolated bungalows with six-foot high chain link fencing and two guard dogs − but down the road and out of sight of any bungalow there'll be a cluster of mailboxes with their flags up, advertising that the mailman has delivered. Are there any checks (cheques) in the post? In the smarter urban areas you'll see dozens of "Neighborhood Watch" signs − but you'll also see homes with the garage door left open, or the caravan ready to hitch up and tow away.

Petty crime. It's very difficult to reconcile these contrasting images of Florida, but all are true. It's even more difficult to come to terms with the natural friendliness of the American people who go out of their way to help anybody, visitor or native, and with this image of a nation on the brink of anarchy. There is a very high level of crime, but at the same time there is limitless scope for the criminal.

My advice, after discussing the point with those in authority, is to take note of the seven warnings given above − and any others you hear − and be on your guard. Certainly lock your car doors when driving at night in any large city, don't walk the streets after dark (this applies in Orlando as much as in Miami; if you're going out, take the car), don't invite crime; don't get careless, and you'll wonder what all the fuss is about.

Big-time crime. Organised crime is altogether different. You could live for years in Miami and not have a hint of the vast amounts of cocaine and crack that come in through the port. Miami Vice? It's a television show, after all.

12: FLORIDA'S WILDLIFE

In Mockingbird State

FLORIDA CAN OFFER SOME OF THE BEST WILDLIFE WATCHING in the United States, yet with conservation and hunting going on almost side-by-side.

The Everglades.

The Everglades National Park is the natural choice for watching wildlife, where you may be obliged to give way to a ten- foot alligator, and where the bird life includes child-high storks, and snake-birds drying their wings like laundry on the line. A full account of the park's wildlife is in the Everglades chapter.

The Florida Keys

Birds predominate in the Florida Keys, with 263 species having been sighted. As you drive down Overseas Highway you cannot fail to notice the thousands of brown pelicans perching on every convenient post and rail or plunging into the sea; the white pelican is rare in the state.

Wildlife Refuges. The magnificent frigatebird (that's its name, not my description) nests on the Marquesas Keys in the Key West National Wildlife Refuge and is an occasional winter resident. The male inflates its distinctive red throat pouch only during courtship.

The great blue heron and its all-white cousin can be seen in the mangrove swamps, standing up to 4ft 6in (130cm) tall, and they have a special haven in the Great White Heron National Wildlife Refuge, which embraces the smaller northern keys from Marathon to Key West.

Other breeding seabirds include the double-breasted cormorant, the little blue and the green heron, the white ibis and roseate spoonbill, the coot-like purple gallinule, and the black-necked stilt. The laughing gull breeds, but three other species are visitors. Ten tern species have been seen here, but only the roseate and the least tern have bred. Noteworthy visitors include the black skimmer which catches fish as it skims the waters.

Among egrets, the great, snowy, reddish and cattle species nest in the Keys, while the osprey, an endangered species in Scotland, is the common fish-eagle that nests on roadside pylons.

TV dinners. The greatest scavengers in Florida, not only on the Keys, are the black vulture and its close relative the turkey vulture. The red-headed turkey vulture or 'tv,' also known as the turkey buzzard, has a six-foot wingspan making it distinctive in flight, but it's often seen feeding on roadside carrion, having its 'tv dinner.'

Land birds on the Keys include the noisy and gregarious red-winged blackbird, and there are swallows, crows, wrens and thrushes similar to those found in Europe.

Bird books. *Birds,* by Zim and Gabrielson (Golden Press, NY, $3.95) is widely on sale in the Keys and Everglades and lists 129 birds of the USA. For more serious work try Peterson's *Eastern Birds,* (Houghton Mifflin, Boston, $12.95) which lists around 390 species of the eastern USA.

Animals. Few wild animals can compete with mankind for space on the Keys, but the endangered key deer have their own national refuge on Big Pine Key. A bridge leads to No Name Key, home to raccoons which may clamber over your parked car around dusk, hoping to be fed.

Central Florida.

Away from the Keys, 'coons and 'possums (opossums) are nocturnal feeders, more often seen on the roadside as yet more tv dinners. Would you believe there are still wild bears in Florida? Black bear from Ocala National Forest range into other lonely parts of the state — and in 1940 they outnumbered humans at Fort Walton Beach in the Panhandle.

Snakes. Florida has several species of poisonous snake: the coral, with distinctive red, yellow and black bands; the cottonmouth water moccasin; the eastern diamond-backed rattler; and the dusky pygmy rattler; as well as 22 species which are not poisonous. Add on a fair number of scorpions and you'll see why you shouldn't poke your hand into the undergrowth without giving its reptilian inhabitants a warning, but in practise it's highly unlikely you'll see any of the undesirables.

Alligators. Those large reptiles, the 'gators, now recovered from near-extermination, aren't confined to the Everglades; you can see them in freshwater creeks anywhere in the state, particularly around Cape Canaveral. The current population is estimated at 1,000,000 and the average adult male reaches 11ft; the longest on record was 19ft 2in (5.85m), found in Louisiana early this century. The female 'gator has strong maternal instincts and can therefore be very dangerous; respect her territory. And remember that while you can hold the reptile's mouth closed with one hand, you can't hold it open; the snap of the jaws exerts a final pressure of 4 tons per square inch.

Great white and great grey: two splendid herons.

The bald eagle, America's national bird, increases its population in Florida with an influx of winter visitors, but the state's resident bald eagles nest in several areas, always in tall trees. The nests are up to 12 feet (4m) across, and with the addition of living branches each year (the bird never uses deadwood) may eventually weight two tons; a medium-sized nest is one of the sights on the Kennedy Space Center tour. Your best chance of a casual sighting is in mid-state; the pair I saw were flying obligingly near Eagle Lake in Polk County.

Florida's state emblem, the northern mockingbird, is not easily seen but in flight is recognisable by large white patches on its wings and tail. You might hear the story of the contest held at Bok Tower in 1931 to decide whether the European nightingale or the mockingbird was the better singer. The nightingale sang first, but when the mockingbird mimicked its rival's song to perfection, it was declared the winner.

Insect life.

Few insects bother the winter visitor, but you need only look at the mosquito mesh fitted at every window to realise there's a major insect problem at some time in the year. Mosquitos — 67 species of them — swarm from spring to autumn. None carries disease, but many can make life irritable, particularly in the Everglades.

You'll not fail to notice the love-bugs that hatch in May and September and stick to everything, and in Miami and the Keys in high summer the householders have to cope with the twin plagues of the so-called termites which can eat a wooden windowframe from inside without damaging the paint, and the palmetto bugs, more truthfully known as giant cockroaches.

Spanish Moss.

Throughout Florida you'll see blue-grey strands several feet long hanging from the branches of trees. This is Spanish moss, an epiphyte which sometimes kills its host by overwhelming it. A legend claims that one Gorez Goz, a Spaniard, bought himself an Amerind maiden but she wouldn't have him. He chased her, following her up a tree from where she escaped — but he was trapped when his long beard caught in the branches. Spanish moss is, of course, his legacy.

The moss was used for stuffing furniture until plastic foam ousted it in the mid-1950s.

Marine life.

The Atlantic and Mexican Gulf waters have a wide range of marine life, including the unusual West Indian manatee, a slow- moving mammal, also known as the dugong and sea cow, which has no natural predator and so hasn't developed the ability to react to sudden danger. The result is that this creature, which is believed to have given rise to the legend of the mermaid, now suffers terrible wounds from propellers of speedboats.

The entire state of Florida is now a manatee sanctuary and boat drivers are under a legal obligation to reduce speed to 'no wake' in designated manatee habitats. If you find a dead or injured sea cow, call the Manatee Hot Line on 1.800.342.1821. Or you can join the Save The Manatee Club for $15 a year and adopt a sea cow; contact the club at 1101 Audubon Way, Maitland, FL 32751.

Manatees spend the winter in the warm-water outflow of power stations, and the summer around the Everglades and in the Banana River Aquatic Reserve between Canaveral Peninsula and Merritt Island. You can usually see them at any time of the year from the comfort of a glass-bottomed boat at Homosassa Springs. Their natural range? From Florida through the Caribbean to Brazil.

Turtles. Sea turtles live in the waters around Florida, the male spending his entire life in the ocean, the female coming ashore only to lay her eggs, by night, on some secluded beach. The young hatch by night eight weeks later and struggle downbeach to the sea, unless distracted by mankind's lights. It's illegal to catch turtles or to trade in anything made from turtle, and if you find a dead or injured one, call the Turtle Hotline on 1.800.432.6404.

A plea for the dolphin. So why does nobody want to know if you find a dead dolphin? If you glance through the brochures of sportfishing boat owners you'll see several offering 'dolphin fishing;' after the initial shock I learned that the prey is not mammalian, but the dolphin *fish*.

Conservation. I suppose that leads to the subject of conservation. Since 1953 it's been illegal to sell tarpon, since '55 you can't sell sailfish, and one by one striped bass, bonefish, marlin and spearfish have joined the list. The first protection for alligators came in 1939; key deer have been protected since '43; goose hunting was abolished in '69; and taking the Key West conch is now forbidden.

Sharks. The coral reefs and keys at the south of the state are home to several species of shark including the tiger, bull, barnet, lemon, nurse and hammerhead. Some of these have been known to attack humans but, despite what you saw in *Jaws,* they seldom do it off Florida. A bull shark bit a snorkeller on the leg in 1983 in the Lower Keys, but the staff at Key West Memorial Hospital, where he was treated, said it was the only instance they could remember.

If you prefer to look at the enemy from the safety of land, visit the Key West Aquarium, the Theatre of the Sea on Key Largo, Sea World near Orlando, or Ocean World at Ft Lauderdale.

Sharks don't have it all their own way. There are stories of fishermen out for tarpon, marlin (whose pointed snout gives us the 'marlinspike'), and swordfish who, on hooking a shark, have chopped off its fins and thrown the rest back to die. The grim evidence has been found on the sea bed in the form of finless sharks scavenging for debris.

Other hazards. There are several other offshore hazards. Barracuda are attracted by bright objects and have attacked divers' jewellery, and the surgeon fish has a scalpel- sharp tail fin. The manta ray is no menace, but its vast size can be daunting.

Walking catfish. Among the other giants of the Florida coasts are jewfish up to 600lb, as well as grouper, kingfish and sailfish, species which have helped make sport fishing extremely popular in these warm waters. And there are the exotics, such as rainbow parrot fish and pufferfish, and the conch which made Key West the capital of the Conch Republic. But that's another story . . . like the walking catfish which tried to invade the state a few years ago.

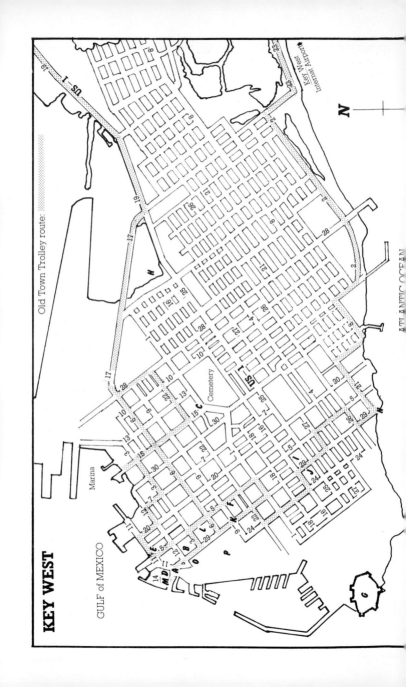

SOUTH FLORIDA:
The Snowbird Scene

13: THE FLORIDA KEYS

Paradise in Peril

THERE IS NOWHERE ELSE IN THE U.S.A. quite like the Florida Keys. I could go further: there is nowhere else in the *world* like the Keys. And there is nowere else in the Keys that is anything like Key West.

KEY WEST

Cayo Oueste or *Cayo Hueso*, 'Key West' or 'Key of Bones,' is what the original Spanish settlers called this outcrop of coral, probably

KEY TO KEY WEST STREETS

1 Angela St	2 Atlantic Blv
3 Caroline St	4 Catherine St
5 Duval St	6 Eaton St
7 Elizabeth St	8 Flagler Ave
9 Fleming St	10 Frances St
11 Front St	12 Greene St
13 Grinnell St	14 Mallory Sq
15 Margaret St	16 Olivia St
17 Palm Ave	18 Petronia St
19 Roosevelt Blv	20 Simonton St
21 South St	22 Southard St
23 South Roosevelt Blv	24 Thomas St
25 Truman Ave	26 United St
27 Virginia St	28 White St
29 Whitehead St	30 William St

KEY TO KEY WEST ATTRACTIONS

A Aquarium	*B* Audubon House
C Bottle Wall	*D* Chamber of Commerce
E Cigar Factory Museum	*F* Fast Buck Freddie
G Ft Zachary Taylor	*H* Glass-bottom boat quay
I Hemingway House	*J* Lighthouse & Museum
K Mile Marker Zero	*L* Oldest House Wreckers' Mus
M Old Town Trolley start	*N* Southernmost Point USA
O Spanish Galleon Treasure	*P* Truman's White Fouse

naming it from the grim remains of a fierce battle fought in the 18th cent by Amerinds (American Indians).

Pirates and wreckers. Pirates from the West Indies hid their ships in the channels around the Lower Keys late in the 18th cent, ready to sail out and attack any vessel that strayed too close.

Havana cigars. The first non-Indian people to settle on the islands themselves were Cubans, who brought the cigar industry in 1820. Soon Key West was the world's largest cigar producer, but fire destroyed the factories in 1870 and the islanders, now including many of English descent, were driven to the growing sponge-gathering industry which had begun in 1849. When that trade was poor, they had no hesitation in encouraging a few unwitting captains to sail too close to the reefs.

Annexation. The 'Island of Bones' was still nominally independent until piracy became such a scourge that the United States could ignore Key West no longer. On 7 February 1822 Lt Matthew Perry arrived aboard the US schooner *Shark* to survey the island and annexe it to the state of Florida: so its Spanish-born owner Juan Pablo Salas sold out to the American John Simonton for $2,000.

Now the USA could really show its strength. Later in the year it sent its West Indian anti-pirate fleet, under Commodore David Porter, to bring order to Key West. He attacked in 1823 with 1,100 men aboard 17 ships and brought the era of piracy to an end.

Salvagers. But the reefs were still a hazard to shipping, and law-abiding salvagers, still known as wreckers, made such a good living that they began building elegant frame houses from the timbers they rescued. Records from the 1840s and '50s show that the people of Key West had the highest standard of living in the USA, and many of their early houses are still standing as mute witness to those times. The enterprising William Curry who appointed himself merchant to the salvagers, became Florida's first dollar millionaire and paid $100,000 for a gold dinner service; his house is open to visitors.

Wreckers' Museum. If you hanker after a glimpse of the old days, call in at 322 Duval St between 1000 and 1600 for a guided tour of the Wreckers' Museum, also billed as the oldest house in Key West and dating from around 1829.

The lighthouses that were built from the late 19th cent made navigation much safer and brought a severe economic decline to Key West, still almost the only island in this coral chain that had been populated.

Conch. And so the people turned to fishing for the conch, pronounced 'konk,' an edible mollusc in a bright pink shell, growing up to a foot (30cm) long and living perhaps seven years in the wild: you can't spend more than an hour in Key West without seeing the shells on sale or hearing the word 'konk' in a score of contexts.

Conch Republic. The conch quickly became the trade mark and the symbol of Key West, and achieved international prominence in April 1982. On the 18th of that month the US Border Patrol put up a road block on US Highway 1 where it came ashore from the Keys, and for the first time in US history a part of the States was treated as foreign soil; people had to prove their identity and were searched before they could come onto continental USA.

At noon on 23rd April the citizens of Key West made their protest by declaring their island independent of the USA, calling it the Conch Republic, hoisting their own flag and naming their own ministers of state. The protest worked, the Border Patrol was recalled – but the Conch Republic remains, now yet another tourist attraction: for $3 you can buy miniature copies of the flag, showing a conch shell inside a sun on a blue ground, and with the legend 'Key West, 1828.'

Sadly, the conch is now an endangered species off the Keys and fishing for them is totally banned in state and federal waters. While restocking progresses, with 10,000 young released into the sea, the conch on your menu is imported, as are the conch shells on sale everywhere: try blowing in one to make your own foghorn.

Two-legged conchs. There's no shortage of conchs of another type: that's what people born in Key West call themselves. And if you manage to stay here for seven years you can call yourself a 'freshwater conch.'

Fort Zachary Taylor. But back in the 1830s, the USA decided to build martello towers at vulnerable points along its coast, much as England had done against the threat of Napoleon. Fort Zachary Taylor, at the south–west corner of Key West, was begun in 1850 and took 16 years to complete; it's now a Civil War Museum. Plain and simple martello towers followed on the south and south–east headlands; the east one is now an art gallery.

Fort Jefferson. In 1846 the federal government began work on the most ambitious of its chain of fortresses, Fort Jefferson, 68 miles (110km) west of Key West on the isolated Garden Key, and was still working on it 30 years later. The hexagonal fort has walls eight feet thick and 50 feet (15m) high and takes up almost the entire island yet still has a moat all around it, separated from the open sea by a breakwater.

It was built to garrison 1,500 men with 450 guns to protect the approaches to New Orleans, but was never used for defence, instead seeing service as a prison. Its most famous and pitiable inmate was Dr Samuel Mudd who received a life sentence for unwittingly setting the broken leg of John Wilkes Booth; Booth had injured the leg on 14 April 1865 when he assassinated Abraham Lincoln. Dr Mudd? He worked through an 1867 yellow fever outbreak and qualified for a pardon.

There's no problem in getting to this remote fort. The Key West

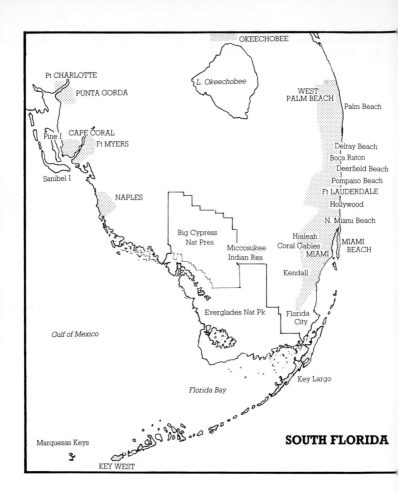

OKEECHOBEE

Pt CHARLOTTE
PUNTA GORDA

L. Okeechobee

WEST
PALM BEACH

Palm Beach

Pine I
CAPE CORAL
Ft MYERS

Sanibel I

Delray Beach
Boca Raton
Deerfield Beach
Pompano Beach
Ft LAUDERDALE
Hollywood

N. Miami Beach

NAPLES

Big Cypress
Nat Pres

Miccosukee
Indian Res

Hialeah
Coral Gables
MIAMI

MIAMI
BEACH

Kendall

Everglades Nat Pk

Florida
City

Gulf of Mexico

Key Largo

Florida Bay

Marquesas Keys

SOUTH FLORIDA

KEY WEST

84

Seaplane Service (✆294.6978), or Air–Sea Key West (✆296.5511) will fly you here in a Cessna with floats and drop you off; you can fly over without landing in a biplane belonging to Conch Classic Air Tours (✆296.0727), or you can charter any of a score of boats. Camping is allowed, but you must take everything you need, including every drop of water.

Dry Tortugas. Garden Key became a wildlife refuge in 1908, home to the sooty tern, and Fort Jefferson has been a national monument since 1935. Nearby Bush Key is closed to human visitors from 1 March to 30 September to allow seabirds to nest. With the neighbouring Loggerhead, Hospital, Middle and East keys, all uninhabited, Garden Key forms the archipelago of the Dry Tortugas, 'dry' for obvious reasons, and 'tortugas' from the turtles that the Spanish explorer Ponce de Leon found here in 1513.

Marquesas Keys. Two-thirds the way back to Key West lie the Marquesas Keys, a larger group of islands forming part of the Key West National Wildlife Refuge. Closer to Key West itself is the quarter-mile-long reef called Ballast Key which has the distinction of being the southernmost point of the United States outside of the Hawaiian Islands.

Southernmost point. So what of that big buoy which was set up at the bottom of Whitehead Street on 10 September 1983, carrying the slogan 'southernmost point of continental USA?' Sorry to disillusion you, but it isn't. For a start, Ballast Key beats it - but you can't easily get there. For another thing, this isn't *continental* USA – we're miles out to sea! And finally it isn't even the southernmost point of Key West – that's in the Ft Zachary Taylor State Park a little to the west. It *is* the southernmost road in the USA outside of the Hawaiian Islands, and it certainly makes an interesting photograph.

'The Railroad that Went to Sea.' Henry Flagler, whose name you'll see in many parts of the state, made his fortune in the oil business. As a diversion he brought the first railway to the Sunshine State, his Florida East Coast Railroad reaching Miami in 1896.

He wasn't content to stop there; he had a dream of driving his tracks on to Key West, in 'The Railroad that Went to Sea,' but which less kindly people called Flagler's Folly. By 1904 his surveying was done and the project began under Joseph Meredith. When Meredith died in 1909 William Krome (you'll see *his* name plenty of times, too) took over. Despite hurricanes, disease, heat, and shortage of water, and at a cost of $50,000,000, the railway reached Key West on 21 January 1912, and Flagler arrived in the city the next day aboard the first train.

Hurricane. Flagler died in 1913, still triumphant. But on 2 September 1935, Labor Day, a hurricane destroyed 41 miles of track and several vital bridges in Flagler's Folly. Engineers estimated the repairs would cost $2,940,000, but the country was recovering from the Great Depression and the bill was too much; there was even a suggestion from the Federal Relief Administration that Key West be abandoned. But the state government moved in, bought everything except the rolling stock for $640,000, and began building a road, which reached Key West shortly before Europe entered World War Two. After the war Key West was back in the tourist business, and now its 34,000 inhabitants play host to a million visitors a year.

Relaxed. Despite this vast influx, Key West genuinely manages to impose its character upon the visitor. This is one of the most relaxed, laid-back cities you'll ever see, and you won't need to be told: somehow the atmosphere envelops you. Is it the old-style architecture? Is it the knowledge you're at the end of the road? Or is it the casual manner of the native 'conchs' as they drift to Mallory Square for the nightly ritual of watching the sun set? The sunset can be spectacular but − don't tell anybody − I've seen much better.

You have to ask around before you learn that Key West had a boom in property prices in the 1980s, and that the city council is so conservation-conscious that it dictates what colour people may paint their houses. The council has also decreed there'll be no more hotels built here after the multi-million-dollar hotel- marina conversion of the Naval Air Base. Key West has "done growin'."

Audubon House. One of those early houses has been foremost in creating the tourist boom and also in preserving Key West's unique architecture. Captain John Geiger was an early 19th cent harbour master and wrecker who built a lavish house on Whitehead and Greene streets, and furnished it with treasures from his and other wrecks. By 1958 the house was near derelict and destined for demolition, but a local historian campaigned to save it. Colonel Mitchell Wolfson, a native conch, bought it and through the Wolfson Family Foundation restored the place. But what should they do with it when it was finished?

John James Audubon was born in Haiti in 1785, son of a French planter and a Creole mother. To avoid being conscripted into Napoleon's army he moved to Pennsylvania and worked on a farm, where he became enchanted with wild birds. Painting them soon became his passion, and Audubon made his reputation from his phenomenal masterpiece *Birds of America,* published in a very limited edition with each book containing 435 hand-painted engravings. Some of the more spectacular engravings were done from sketches made in Captain Geiger's garden.

That was the answer. Geiger's restored home became the Audubon House, furnished with the best the early 19th cent could produce, including Chippendale chairs, a Sheraton table and Crown Derby pottery, plus some original Audubon paintings. The house is now open 0930-1700 every day of the year, for $4.50.

The restoration of Geiger's old house caught the nation's imagination and started a wave of renovation in Key West, which is still going on, financed now by income from all those visitors.

Hemingway. And while you're looking at restored houses, call in at the Ernest Hemingway Home and Museum at 907 Whitehead St, open 0900-1700 daily for $5 (children $1). Papa Hemingway bought the coral-rock house in 1931 and died there in July 1961, meanwhile writing several of his best-known books in his poolhouse loft: *A Farewell to Arms, Death in the Afternoon, The Snows of Kilimanjaro, For Whom the Bell Tolls, Green Hills of Africa,* and others. Hemingway, known also for his love of alcohol, ended each day on his reserved bar stool in Sloppy Joe's on Green and Duval, listening to Joe's fanciful tales of the sea. Maybe Hemingway picked up a few ideas for his books from poor old Joe? But we mustn't forget Cap'n Tony's Saloon at 428 Greene St, another of Papa's watering holes.

Cats. Hemingway's other love was cats, and he had up to 50 around the house at the same time, some of them with six toes on their front feet; the six-toed felines that still live at 907 Whitehead St are arguably their descendants.

Tennessee Williams. America's favourite playwright, Tennessee Williams, came to live in Key West in 1930, and is remembered in the Tennessee Williams Fine Arts Center on Stock Island. Harry Truman came to Key West in 1946, liked it so much he had a little house here — it's beyond the south end of Caroline St — and made 11 visits while he was President of the USA.

Curry Mansion. You want more affluence? Then visit the Curry Mansion at 511 Caroline St, former home of the city's first millionaire and open daily 1000-1700. Here you can see how the millionaire class lived from 1906, when the house was built; 20 rooms of lavish elegance await your sighs of envy.

Treasure trove. For the last word in affluence cross Whitehead St from the Audubon House and visit Mel Fisher's Maritime Museum at 200 Green St, open daily 1000-1600 for $5 (children $1). Mel is a modern-day wrecker who spent 16 difficult years searching for the Spanish galleons *Nuestra Señora de Atocha* and *Santa Margarita* which were driven onto reefs by a storm on 6 September 1622. On 20 July 1985 Fisher's son Kane found the first wreck and reported: "It's here! A wall of silver five feet high! Today's the day!"

The *Atocha* alone held around $400,000,000 in treasure, a portion of which is on display — and some is even for sale. Do you fancy a $1,200 gold coin as a souvenir?

Lighthouse. And a final building to see: the 110-foot (34m) lighthouse at 937 Whitehead St and its military museum showing, among other exhibits, a two-man submarine.

Bottle wall. Among Key West's unusual attractions there's now

Carolyn Fuller's bottle wall, at the corner of Margaret and Angela streets. Ms Fuller, 66, spent years trying to keep cars and people out of her garden, so she built a wall of empty bottles. She then spent years trying to get the city fathers to legalise the thing – and succeeded in November 1988. Contributions are welcome, preferably empty.

USS Maine. Opposite Ms Fuller's house is the City Cemetery with above-ground vaults – Key West is only six feet above high tide – and the bodies of the victims of the *USS Maine*, sunk in Havana during the Spanish-American War.

Aquarium. And in this bizarre city, if you feel you'd like to stroke a living shark, come to the aquarium at 1 Whitehead St, backing onto Mallory Square.

Mallory Square. Mallory Square is the centre of interest in Key West, not only for the daily spectacle of applauding the setting sun but also for its shops, sponge market, and small cafés.

Shopping. Key West is a shoppers' paradise, particularly along Duval Street down from Mallory Square. Among the usual array of

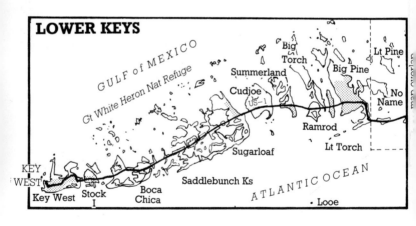

restaurants and souvenir shops you'll find Hemingway's haunt, **Sloppy Joe's Bar,** and at 500 the shop they call the Bloomingdale's of Key West, **Fast Buck Freddie's,** selling anything and everything. At 612 the **Greenpeace** shop sells environmentally acceptable items, and campaigns against keeping killer whales and dolphins in captivity to perform for mankind. And don't forget **Croissants de France** on Duval for probably the best bread in Florida.

Getting around. Back at Mallory Square is where you can catch the city's unusual public transport, either the **Conch Tour Train** (0900-1600, 90-minute trips for $7), one of several tractor-drawn road trains, or its rival the **Old Town Trolley.** Both offer guided tours of the old town and the remainder of the island. Or you can **hire a cycle** for $5 a day from Bubba's Bike Rental, 705 Duval St, ✆294.2618; Ray's Bike Shop, 1200 4th St (in the middle of the island), ✆294.0553; or Moped Hospital, 601 Truman Ave (by Simonton St), ✆296.3344.

The gay life. Another of Key West's unusual traits is its large homosexual community, both male and female, with virtually all the hotels and guest houses openly welcoming gay guests. Some, indeed, are exclusively gay, usually catering for men only, and here — if you fit the description — you can swim and sunbathe in the nude. The gays are so discreet that the heterosexual community is scarcely aware of them. Perhaps its inevitable, but at 2700 Flagler Ave there's Aids

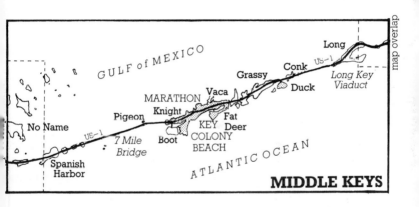

Help, Inc, working with the victims of the gays' disease.

VERDICT. Key West is unique in many respects, is truly fascinating, and with its tropical climate and vegetation is one place you should not miss. Traffic jams waste a lot of time, parking can be a nightmare, and wheelchair visitors can't go to a lot of places.

The **beach** is on the south-east of the island, near the airport, with good sand but no overnight parking.

The **Chamber of Commerce,** open 0900-1700, is on Wall St, near the Conch Train starting point, ✆294.2587; ask here for details of hotels and restaurants or with time to spare contact the rival Key West Business Guild at PO Box 1208, Key West, FL 33041, ✆(305).294.4603.

Acommodation is plentiful but expensive; here's a random selection with winter (high season) rates per room:

Atlantic Shore Motel, 510 South St, ✆296.2491; $40-$110; pool, nightclub, fun.

Best Western Key Ambassador Resort Inn, 1000 S. Roosevelt Blv, ✆296.3500; $115-$185; top class.

Blue Parrot Inn, 916 Elizabeth St, (✆296.0033); from $40; homely, gay, and the cheapest hotel in town, built 1884.

Key Lime Village, 725 Truman Ave, ✆294.6222; from $42.

Key West Hostel, 718 South St, ✆296.5719; $12.25 non- members per person; youth hostel.

Pegasus International Hotel, 501 Southard St, ✆294.9323; $59.99; in Old Town.

Southernmost Motel in USA, 1319 Duval St, ✆296.6577); from $70; name-claim is genuine, a so-called 'gingerbread' house.

Tilton Hilton Guest House, 511 Angela St, ✆294.8697; from $40; beside Greyhound bus station.

Camping and RVs allowed only at recognised sites, of which this is a sample with prices per person:

Boyd's Key West Campground, 6401 Maloney Ave; $20; near beach.

Leo's Campground & RV Park, 5236 Suncrest Rd; from $15; near beach.

Boat charters. Scores of boats for hire or charter; here's a selection:

Captain Nemo, Galleon Marina, ✆294.8865; cruises 1000, 1200, 1400, 1600.

Clione, 631 Greene St, ✆296.1433; day or night reef snorkelling; gay owner, go nude if you like.

Escape Cruises, Garrison Bight Marina, ✆296.4608; men only, to uninhabited keys.

Women of the Water, PO Box 502, ✆294.0662; women only.

Festivals. Key West has a festival at the least excuse – or no excuse at all. But the Festival of the Continents is a series of major arts performances spread through the winter season. Contact Suite 305, 0 (yes, zero) Duval St, FL 33040, ✆296.5882.

THE BRIDGES

Milemarkers. Milemarker Zero is at Whitehead and Fleming streets, Key West, from which point all distances along US-1 are measured to MM 126, south of Florida City; MM 107 on Key Largo near Jewfish Creek marks the end of the Overseas Highway. The only marker stone remaining from Flagler's railroad is near MM 31 on Big

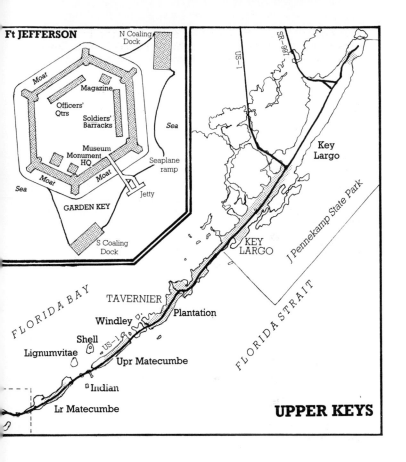

Ft JEFFERSON

N Coaling Dock

Moat

Magazine

Officers' Qtrs

Soldiers' Barracks

Sea

Museum
Monument
HQ

Seaplane ramp

Sea

Moat

Moat

Jetty

GARDEN KEY

S Coaling Dock

US-1

SR-905

Key Largo

KEY LARGO

J Pennekamp State Park

FLORIDA BAY

TAVERNIER

Plantation

Windley

FLORIDA STRAIT

Shell

US-1

Lignumvitae

Upr Matecumbe

Indian

Lr Matecumbe

UPPER KEYS

Pine Key.

Bridges. The Overseas Highway is unique; who but the Americans would build a road 100 miles out to sea spanning a chain of islands to end at a jetty? The 42 bridges which make the links are an engineering feat in their own right. Here they are, reading from Key West to the mainland, with their length, though you'll find some authorities quote different lengths: maybe the surveyor had a knot in his tape?

Key West Channel, 159ft (48m); Stock Island Channel, 360ft (109m); Boca Chica, 2,730ft (832m); Rockland Channel, 1,280ft (390m); Shark Channel, 2,090ft (637m); Saddle Bunch 5, 900ft (274m); Saddle Bunch 4, 900ft (274m); Saddle Bunch 3, 760ft (231m); Saddle Bunch 2, 660ft (201m); Lower Sugar Loaf, 1,210ft (369m); Harris, 390ft (119m); Harris Gap, 390ft (119m); North Harris Gap, 390ft (119m); Park Key, 880ft (268m); Bow Channel, 1,302ft (397m); Kemp's Channel, 992ft (302m); Nile's Channel, 4,433ft (1,350m); Torch-Ramrod, 720ft (219m); Torch Key Viaduct, 880ft (268m); South Pine Channel, 806ft (246m); North Pine Channel, 620ft (189m); Spanish Harbor, 3,311ft (1,009m); Bahia Honda, 6,734ft (2,052m); Ohio-Bahia Honda, 1,005ft (349m); Missouri-Ohio, 1,394ft (425m); Little Duck-Missouri, 800ft (244m); Knight's Key (Seven-Mile Bridge), 35,716ft (10,883m); Vaca Cut, 300ft (91m); Tom's Harbor 4, 1,395ft (425m); Tom's Harbor 3, 1,209ft (368m); Long Key, 11,960ft (3,644m); Channel 5, 4,516ft (1,376m); Channel 2, 1,720ft (524m); Lignumvitae, 790ft (241m); Indian Key, 2,004ft (611m); Teatable, 614ft (187m); Teatable Relief, 226ft (69m); Whale Harbor, 616ft (188m); Snake Creek, 192ft (58m); Tavernier Creek, 133ft (40m); Key Largo Cut, 360ft (109m);

and Jewfish Drawbridge, 223ft (68m), which crosses the Intracoastal Waterway.

THE LOWER KEYS

Just across that first bridge, you're in **Stock Island,** which took its name from the cattle and pigs that were raised here in the old days. The isle now holds the hospital, the Tennessee Williams Fine Arts Center, a college, golf course, and the overflow population from Key West.

Most of **Boca Chica Key,** including its US Naval Air Station, is part of the Great White Heron National Wildlife Refuge. The army took over the beginnings of a municipal airport in 1941, as the USA headed towards World War Two; the Navy borrowed it in 1943 and hasn't yet returned it. Conchs from Key Largo to Mallory Square should be grateful that the need for drinkable water for the base prompted the laying of the 30-inch pipeline from Florida City; keys' water is now chlorinated instead of marinated.

The almost uninhabited **Saddlebunch Keys** are also included in the Great White Heron National Wildlife Refuge, which therefore takes in the naval radio station at its northern tip. US Highway One cuts straight across these keys, though the old state road, SR-939, winds along the southern reef and joins US-1 on **Sugarloaf Key.**

Sugarloaf takes its name from the shape of an ancient Amerind midden (rubbish tip), but the key's main attraction is Richter Perky's bat tower, built in 1929 as a roost for bats which Perky hoped would eat the millions of mosquitos. They didn't. Perky bought his stake on the key from the Englishman C. W. Chase who harvested sponges here from 1910 until unscrupulous neighbours plundered the sponge beds.

As you cross **Cudjoe Key,** whose name is said to be a corruption of 'Cousin Joe,' look to the north for a glimpse of Fat Albert, a remote-controlled tethered airship which flies from the Air Force base at the tip of the island. Albert is a podgy 250,000 cubic feet of helium and air on a 25,000ft (7,600m) cable, and since 1980 his radars have been spying for enemy intruders — nowadays mainly drug smugglers.

Half of Cudjoe's 3,330 acres (13 sq km) are in the National Key Deer Refuge, which takes in a dozen other islands including **Big Torch Key,** bypassed by US-1, and **Middle Torch Key.** The Torches — there's a **Little Torch Key** as well — take their name from the native torchwood tree which burns very easily, green leaves and all. By the way, Stan Becker runs canoe tours from Little Torch Key; for $50 per person, minimum four, you can explore the keys and mangrove swamps; Stan is at PO Box 62, FL 33043, ✆872.2620.

Summerland Key has a small landing strip, one of three civil airfields in the Keys, the others being at Key West and Vaca Key. Six miles south of Summerland, on the edge of the continental shelf, lies **Looe Key,** named from the British frigate *HMS Looe* which was wrecked here in a storm in 1744.

The island is now awash at high tide, but the surrounding reefs are a paradise for scuba divers and come in the 5.3 square mile Looe Key National Marine Sanctuary, home to four-eyed butterfly fish, Spanish hogfish, queen and French angelfish, dolphin fish, king mackerel, grouper, yellowtail snapper and the endangered queen conch.

Big Pine Key is one of the largest islands, covering 6,524 acres (26 sq km), and is the main refuge for the endangered key deer, a diminutive subspecies of the Virginian white-tailed deer of the mainland. A minor road leads to **No Name Key,** home to raccoons, while ahead lie the **Spanish Harbor Keys** which had the best deep-water sheltered anchorage when Florida was ruled by Spain. More reminders of Spanish days are in the tiny **Don Quixote Key** nearby, and in **Bahia Honda Key,** whose name means 'deep bay.'

Bahia Honda is now a state recreational area with three campsites, and the remains of one of Flagler's railroad bridges. Beyond, Ohio Key, like neighbouring **Missouri Key,** was given its name by homesick railway builders. Ohio has recently been renamed **Sunshine Key** and its 75-acre campsite has pitching for 400 tents or small RVs.

THE MIDDLE KEYS

The spectacular **Seven Mile Bridge,** claimed to be the world's longest multi-arch bridge, was completed in 1982; since 1937 traffic had to use Flagler's converted and repaired railway bridge which now runs alongside and provides the only access to Pigeon Key, from the east. To the west, Flagler's bridge is now billed as the world's longest fishing pier. When you begin the crossing of the Seven Mile, with the Atlantic on one side, the Gulf of Mexico on the other, the two waters meeting beneath you, and no land in sight ahead, you could imagine yourself in a Disney fantasy film. But it's real!

The Spanish came to **Pigeon Key,** calling it *Cayo Paloma* from the hundreds of birds that nested here. Audubon painted them for his *Birds of America,* and they're now on the endangered-specie list under the name of white-crowned pigeon. If you see any birds on the railroad girders they're almost certainly domestic pigeons gone wild.

Pigeon Key has its place in the record books. The largest fish ever caught (so they say) was taken near here in June 1912, a 45- ft whale shark estimated to weigh 27,000lb (12,000kg). And did you see the James Bond film, *Licence Revoked*? Part of it was shot here on Pigeon Key amid the deserted houses that were recently leased by the University of Miami.

The Overseas Highway now travels on land for several miles, crossing tiny **Knight's Key,** where Henry Flagler housed up to 5,000 railway workers in 1908 while they built the original Seven Mile Bridge, and then the highway takes the causeway to **Hog Key** and so to **Vaca Key,** 'cow key,' named from the manatee or sea cow which the Spanish discoverers found here; the mammal is now a very rare visitor.

Marathon. Here on Vaca Key stand the towns of Marathon and Marathon Shores, with Marathon Airport which parallels the road. Marathon is a busy place which owes its origins and its name to Henry Flagler's railway builders who stayed here awhile. As the railroad gradually whittled away their livelihood, ferries from No Name Key and Key West called at Vaca, and the tiny fishing village of the 1880s became a boom town. One of the railmen referred to their work as a 'marathon' task — and so the town had a new name.

Marathon claims to have virtually everything the visitor may need, and its special events include an air show and powerboat race in

May, and in April 1,500 people enter the Seven Mile Bridge Run, too short to be classed as a 'marathon.'

South of Marathon lies **Boot Key,** base for a large marina and now linked by a bridge, but in Flagler's day the key had several shops which brought their customers over by boat.

Short bridges, not worthy of inclusion in the list, alternate with short causeways in linking Vaca with **Fat Deer Key** where, south of US-1, stands Key Colony Beach, the only 'incorporated city' between the mainland and Key West and home to the wealthy retired with a love of golf. **Long Point Key** leads to **Crawl Key,** supposedly named from the turtles formerly kept here in 'crawls' — corrals or maybe even kraals — until they were needed for the kitchen.

Grassy Key has the Dolphin Research Center which has evolved from Flipper's Sea School where Flipper, one of the first dolphins to be taught to perform in captivity, went through its act for the early cinema. And talking of cinemas, Tavernier Key on Key Largo, got its first in 1980.

A short causeway connected **Duck Key** to US-1 in 1955, and now the small island has some of the smartest homes in the Keys. Duck Key had been uninhabited since 1937, when a salt—drying business collapsed. A long causeway spans the small **Conch Keys** and leads to Long Key Viaduct and the Upper Keys.

THE UPPER KEYS<

Much of **Long Key** is mangrove swamp, with a state recreation area sandwiched between it and the highway, but there is a little community called Layton. Del and Mary Layton came here in 1946 to retire from their Miami grocery business, but Del couldn't relax. He bought some ex-army cabins, expanded it into a motel, added a dock which grew to a marina, then sold off his spare land which grew into the town of Layton.

Still Del couldn't rest. As well as running the cruise business (Mary ran the motel), he became postmaster, police deputy, fire chief, church deacon and in 1963 Layton City's first mayor. He died in 1986, still holding top office.

From **Lower Matecumbe Key** US-1 leads to 10-acre (4ha) **Indian Key,** not to be confused with the 12-acre island of the same name a mile away to the south and accessible only by boat. It was to this southern and isolated **Indian Key** that John Housman moved in 1831 and built a mini-empire based on wrecking, eventually sharing the island with 400 people. The Dade County seat was established here in 1836 (the Keys are now in Monroe County) but on 7 August 1840 Indians attacked in the Second Seminole War and burned everything. This Indian Key has been deserted ever since, but traces of Housman's village remain.

To the north lies **Lignumvitae Key,** named from the *lignum vitae* or 'tree of life,' yielding an extremely hard pale-yellow wood which sinks in fresh water. Plumbers used tools of lignum vitae before plastic replaced lead, bowling balls are turned from it, roller bearings were carved from it during World War Two, and it even outlasts bronze on boats.

This is one of more than 70 species of tree found on the 280- acre (113ha) island now designated a botanical garden; you can also find the gumbo limbo, Jamaican dogwood, mahogany, pigeon plum, poisonwood, and a tree called blolly.

The first settler on Lignumvitae was William Bethel in the 1850s who raised a few crops, but in 1919 W.J. Matheson built a coral-rock house with a 12,000-gallon (45,000-litre) rainwater tank and a windmill to supply electricity. The State of Florida bought the island in 1971 and it's now uninhabited, but the Matheson house survives intact; you can see it for $1 on a guided tour aboard *MV Monroe* from MM78.5 on Upper Matecumbe Key, by courtesy of the Florida Park Service; ✆664.4815.

Upper Matecumbe Key has the town of Islamorada, supposedly taking its name from the Spanish *isla morada,* 'purple island,' from the colour of its sea snails, but it can equally translate as 'island sanctuary.' Oddly, the 's' in the name is mute.

The 2,196-acre (888ha) island was deserted when Flagler brought his railway here in 1906, but more than 2,000 people now live in the town. The Chamber of Commerce is in a distinctive bright red caboose — railway wagon — still on Flagler's original tracks, but public transport now relies on the Islamorada Trolley which runs between mile markers 80 and 103, the south of Upper Matecumbe Key to the middle of Key Largo.

Theatre of the Sea. ♿ Henry Flagler quarried coral rock on Upper Matecumbe, leaving a saltwater pool which, in 1946, became the basis for the world's second marine park, now trading as the Theatre of the Sea. For $12 ($8 for children) you can pick up the continous show and see sharks, a 200lb (90kg) jewfish, barracuda, surgeon fish, a turtle that lost one flipper to a shark, and the star attraction, the performing dolphins. For $50 and a liability waiver you can even swim with the dolphins.

Flagler dug another quarry on **Windley Key,** which is two islands joined by a causeway. This quarry is now a nature reserve, and the slag tip is claimed to be the highest point in the Florida Keys. **Plantation Key** had a thriving pineapple plantation on it in the 19th cent, but its 3,183 acres (13 sq km) are now devoted to real estate, with a little bit left for mangrove swamp.

The real **Tavernier Key** is a small island north-east of Plantation Key, but **Tavernier** is also a town on the southern tip of Key Largo,

Pelicans are almost too tame.

John Ringling, ancestor of the Ringling Brothers of circus fame, built this $2,000,000 mansion in Sarasota in 1920.

Now showing in Miami: H.M.S. Bounty, by courtesy of Metro-Goldwyn-Mayer. Airship by courtesy of Goodyear.

Naples - but different from the one in Italy.

where early settlers grew pineapples and coconuts.

The Spanish *Cayo Largo,* 'long island,' became **Key Largo,** at 5,186 acres (20 sq km) the largest as well as the longest of the keys and now has a bustling population of 11,000 concentrated in the southern half. Humphrey Bogart popularised the place with his 1948 film, *Key Largo,* but its attractions today, apart from charter boats, are the submarine hotel and the nearby John Pennekamp Coral Reef State Park. The *African Queen,* used in Bogart's film of the same name, is usually on view around MM 100 but may be away on loan.

In the mid-70s, scientists studied the living coral and the marine environment from what they claimed was the world's first underwater laboratory, built on the reef 30 feet (10m) below the surface. The lab has now been converted to the world's first underwater hotel, **Jules's Undersea Lodge,** where six people at a time can stay in the three air-conditioned suites and enjoy most of the conveniences of a top motel, plus an escape hatch in the floor through which they can glide out and explore the reef: they can even watch fish swimming past the bedroom window.

Non-certificated scuba divers must take a four-hour lesson in tethered-airline diving before signing the hotel register, then all that remains is to pay the bill: a mini-tour costs $50, with full board going for $295, per person. Contact Jules's Habitat Inc, PO Box 3330, Key Largo, FL 33037, ✆451.2353.

John Pennekamp, former editor of the *Miami Herald,* was con-

Just 90 miles to Cuba.

cerned that the largest living coral reef in the Americas had no legal protection. He campaigned through the press and the state legislature until in 1960 he achieved his dream, the creation of the **John Pennekamp Coral Reef State Park,** 21 miles long by four wide. It's a wonderland for divers, inhabited by more than 650 species of fish in waters no more than 40ft (12m) deep.

The park gates are open from 0800 to sunset and out-of-state visitors pay $2.50 for driver and car, plus $1.50 for each passenger. A glass-bottomed boat sails daily at 0900, 1200 and 1500, and there are snorkelling tours at the same times, for up to $18 per person; ✆451.1621 or 1.800.432.2871 for details.

On the seaward side of John Pennekamp's park, the **Key Largo National Marine Sanctuary** takes the protected area up to seven miles futher into the Florida Strait, and well into the Gulf Stream.

US-1 swings sharp left at the edge of Key Largo town and heads through the mangrove swamps to the mainland, via Jewfish Draw-bridge which crosses the Intracoastal Waterway. Alternatively you can veer right onto SR-905 through totally uninhabited terrain before plunging into the mangrove for the hump-backed toll bridge – $1 per car – over Card Sound. This is backwoods country, and the fishermen's shacks by the bridge are in stark contrast to the luxury mansions down at Key West.

Biscayne National Park. The Florida Keys extend northwards through the near-uninhabited Elliott Key, then burst into life again with Key Biscayne before running parallel with Florida's Atlantic coast as Miami Beach and those other world- renowned resorts. Biscayne National Park is 181,500 acres (734 sq km or 283 sq miles) of ocean bed, plus Elliott Key and miles of vital coastal mangroves, extending north from Key Largo through Biscayne Bay. It's part of the keys, though access is from SW 328th St, Homestead, or Tallahassee Road, Miami, to the Convoy Point Information Station.

The park is open daily from 0800 to sunset, and the Information Station on the mainland and the Elliott Key Visitor Center are open from 0900 to 1700 for books and other information, though the Visitor Center is seldom open outside weekends.

Biscayne is a wildlife and historic preserve and the only things visitors may take away are the game fish they catch (subject to limits on size, specie, season and number) – and all their rubbish. Elliott Key's harbour has free mooring, but overnight stays must be reserved in advance; the key's campsite is also free and campers are accepted on a first-come, first-served basis. Back-country camping is by licence only.

The park offers cruises in 53-ft glass-bottom boats every day, plus snorkelling, scuba diving, visits to Elliott Key, and canoe trips. For more information, times and prices, ✆247.PARK or ✆247.7275; if you want to hire a canoe, ✆247.2400.

Diving in the keys. There are more diving schools and diving shops per square mile in the Florida Keys than anywhere else on earth. Among the schools, Hall's Diving Center at 1994 Overseas Highway, Mile Marker 48, ✆743.5929, offers instruction at all levels, from a one-day scuba course at $150 to an 18-day professional course at more than $1,500, plus package holidays for divers. Other schools such as Admiral Dive at 103190 Overseas Highway, MM 103, Key Largo, ✆451.1114, and Florida Keys Dive Centre at MM 90.5, Plantation Key, ✆852.4599, specialise in instruction at non-professional level. The dive shops begin at Key Largo and run to Stock Island; take your pick along the roadside.

Diving flag. When you're diving around the keys you'll drop a marker buoy carrying a red flag with a diagonal white stripe. And when you're boating, keep a good lookout for diving flags — and for the occasional manatee.

There is plenty for divers to see. The main reef is on the rim of the continental slope, about three miles into the Florida Strait, with three lighthouses marking the areas most dangerous to shipping and therefore most interesting for wreck-hunters. The lights are named from ships lost at those spots: Tennessee, off Long Key; Alligator, off Indian Key; and Molasses off Key Largo. Less dangerous but equally interesting reefs mark the continental slope from the Marquesas to Key Largo, with the popular Hen and Chickens, off Plantation Key, standing in the shallower waters of the older reef.

Wrecks. Wrecks make particularly interesting diving, not only for the hulks themselves and what they might yield, but also for the marine life they attract. You'll certainly hear of the Spanish treasure fleet which sailed from Havana on 13 July, 1773, a Friday (the Spanish believe that *Tuesday* the 13th is unlucky). All but one of the 21 ships were wrecked on the Keys the next day and while the Spaniards managed to salvage seven, 13 remained. They've all been located and identified and the *San Pedro,* lying off Indian Key, is to become an underwater state park.

In recent years the Florida Keys Artificial Reef Association has been sinking worn-out ships in designated spots to increase reef life and take the pressure off the older wreck sites, but FKARA was not responsible for the sinking of the so-called *Cannabis Cruiser,* caught while running drugs and scuttled by her crew. FKARA is at PO Box 917, Big Pine Key, FL 33043.

VERDICT. A drive down the Keys is an experience of a lifetime; you'll see thousands of brown pelicans so tame you can scratch their head and, if you stop in the right places, plenty of other wildlife. For divers, these reefs are almost as good as those in the Red Sea although the waters are not as warm and, on the Atlantic side, there is the Gulf Stream to contend with.

Other watersports. Every watersport you could wish for is here, except surfboarding, as the Atlantic rollers seldom come south of the Bahamas. You can take your choice from sportfishing charters and windsurf hirers as you drive past, or contact the relevant Chamber of Commerce for detailed information: addresses are in Chapter 4.

Accommodation is expensive, but not as dear as in Key West, and you shouldn't camp by the roadside although many do. If you're looking for motels, concentrate on Big Pine Key, Marathon, Islamorada and Key Largo town.

Paradise in peril. There are problem spots. Every household on the Keys is obliged to have a septic tank but as it's utterly impossible to service them all there is consequent pollution. In isolated places the smell of hydrogen sulphide is overpowering, and a few householders have complained that the gas strips the paint off their properties.

Wildlife on the Keys is seldom intrusive, but remember the love bugs, the palmetto bugs, and the mosquitos.

This is a selection from hotels and motels:

Big Pine Key:
Big Pine Resort Motel, MM 30.5, ✆872.9090; from $40; pool and restaurant.

Deer Run Bed & Breakfast, MM 33, ✆872.2800; $50; an old 'conch' house.

Parmer's Place, MM 28.5, ✆872.2157; from $45.

Islamorada:
Bed & Breakfast of Islamorada, MM 81, 81175 Old Hwy, ✆664.9321; from $45; cycle hire available.

Key Lantern Motel & RV Park, MM 82.1, 82150 Hwy-1, ✆664.4572; from $35.

Palms of Islamorada, MM 80, 79901 O'seas Hwy, ✆664.8000; from $1,000; spa, sauna, health farm.

Shoreline Motel, MM 81, ✆664.4027; from $42; gulfside; watersports.

Key Largo:
Bay Cove Motel, MM 99.5, 99446 O'seas Hwy, ✆451.1686; from $35; oceanside waterfront.

Hungry Pelican, MM 99.5, ✆451.3576; from $40; gulfside waterfront.

Neptune's Hideaway, MM 104.2, ✆451.0357; from $55; near John Pennekamp entrance; thatched hut accommodation.

Little Torch Key:
Little Palm Island Beach Club, MM 28.5, ✆872.2524; $300.

Marathon:
Anchor Lite Botel, MM 53, 11699 O'seas Hwy, ✆743.7397; from $40; on oceanside waterfront.

Bed & Breakfast of Florida Keys, MM 50, 5 Man-o'-War Dr, ✆743,4118; from $45; oceanside waterfront.

Casa Clara Condos, MM 54.5, 201 E Ocean Dr, Key Colony Beach, ✆289.1791; $1,350 for 2 weeks.

Faro Blanco Marine Resort, MM48, 1996 O'seas Hwy, ✆743.9018; from $45; gulfside waterfront.

Floating Sea Cove Motel, MM 54, 12685 O'seas Hwy, ✆289.0800; from $25; basic room, efficiencies dearer. Oceanside waterfront.

Jolly Roger, MM 59, PO Box 525, ✆289.0404; from $15; gulfside waterfront.

Longhorn Lodge, MM 53.5, 12550 O'seas Hwy, ✆743.2680; $40; gulfside waterfront.

Pelican Motel & Trailer Park, MM 59, ✆289.0011; from $38; gulfside waterfront.

Seacove Motel, MM 54, 12685 O'seas Hwy, ✆289.0800; $20; oceanside waterfront.

Siesta Motel, MM 51, 7425 O'seas Hwy, ✆743.5071; $35.

Boat rental:
Buccaneer Resort, 2600 O'seas Hwy, Marathon, ✆743.9071: variety of small boats and windsurfers for hire.

Roma, 32ft sloop based at Buccaneer Lodge, Marathon Key (2600 Overseas Highway, FL 33050, MM 48.5), whose skipper will let you try your hand at sailing even with no previous experience. The rate is $30 for a half-day.

Guide book. For the latest information try to get a copy of Humm's *Guide to the Florida Keys,* issued quarterly, free, by Monroe County; it should be at chambers of commerce, boatyards, motels and larger reataurants. Humm's *Reefs & Wrecks,* invaluable for the serious diver, is available from PO Box 2921, Key Largo, FL 33037, if you enclose international reply coupons for 160 grams (or 200gm printed paper rate). Teall's large-scale maps of the Florida Keys are excellent for motoring and planning boating trips, but they are no substitute for charts when you put to sea.

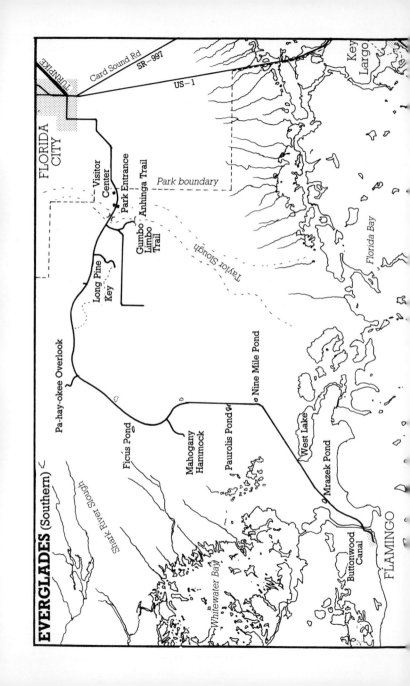

14: THE EVERGLADES
River of Grass

THE EVERGLADES IS ONE OF THE MOST FRAGILE ENVIRON-
MENTS in the world, a sea-level plateau where the tropics meet the
temperate climes and where freshwater merges with saline. Before
the Europeans settled in Florida, the 60 inches (1,500mm) of summer
rains that fell on Lake Okeechobee, spilled over the southern rim and
flowed, imperceptibly slowly, through the standing grass until 100
miles to the south they trickled through the mangrove swamps and
entered the Gulf of Mexico.

The 'river of grass' was 50 miles (80km) wide and six inches
(150mm) deep, and nourished the grasslands for weeks, supple-
mented by the rain which fell directly onto it.

And then came the white man. Within a lifetime he had altered the
balance that nature had taken thousands of years to establish. He put
an embankment all around Lake Okeechobee. He cut canals from the
lake to Miami and to Boca Raton. He cut another canal from Naples to
Miami. He began growing thirsty sugar cane south of the lake, and he
sucked up vast amounts of water to supply the expanding city of
Miami. He built roads across the Everglades, funnelling the 50-mile-
wide slough into a few culverts.

Finally he realised what was happening to the 'Glades and, barely
in time, he became conservation-conscious. The Everglades have
been saved — but only just. Yet even now their survival is in doubt,
threatened by every new swim pool in Miami, every tourist taking a
shower in Key West, draining water that might have gone into the
'Glades.

National Park ... The Everglades National Park received federal
approval in 1934 but wasn't established until 1947 and its boundaries
weren't fixed until 1958. Its original purpose was to provide a
protected habitat for herons and ibises that had been persecuted for
their plumage, but people soon realised the park would need to do
much more. Barron Collier, who owned much of Collier County and
whose name lives on in the Collier-Seminole State Park, gave large
tracts of land for the 'Glades which now covers almost 1,400,000 acres
(5,660 sq km, 2,190 sq miles), including all of Florida Bay and its many

mangrove keys — but does not take in vast areas of the river of grass to the north.

... and National Preserve. But still there was economic pressure. Oil was found in 1943 north of Alligator Alley. Loggers moved in to the Big Cypress Swamp. Land speculators followed. As recently as 1968 other speculators planned a major airport slap in the middle of the river of grass: the first runway was built and is now the Dade-Collier Training Airport. And so the Big Cypress National Preserve was created on the Everglades' north- western rim to save more fragile land.

Big Cypress National Preserve. Big Cypress, named from the size of the swamp and not the stature of the trees, took in 2,400 sq miles (6,200 sq km) of the swamp, while the much smaller Fakahatchee Strand State Preserve, the Collier-Seminole State Park and the Ten Thousand Islands Aquatic Preserve have increased the area that's now protected. But it's still not enough; the headwaters of the river of grass, the Shark River Slough (slough is pronounced 'slew'), are still vulnerable.

When to visit. As south Florida is a winter resort, most people visit the 'Glades from November to March when the grasslands are drying, forcing the wildlife to congregate around the few all-season pools. In short, they see the 'Glades at the most convenient time, when it's possible to walk rather than wade, when they can do all their bird-watching from one spot — and when the mosquitos are less of a menace. True, these insects are a nuisance in November but by the average February they have vanished.

In summer, the birds and reptiles are distributed across the vast expanses, the rain may come tumbling down — and the mosquitos can make life almost intolerable.

THE EVERGLADES PARK

The main entry to the Everglades is from Florida City along SR-9336, though fields which yield much of the state's crop of winter tomatoes: stop for some U-pick and notice the limestone bedrock poking through the thin sandy soil. This same rock stretches across the 'Glades and Big Cypress, varying only a foot or so in elevation — but that foot is vital.

Visitor Center. The Visitor Center is open daily 0800- 1700 and is a useful stop for information, books, and the National Park Service's excellent free map. The entrance is a little further, open day and night; it'll cost you $5 for the car and everybody in it, and keep your ticket because it's valid for seven days and allows free entry into the Shark Valley trail.

The tarmac road winds for 38 miles (61km) through several vegetation zones to reach the Flamingo Visitor Center on Florida Bay,

The anhinga or snake bird spends hours drying its wings.

but the main interest lies in the walking trails that lead off this road.

ANHINGA TRAIL. ♿ Half a mile of tarmac path over firm ground, and elevated boardwalk over permanent pools, allow you to enter the territory of a variety of wild creatures who scarcely bother to move away at your approach. The anhinga, also called the snake bird, Grecian lady, water turkey, water crow, darter (which it is not), and whang doodle, spends hours holding its wings outstretched to dry its plumage. Here, too, are the purple gallinule, a relative of the moorhen; the 4ft 6in (130cm) tall great blue heron which will eat baby 'gators; the six-inch (15cm) pig frog named from its grunt; and, of course, the alligator.

You may also see turtles, marsh rabbits, egrets, the occasional raccoon — raccoons are known to carry rabies so don't break the no-feeding laws — and perhaps the Florida cottonmouth, one of the four poisonous snakes in the 'Glades. Vegetation includes the pond apple or corkwood whose fruit, I'm told, tastes like turpentine. Or there's the coco plum whose fruit is a mild narcotic.

This is the most popular and the most rewarding trail: come early in the day before the crowds arrive.

GUMBO LIMBO TRAIL. ♿ (with difficulty). The Gumbo-Limbo trail starts from the same car park as the Anhinga Trail, but takes you for half a mile along tarmac paths through a hardwood hammock, past trees with exotic names and no less exotic shapes: the tall royal palm,

105

the squat gumbo limbo, as well as wild coffee, with epiphytes (non-parasitic plants) growing on their branches.

The hardwood manages to survive because here the limestone base rock is up to three feet (1m) higher than the surrounding slough: this is a 'hammock.'

LONG PINE KEY. The next turn off the main road leads to the Long Pine Key campsite with toilets, and the start of an unpaved track wandering for 7 miles (11km) through the pine forest and rejoining the main road; one member of your party might give you a two-hour start before driving along to meet you at the other end.

This trail takes you across a pine forest hammock where lightning-strike fires have kept the dry undergrowth in check, allowing the survival of 200 species of plants including 30 found nowhere else on earth. Here you are in the territory of the whitetail deer, a relative of the key deer, and its predator the endangered Florida panther, now down to around 30. This beautiful animal was hunted for bounty until 1950, was added to the no-hunting list in '58, and classed as an endangered species in '67.

PINELAND TRAIL. ♿ (with care) The Pineland Trail is half a mile of tarmac path through more slash pine, Florida's only native conifer, with an undergrowth of palmetto. Signs point out the poisonwood tree, whose leaves cause a skin rash.

On this trail you can see the limestone bedrock, riddled with 'solution holes' caused by acid erosion of the calcium; you can appreciate how difficult it was for loggers on foot to penetrate this far.

PA-HAY-OKEE OVERLOOK TRAIL. ♿ (up to the tower) Beyond the Rock Reef Pass, 'elevation three feet,' is the Pa-hay-okee Trail, a quarter-mile long boardwalk ending in an observation tower on stilts, from where you can see the 'river of grass' — *pa-hay-okee* in the local Amerind language. This is the essence of the Everglades, bone dry in late winter and with passing birdlife, and waterlogged in summer. You'll recognise the sawgrass which covers acres of the dead-flat landscape, because the edges of its leaf-blades have tiny saw-teeth which can lay your flesh open. The Indians say that when the sawgrass — which is a sedge rather than a true grass — is in flower, a hurricane is coming. The whitetail deer say nothing: they just eat the stuff.

MAHOGANY HAMMOCK TRAIL. ♿ Two ponds, Sisal and Ficus, offer a glimpse of birdlife before you reach the dense jungle-like undergrowth of the Mahogany Hammock Trail, where the boardwalk is six or seven feet (2m) above the bedrock. The trail passes within touching distance of the largest surviving mahogany tree in the United States which isn't impressively large. Tree snails, golden-orb weaver spiders, green lizards and barred owls are among the notable wildlife.

WEST LAKE TRAIL. ♿ More small ponds herald your entry into the mangroves where the half-mile West Lake Trail takes you over the swamp to see the strange aerial roots of these salt-tolerant trees.

MRAZEK POND. ♿ Near journey's end you come to Mrazek Pond, an ideal spot for seeing pelican, egret, flamingo, coot, moorhen and spoonbill feeding side by side, while alligators bask on the nearby brick-red mudbanks.

FLAMINGO. ♿ Flamingo is a tiny village, but it's the *only* community in the 2,000 or so square miles of Monroe County which lie on the mainland: the rest of Monroe's people live in the Florida Keys.

Flamingo has an RV and camp site, a marina for houseboats, a grocery store which is open 0600-2000 and stocks all the essentials of life except alcohol, a gift shop open 0800-2000, a restaurant, petrol station, and the Flamingo Inn motel (PO Box 428, FL33030, ✆253.2241) which charges from $65 per room in high season.

It's a pleasant place to relax for a day in midwinter — the mosquitos are a nuisance in summer causing most activities to wind down — and is the place to come for boat excursions to Florida and Whitewater bays.

Pa-hay-okee Overlook in the Everglades; you watch the birds, the mosquitos watch you.

The **Flamingo Visitor Center** is open 0800-1700 daily for information, for the backcountry permits which are essential if you plan to spend a night in the wilds, and for arranging to go on ranger-organised expeditions such as canoe safaris or wilderness walks. ✆695.3101 ext 182 for latest information and reservations. Here, or in the grocery store, you can stock up on waterproof charts at $14.50, or invest $49.50 in the *Waterways Guide Chartbook of Lower Florida and the Keys* or $9.95 in Wm Truesdell's *Guide to Wilderness Waterways* (University of Miami Press).

It's illegal as well as irresponsible to feed any wildlife in the 'Glades, and there's the threat of a $500 fine on conviction. There's also a daytime ban on fishing in Flamingo as pelicans are liable to go for your catch and swallow the hook.

Wilderness Waterway. With your own sailing yacht or canoe and the necessary backcountry permit, the wilderness is yours, particularly the 99-mile (160km) Wildernes Waterway through the mangrove swamps up to Everglades City. By canoe it's a leisurely seven-day adventure of a lifetime, with designated campsites. Take absolutely everything you'll need, and bring back every scrap of litter.

But for those people who couldn't bring a 20-foot canoe on the plane, hiring or chartering is the only alternative. Join the backcountry cruise to Whitewater Bay, two hours for $7.25; go schooner sailing for 90 minutes and $10; or hire a canoe for $10 a half day, $15 the day. A motor skiff is yours for the day at $55; three of you can take a day-long fishing charter for $215 — or you can hire a houseboat: contact Flamingo Lodge Marina & Outpost Resort in person or at PO Box 428, Flamingo, FL 33030, ✆(305)253.2241.

SHARK RIVER. &. Your entry ticket for the road to Flamingo is valid for seven days and lets you into the Shark Valley trail; access is off US-41, the Tamiami Trail. Here the Visitor Center is open 0830-1715 daily, and you have the option of walking some way down the 15-mile trail to a 65-ft (20m) observation tower in the Shark River Slough, the 'river of grass' or, for $5, taking the two-hour 'tram' ride, or hiring a cycle. The tram leaves on the hour from 0900 to 1600 every day.

You'll see alligators, plenty of bird species, and probably a bobcat.

EVERGLADES CITY. &. In the far north-west corner of the Everglades National Park is Everglades City, population 344 including Chokoloskee village on Sandfly Island. I found the Visitor Centre here to be open 0900-1700 but its official hours are listed as 0800-1630, daily.

The city itself has an RV camp, condos for rent, a restaurant and deli, a 70-ft (22m) observation tower, an oversized city hall — and an airport.

Ten Thousand Islands. The 20 miles of coast nearby is a vast mangrove swamp that's virtually unmappable; no wonder it's called the Ten Thousand Islands. Sammy Hamilton has a National Parks concession to operate two boat safaris, the Mangrove Wilderness Trip and the Ten Thousand Islands Trip, lasting from 100 to 180 minutes, time and route depending upon prevailing conditions. You can contact Sammy at PO Box 119, Everglades City, FL 33929, ✆(813)695.2591 or 1.800.445.7724, or through the Visitor Center.

Florida Boat Tours operates airboats on Chokoloskee Bay but doesn't enter the park where these craft are banned; the trips introduce you to pelicans and let you feed them – also banned in the park. Contact Captain's Table Marina, Collier Blv. ✆1.800.282.9194. Wooten's Everglades Airboat Tours offers similar trips; ✆695.2781. Or hire a canoe for $18 a day, $12 a half-day, at the Glades Haven Store.

The privately-owned and run Everglades Wildlife Sanctuary is on the approach to Everglades City and offers cruises over much the same routes in the catamaran *Jungle Queen.* Your ticket also includes admission to the zoo, which has a captive panther. Open daily 1000-1700; ✆695.2800 or 1.800.543.3367.

Florida Boat Tours on ✆695.4400 or 1.800.282.9194 operates pontoons among the islands and airboats into the backwaters.

Chokoloskee Island. The road continues on a causeway to Chokoloskee Island, a 135-acre (0.5 sq km) 20-foot-high heap of seashells discarded by the Amerinds. Chokoloskee village is a scattering of small bungalows and fishing cottages.

OUTSIDE THE PARK

Ten miles west along the Tamiami Trail is Port of the Isles Resort, a splendid 200-room hotel with tennis courts and marina – and Island Nature Cruises which will take you to the Ten Thousand Islands aboard the cat-pontoon *Island Princess.* Port of the Isles is at 25000 I-41, Naples, FL 33961, ✆394.3101 or 1.800.282.3011.

Airboats. Airboats are not allowed in the Everglades National Park, nor a central section of the Big Cypress National Preserve, as they're noisy and scare the wildlife. Nonetheless, there are several chances to try this unusual form of transport, either along the Tamiami Trail – the name comes from Tampa and Miami, the cities at the trail's ends – or at the Everglades Holiday Park on US-27 just south of its junction with Alligator Alley, I-75. The holiday park has the world's largest, and probably noisiest, twin-engine airboat as well as a campsite and zoo. Address? 21940 Griffin Rd, Ft Lauderdale, FL 33332, ✆434.8111 in Broward County, ✆621.2009 in Dade.

MICCOSUKEE INDIAN VILLAGE. ♿ Half a mile west of the Shark Valley Visitor Center on the Tamiami Trail you'll find one of the smallest of the North American Indian tribes, the 500-strong Miccosukees. After the 19th-cent Indian Wars the majority of the Seminoles were forcibly moved out of Florida, but a few families escaped the round-up and lived in seclusion in the Everglades.

When the Tamiami Trail was carved through their wilderness in the 1930s, the Miccosukees came out of hiding and decided to accept some of the conveniences of modern life while still keeping their tribal traditions and living in their thatched huts, *chickees*, in the swamplands.

The tribe gained federal recognition in 1962 and now has its own reservation amid the river of grass and spanning Alligator Alley; the Miccosukee elect their own council, publish their own newspaper and speak their own language, but their main source of income these days is in throwing their village on the Tamiami Trail open to paleface visitors, selling crafts and souvenirs (some are excellent Indian works but others are mass-produced plastic), operating airboats, and holding alligator-wrestling displays. By the way, a 'gator has extremely powerful muscles for closing its jaws but very weak ones for opening them.

The Miccosukee Tribe of Indians is at PO Box 440021, Tamiami Station, FL 331144, ✆223.8388; admission to the village is $5.

VERDICT. Did you come to Florida to see Walt Disney World, the Kennedy Space Center and Palm Beach? If so, the Everglades may be a waste of your time. But if you love the wilderness and all wild creatures, the 'Glades offers an experience you'll long remember; you could easily spend a week here, but if time is short concentrate on the Anhinga Trail. Do remember the mosquito menace from Easter to Christmas, as well as the alligators, the few crocodiles on the coast, and the snakes: in other words, don't go swimming.

15: MIAMI

The Tuttle-Flagler Extravaganza.

MIAMI IS BIG, BRIGHT AND BRASH. It calls itself the 'sophisticated tropics' and among its claims to fame are: it's the only US city created by a woman; it's the busiest cruise port in the world; it has the oldest building in the New World; at Miami Beach is the world's largest concentration of art deco buildings; its airport has the USA's greatest number of international flights; at Coral Gables it has the first planned community in the USA; it has the tallest skyscrapers south of New York and east of Chicago; it holds the USA's largest banking community outside New York; it has the largest botanical garden in continental USA — and it was where the Beatles made their US debut, on the Ed Sullivan Show.

True. Sadly it's also the world's largest illegal importer of hard drugs and it has a couple of night-time no-go areas — Liberty City and the Biscayne district.

Oldest building? And the claim about the New World's oldest building needs clarification: the **Monastery of St Bernard** was built in Segovia, Spain, in 1141. Newspaper millionaire William Randolph Hearst shipped it to the USA in 1929 in 10,000 crates destined for San Simeon on the Californian coast, but the stones became mixed when customs officers demanded the straw packing be burned. It was eventually reassembled in 1954, at 16711 West Dixie Highway here in Miami, and it's open Mon-Sat 1000-1700 (Sunday 1200-1700) for $3 a tour. Continental North America's oldest native building is in the north of the state at St Augustine, but the New World's oldest surviving building is arguably in the Dominican Republic.

Julia Tuttle. So let's begin at the beginning. In 1870 the entire population of Florida between Lake Okeechobee and Key Largo was 85. Then in 1891 Clevelander Julia Tuttle came by mailboat to the tiny township that still had its Seminole Indian name, Mayami. She decided Miami should be a big city, and that *she* would mastermind the transformation.

Henry Flagler. Soon she realised she needed the railway if her dream were to come true. But railroad magnate Henry Flagler wasn't interested in her offer of 300 free acres. During the big freeze of 1893-

94, Mrs Tuttle sent Flagler an orange branch in full blossom, and Flagler saw the prospect of freighting fruit to the frozen north: a year later the Florida East Coast Railroad reached Miami.

Flagler joined Mrs Tuttle in promoting 'the city that never was a town.' He built the Royal Palm Hotel and brought down the country's most influential figures to see for themselves. Soon elaborate homes were going up on Brickell Avenue, today the heart of downtown Miami.

Vizcaya. James Deering, vice president of International Harvester, engaged 1,000 men for five years to build the most luxurious house conceivable, a 34-room mock-medieval Italianate mansion which he called Vizcaya, the Spanish word for Basque and with the same roots as 'Biscayne.'

During the construction, Deering lived in the 380-acre (154- ha) forested grounds in a stone house that had nothing which could burn, and his art collection was kept in a room without windows (this house has now been converted into efficiencies). His new winter home, completed in 1916 in unashamed extravagance, used genuine 16th- and 18th-cent interiors from European palaces — and it's still in that condition today though it's now the **Vizcaya Museum and Gardens** at 3251 S Miami Ave, ✆579.2813, open daily except Christmas 0930-1700 for $5 admission. More than 250,000 people visit the mansion each year.

The amazing banyan tree can almost turn itself into a forest; perhaps they'll take over Miami's Coral Gables one day?

The ultimate dream? No – only 'Song of America' in Miami.

So you want to discover the thrill of scuba diving? Or are you studying colonial architecture in Key West?

Air boats don't harm the marine life, but they're not easy on the ear.
Interior of the Audubon House, Key West.

Boomtown. Miami was one of America's top boom towns in the 1920s, with property touts selling their real estate to eager crowds on the street. As tourists and would-be speculators flooded in, the hotels developed the 'hot bed system,' renting a room for just half a day.

Coral Gables. George Merrick planned and built a garden city and named it Coral Gables from the main feature of his house there; he sold the first properties in 1921. Coral Gables is now almost a city within a city, surrounded by a mock-medieval wall pierced with elegant gates, watered by miles of grid-plan canals, divided by avenues shaded by some of the largest banyan trees you're likely to see, and now forming one of Miami's most select areas, bounded by SW 8th St — the famed Calle Ocho — and SW 72nd St, Sunset Drive. The Venetian Pool is a popular beauty spot and Main Street is better known as Miracle Mile from its smart shops.

Fairchild Tropical Gardens. (&. in part.) And in Coral Gables, the USA's first planned community, are the largest botanical gardens in continental USA, the 83-acre Fairchild Tropical Gardens, recreating tropical rain forest and palmy glades and also featuring a hot house to combat those rare Florida frosts. Find the gardens at 10901 Old Cutler Rd, ✆667.1651, open daily 0930-1630 for $4.

Hialeah. Aviation pioneer Glenn Curtiss, whose firm built the first flying-boat to cross the Atlantic, created Hialeah and Miami Springs as winter havens for wealthy northerners, the forerunners of the 'snowbird syndrome.' Hialeah is home to a 'higher layer' of society, and that's how to pronounce its name. On the north-east of Okeechobee Rd, it now has what's claimed to be the most beautiful horse racetrack in the world at Hialeah Park, and the park's flock of 400 flamingos sometimes features in the credits for the TV series *Miami Vice.* And at Miami Springs on the south-west of Okeechobee Rd the main attraction is the **Miami Jai-Alai Fronton,** where the Basque sport of pelota made its landfall in the New World.

Opa-locka. Then in 1926 Curtiss went on to create the exotic Opa-locka district just above Hialeah, reproducing all that's best in the architecture of the Arab world. The district's centre is built around an Islamic crescent moon, with radiating streets named from characters out of *The 1,001 Tales from the Arabian Nights.*

Amelia Earhart. As a point of interest, America's favourite female flyer, Amelia Earhart, took off from Opa-locka Airport in 1937 for her round-the-world flight. She was lost in the South Pacific in July, three weeks before her 39th birthday.

Bust. A hurricane struck Miami in 1926, causing people to reconsider their plans for this subtropical paradise. Three years later the Wall Street Crash turned many Miami millionaires into paupers, but the building boom merely went into lower gear.

Miami Beach. In the early years of the century a simple wooden

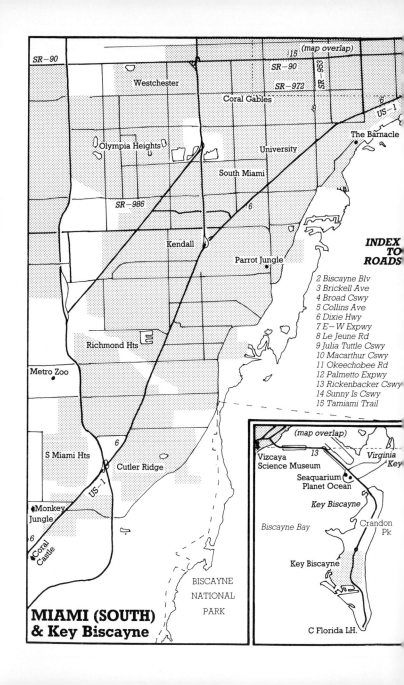

INDEX TO ROADS

2 Biscayne Blv
3 Brickell Ave
4 Broad Cswy
5 Collins Ave
6 Dixie Hwy
7 E—W Expwy
8 Le Jeune Rd
9 Julia Tuttle Cswy
10 Macarthur Cswy
11 Okeechobee Rd
12 Palmetto Expwy
13 Rickenbacker Cswy
14 Sunny Is Cswy
15 Tamiami Trail

MIAMI (SOUTH)
& Key Biscayne

bridge linked northern Miami Beach to the mainland, allowing avocado farmer John Collins to get his crops to market. Tired of the graft, Collins sold his 1,600 acres of sand to Carl Fisher who had earned his fortune by making car headlights and had already built the Indianapolis Speedway. Fisher pumped sand from the bed of northern Biscayne Bay and dumped it onto Collins's former avocado farm, raising the altitude of Miami Beach to five feet above sea level and turning it into useful real estate.

Fisher began building hotels and golf courses, publicising them with stunts such as providing a baby elephant as caddy for President Harding's golfing holiday on the Beach.

Al Capone. But Chicago gangster Al Capone heard of the stunts and decided that Miami was ready to receive his protection rackets. Capone soon left, but the mobs stayed on until Senator Kefauver's much-publicised clean-up in 1950 sent them to Havana, and ultimately to Fidel Castro.

Art deco. Meanwhile, Miami Beach continued to prosper, despite the Depression. Perhaps as a result of the general gloom the Beach's architects exaggerated the current art style and adapted it to buildings, creating what we now call *art deco*. Walk north along the Beach's Collins Avenue today — it's often quicker than driving — and you can see block after block of sugar-candy apartments and hotels painted in pastel tones.

As you approach a zigzag you get a marvellous view of the 12-storey Fontainbleau Hilton, built in 1954 on 20 acres of seafront. This particular view is framed by an art deco arch, but as you draw closer you realise the perspective isn't changing and that you're looking at the ultimate in murals, covering 13,000 sq ft (1,400 sq m) of blank wall.

During the Second World War Miami became a major military base, but in the early '50s the fast-talking property salesmen were back again, offering big discounts to hesitant buyers provided they snatched the bargain within 15 minutes. Television helped promote the resort first by networking the most popular programmes from here, such as Ed Sullivan's interview with the Beatles, and later by turning the cameras on the city itself, as in *Miami Vice*. Meanwhile, tourism was entering its boom years with airlines replacing Flagler's railroad, south Florida became the nation's retirement home — and refugees poured in from the Caribbean, 265,000 from Castro's Cuba, 150,000 from Papa Doc's Haiti, and now a steady stream from Nicaragua and other Central American states.

Modern Miami. Modern Miami is therefore a very cosmopolitan society. Overtown was the city's first black community and the starting point for jazz musicians Nat King Cole and Louis Armstrong, but the former Lemon City has now become Little Haiti. Bounded by Biscayne Blv, North-South Expwy, Airport Expwy and NE 79th St, this is the place to come for Creole food and music.

Cuba's exiles gathered in Little Havana, centred on SW 8th St, *Calle Ocho,* where Spanish has ousted English and where men roll Havana cigars in small back-street factories. Here you'll find paella, flamenco, the Cuban Memorial Boulevard commemorating the Bay of Pigs invasion and, every March, the *Carnaval Miami,* its million participants making it the biggest Latin-American festival in the USA.

OTHER MIAMI SIGHTS

BRICKELL. The downtown area of Miami is overshadowed by its skyscrapers, yet there's still a sense of space and daylight down at street level. The tallest scraper is the 55-floor Southeast Financial Center of glass and granite and with 1,150,000 sq ft (100,000 sq m) of floorspace. I took the skyscraper photograph from the **Visitor's Bureau** on the 27th floor of the Barnett Bank at 701 Brickell Ave, which is where to come for specific tourist information.

Bayside. Nearby is Bayside, a modern shopping mall with its own adjacent car park; trouble is, the park is usually full. Bayside has plenty of boutiques and up-market shops, a selection of 30 places to eat, and an intriguing craft market where you can watch, among other activities, glass-blowers at work. It's strange to recall that just 12 miles from here you could be standing in the Everglades.

H.M.S. Bounty. On the waterfront you might see the full-scale replica of Captain Bligh's *H.M.S. Bounty,* built by MGM in Lunenburg, Nova Scotia, in 1960 for film work. The ship had cruised 70,000 miles via Tahiti and the Pool of London before mooring at Bayside where she's open to inspection Sun-Thurs 1200-2000, Fri 1200-2200, Sat 1000-2200, for $3.50, reductions for under 12s and over 50s. But don't blame me if she's not there; she came round from Tampa and she'll doubtless move on again.

Bal Harbor. At the northern end of the island of Miami Beach, Bal Harbor is a haven for the well-heeled, and the beach on which GIs trained during World War Two now has smart gardens sprouting from the sands. This is exactly where you would expect to find top-market hotels such as the recently-refurbished Sheraton Bal Harbor (9701 Colline Ave, ✆865.7511) which has an enclosed two-storey fountain and the Bal Masque showgirl revue.

Coconut Grove. On the S Dixie Hwy south-east of Coral Gables, Coconut Grove is one of the older districts that expanded beyond Deering's Vizcaya. Queen Victoria was already dead, but Victorian England has been preserved in much of the architecture and some of the street lamps.

Commodore Ralph Munroe, one of the first to move in, built an elegant house at 3485 Main Hwy which he called The Barnacle; the house was high off the ground to allow air circulation and as

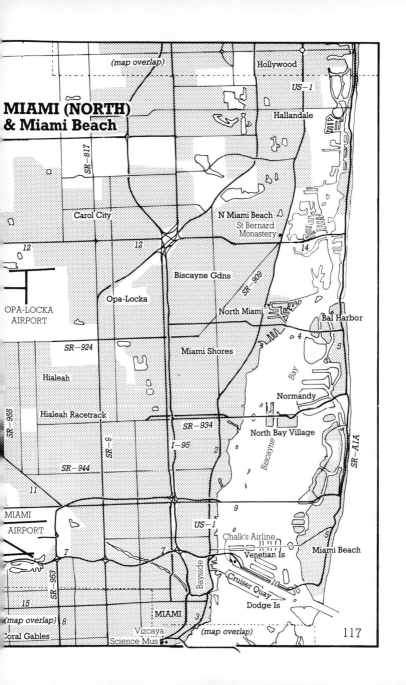

MIAMI (NORTH)
& Miami Beach

(map overlap)

Hollywood

US−1

Hallandale

SR−817

Carol City

N Miami Beach
St Bernard
Monastery

12

12

14

Biscayne Gdns

SR−909

OPA-LOCKA
AIRPORT

Opa-Locka

North Miami

Bal Harbor

SR−924

Miami Shores

4

5

Hialeah

Bay

Normandy

SR−955

Hialeah Racetrack

SR−934

North Bay Village

SR−9

I−95

2

SR−A1A

Biscayne

SR−944

11

9

MIAMI
AIRPORT

US−1

5

Chalk's Airline

7

7

Venetian Is

Miami Beach

SR−953

Bayside

Cruiser Quay

15

Dodge Is

(map overlap)

8

Coral Gables

MIAMI

3

Vizcaya
Science Mus

(map overlap)

117

protection against floods. Now restored to its turn-of-the-century grandeur, **The Barnacle** is open to view 0900-1700, Wed- Sun; ☎448.9445.

Back to Vizcaya for the **Museum of Science** and **Space Planetarium,** at 3280 S Miami Ave, ☎854.4247, (854.2222 for times of planetarium special shows), billed as a children's museum but equally entertaining for adults. Popular science is brought to life here, and you can do a number of the experiments yourself, if you can find elbow space.

Virginia Key. Cross the Rickenbacker Cswy to Virginia Key for **Planet Ocean,** open daily from 1000, last admissions 1640, entry $6.50, ☎361.9455. This is more an experience than a museum, allowing you to touch an iceberg, create a hurricane, step inside a drop of water, and follow the Gulf Stream back to Europe. You can also see *April Fool*, a boat less than six feet long, which sailed across the Atlantic.

The Rickenbacker Cswy leads on to the **Miami Seaquarium** (☎361.5703) and its continuous performances by dolphins, sealions and a killer whale, and you can study manatees, sharks, turtles and tropical fish. The site covers 60 acres (25ha) with transport by the aquarium's own monorail. Open 0930-1830, last admissions 1700, fee $12.

Key Biscayne. Bear Cut Bridge leads on to Key Biscayne, home of unashamed opulence and world-famous sporting centres such as the Key Biscayne golf course and tennis courts – but beware the morning and evening rush hours. The Bill Baggs Cape Florida State Recreation Area is a 400-acre (160ha) park at the key's southern end, from where there are superb views of Miami. Here, too, is Stiltsville, a tiny community of homes set on legs rising from the sea. And there's a good beach, too.

Miami Beach. From an avocado farm and natural coconut groves to a bustling seaside resort in ten years; that was Miami Beach's origin in the 1930s. Fisher raised the island above flood level, but since then millions of tons of sand have been dredged up to make the Beach's beach, which is now wide, white, and fine-grained. Incidentally, it's officially closed from midnight to 0500.

You'll come here not only for the sands and the art deco – get a map of the art deco district from the Miami Design Preservation League at Room 11, 1236 Ocean Dr, ☎672.2014 – but also for the atmosphere; be lucky with your timing and you'll see people in 1930s costume reviving the old days. Only the crush of traffic reminds you that this is the 1990s.

Parking your rented car is not easy and will cost 25¢ at a Collins Ave meter, but don't be tempted to park in the seedier backstreets if you want to see the car again. Española Way, south of 15th St, isn't seedy any longer; it looks a cross between small-town Spain and a Hollywood film set, and is home to a growing colony of artists.

You can reach Miami Beach suggestably by the Macarthur Cswy from near Bayside, crossing Wilson's Island, home of Chalk's International Airline, and from where you have a wonderful view of the cruise liners at their Dodge Island quays. North of the causeway are three man-made islands protected by barriers and security guards; you're allowed in to drive past the homes of the super-affluent.

Sunny Isles. You can then come off the Beach over the Julia Tuttle Cswy to Biscayne Blv; northbound this leads to North Miami Beach, which is on the mainland, and the Sunny Isles, where lower priced hotels and condos cluster around the man-made beach, and St Bernard Monastery is nearby.

Take US-1, the S Dixie Hwy, out of town for the remaining tourist attractions. Turn off left onto SW 57th Ave for **Parrot Jungle,** at number 11000, open daily 0930−1700 (∅666.7834), entry $6. Parrots, cockatoos and macaws go through their routines while flamingos and other birds stroll around the showpiece grounds. SW 112nd St takes you back to US−1, southbound.

Turn right onto SW 128th St for the **Weeks Air Museum,** ∅233.5197, at number 14710, the Tamiami Airport. The museum is open 1000-1700 Wed-Sun for $4 and displays more than 30 aircraft from the early days of aviation to 1945, most of them in airworthy condition. The non-profit organisation which started this venture in 1987 has some good WW2 veterans as well as an early Boeing biplane.

A good map will help you short-cut to the **Metrozoo,** ⅃ in part, or you can approach it from US-1 westbound along SW 152nd St, Coral Reef Drive, to number 12400, ∅241.0400. This zoo has the right approach in that humans are behind wire mesh while the animals are for the most part free to roam; there are around 3,000 residents in 285 acres, which makes this the USA's largest zoo as well as the newest. Big cats in a Thai temple, the fauna of the Kenyan grasslands, rare and endangered species, and a breeding programme, all go to make this a zoo with a difference assuming you must have captive creatures. Metrozoo is run by Metro-Dade Parks Department, open daily 1000-1730 (last tickets 1600) for $6.

That good map could also short-cut you to **Monkey Jungle,** otherwise you'll need to take SW 216th St, Hanlin Mill Dr, to number 14805, ∅235.1611. Monkey Jungle was founded in 1935 and was a pioneer of the policy of caging the visitors to let the animals roam free, and it has recently released captive- bred primates back into the wild. You can stroll through tunnel- cages to see most of the primates, from gorillas and mandrills to baboons, marmosets and chimpanzees − and a few alligators in the 30-acre (12ha) jungle. Open daily 0930-1700 for $6.

Your next call is at **Orchid Jungle** ⅃ on SW 157th Ave, Homestead, ∅247.4824, open daily 0830-1730. This jungle gives free advice on growing orchids and allows you to see its tissue-culture laboratories.

It's easy to find **Coral Castle** ♿; look on US-1's northbound lane between SW 280th and 288th Sts, or look for SW 157th Ave (Streets are east-west, don't forget). And it's in Homestead, not Miami.

Edward Leedskalnin was a five-foot Latvian who used hand-tools to carve more than 1,000 tons of the hard coral rock, and hand-operated pulleys and levers to manoeuvre it into place; no mean feat considering that some stones weigh 30 tons! Ed was interested in astronomy and magnetism, and built his hobbies into this fantastic coral castle which was, presumably, to be his marital home. But his intended bride jilted him the day before the wedding and in 1920 Coral Castle became Florida's first tourist attraction. One of the oddities, a nine-ton gate that a child can push open, has helped put the castle in several record books. It's open daily 0900-2100 for $6.50; ✆248.6344.

The 2,000-square-mile (5,000 sq km) conurbation of Greater Miami finishes at **Florida City,** a quiet community whose entire economy rests on the cultivation and marketing of tomatoes. They're harvested nine months of the year, omitting only high summer when it's too hot and the market is glutted.

The 'Heritage of Miami' is yours for $20 — but you must give it back after four hours.

MIAMI FACTFILE

(See also chapters 4, 5, and 7 for tourist contacts, sports, car hire and public transport in Miami.)

Travelling in Miami: on land. Apart from the functional public services there are the fun ways to travel. **Old Town Trolley Tours** operates from offices at 650 NW 8th St, ✆374.TOUR, with trolleys covering Miami and, separately, Miami Beach, with Bayside their common point.

Services run from 0900-1600 daily, with trolleys at 30-minute intervals. The fare is $11 for each tour, or a $16 ticket takes you on both. You can pick up anywhere on the route and drop off to see the local sights before catching the next trolley. If you happen to be carless this is the best way of visiting the tourist attractions.

The Miami route is: Bayside – Hyatt Hotel – Sheraton Brickell – Miami Seaquarium (Virginia Key) – coast road to Vizcaya – Mayfair – Fairchild Tropical Garden – Parrot Jungle – north to Biltmore Hotel (1200 Anastasia Ave, Coral Gables) – Venetian Pool, Coral Gables – Hyatt Coral Gables – Tamiami Trail, 'Calle Ocho' – Biscayne Bay Marriott – Bayside.

The Miami Beach route is: Bayside – Macarthur Cswy to Penrods (south end of Ocean Dr) – north to 13th St – Shelborne Hotel and Seville Hotel (both on Collins Ave) – Fontainbleau Hilton – Eden Roc – Doral – Seacoast Towers – south to previous three stops – western Miami Beach to Miami Beach Colony – Lincoln Rd Mall – Bayside.

Travelling in Miami: by boat. There are numerous ways of seeing Miami from the water. *Heritage of Miami II* is a two-mast schooner moored at Bayside which takes twice-daily parties at $20 a person; ✆858.6264.

Hire yourself a motor-boat from **Beach Boat Rentals** at 2380 Collins Ave, FL 33139, ✆534.4307. Rates range from $45 for one hour to $175 for eight, with a credit-card deposit of $250.

Easy Sailing at Dinner Key Marina, Coconut Grove, ✆858.4001, has 19ft and 22ft sailing boats for hourly or daily rental. Reservations required.

You can be a passenger aboard **Pier One Charter Service**'s *Celebration* for a half-day or full-day cruise: contact Suite 9, 3239 W Trade Ave, Coconut Grove, ✆444.2778.

For group charters and private charter of luxury yachts, contact the Chamber of Commerce.

HOTELS and MOTELS. It is utterly impossible to give a complete list of Miami hostelries. As the average European visitor is more money-conscious than the American, motels are usually the answer. In Miami, look along the Tamiami Trail, or go to Homestead and

Florida City along SR-997. But if you're in the market for luxury at any price, here are some of the top Greater Miami hotels which are also tourist attractions, with daily rates:

The **Biltmore Hotel,** 1200 Anastasia Ave, Coral Gables, FL 33134, ✆445.1926. The phone number is the year the hotel was built, and early guests include Bing Crosby, Ginger Rogers and Johnny Weismuller. It became a World War Two hospital and was then closed in 1968 with the threat of demolition. It was saved, restored at a cost of $40,000,000, and it reopened in 1986. Front door rates start at $150 per room, but you might get in cheaper in a package deal.

At 700 Biltmore Way, Coral Gables, FL 33134, is the **David William Hotel,** ✆445.7821, for an extravaganza of keep-fit equipment, presumably for use after you've tried the food which gourmets rate among the city's best. The tariff isn't too bad, starting at $100.

Mutiny in Sailboat Bay really is the name of a hotel! It's at 2951 S Bayshore Dr, Coconut Grove, FL 33133, ✆442.2400, and its decor must surely be the ultimate in psychedelic design. Staying here is an experience in its own right, regardless of the bill of around $140.

Go for art deco in the **Cardozo Hotel,** 1144 Ocean Dr, Miami Beach, FL 33139, ✆534.2135. This is the best of several renovated hotels that have preserved the 1930s style down to the last detail. The price isn't bad at $65, high season.

The ultimate in luxury awaits you at the **Fontainbleau Hilton Resort and Spa** at 4441 Collins Ave, Miami Beach, FL 33140, ✆538.2000. This is the subject of that vast mural along Collins Ave, but no picture can tell of the $60,000,000 refit when the Hilton chain took over. The hotel has 1,200 rooms, two pools, 11 restaurants, and a staff of more than 400. Past guests include Cary Cooper, Frank Sinatra and Lana Turner, and the hotel featured in the Bond movie *Goldfinger*. Rates start at $150.

RESTAURANTS. My comment on hotels is even more apt when applied to restaurants. You can find good, clean eating houses *anywhere* in the city, at all reasonable hours and many that are unreasonable. You can eat traditional American, new American, regional American, Argentinian, Basque, Bavarian, Brazilian, Caribbean, Chinese, Colombian, Cuban, Danish, French, German, Greek, Haitian, Hungarian, Indonesian, Indian, International, Italian, north Italian, Jamaican, Japanese, Korean, Kosher, Mediterranean, Mexican, Nicaraguan, Puerto Rican, Spanish, Swiss, Thai, Turkish, West Indian or Vietnamese . . . but no English. You can have fast food, sea food, vegetarian food. And you can spend anything from $2 to a month's salary.

In the circumstances, no recommendations, no listings. Go find your own.

NIGHTLIFE. Not surprisingly, you're spoiled for choice once more. If you're plannng to get the best, look for *This Week in Miami* and similar freesheets, normally available in hotel receptions and at the desks in the better motels.

Alternatively, call American Sightseeing Tours, Inc, either through your hotel reception or direct on ✆681.4500. ASTI will pick you up at your hotel by coach, give you a choice of the latest entertainment, add in dinner, taxes and tips – and bill you from $35, which is very reasonable considering that the deal may include such shows as the Fontainbleau Hilton's High Society nightclub and variety show, or the Sheraton Bal Harbor's Las Vegas-style revue.

For go-there-yourself entertainment you might consider **Cherry's Lounge** at 14670 W Dixie Hwy, N Miami, ✆944.2221, for 'adult entertainment' in a go-go bar. **Les Violins Supper Club** at 1751 Biscayne Blv, has top-class floor shows, but you must phone ✆371.8668 for the latest times, and make a reservation.

The **Jackie Gleason Theater** at 1700 Washington Ave, Miami Beach, ✆673.8300, puts on Broadway shows during the winter season, while the **Coconut Grove Playhouse** at 3500 Main Hwy, Coconut Grove, ✆442.4000, brings over shows from London's West End as well, for its October to June season.

Ballet, opera, symphony and concert music, pop groups and Broadway stars in one-man or -woman shows, complete the high-season attractions. Prices? For these shows the tickets cost from a few dollars to a few hundred.

Miami Grand Prix. Finally, if you come to Miami in February, don't forget it's Grand Prix time when part of Biscayne Blv becomes a racetrack for one of the richest meetings in the USA's motor racing calendar. And in the autumn the Nissan Indy Challenge is held on public roads around Tamiami Park.

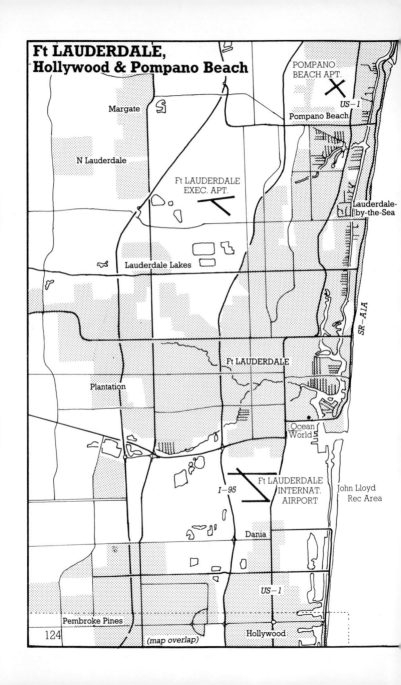

Ft LAUDERDALE, Hollywood & Pompano Beach

POMPANO BEACH APT.

Margate

Pompano Beach

US−1

N Lauderdale

Ft LAUDERDALE EXEC. APT.

Lauderdale-by-the-Sea

Lauderdale Lakes

SR − A1A

Ft LAUDERDALE

Plantation

Ocean World

I−95

Ft LAUDERDALE INTERNAT. AIRPORT

John Lloyd Rec Area

Dania

US−1

Pembroke Pines

124

(map overlap)

Hollywood

16: Ft LAUDERDALE to PALM BEACH

The Gold Coast

WHEN A TOP SOCIETY MAGAZINE gave the resorts along this coast a carat rating as if they were gold ingots, Ft Lauderdale came out at 18-carat, Coral Gables and Coconut Grove in Miami were 20 and 23 carat, but Palm Beach was pure gold, 24-carat.

They couldn't call this strip of seashore anything but the Gold Coast. The beaches are golden, the sunshine is golden, and you need a few bars of the stuff to contemplate buying your way in to Palm Beach, one of the wealthiest and most exclusive towns in the world. Property is so expensive here that Sothebys of London, better known as fine art auctioneers, have moved in as realtors.

Today the carat rating still holds true. Ft Lauderdale has more panache than downtown Miami, Boca Raton (the name means 'Rat's Mouth,' but don't tell anybody) lives and breathes money — but Palm Beach is the last word in sophistication, the East Coast's answer to that other Hollywood in California. In Palm Beach it's illegal to hang out a clothesline, to wash your car in public, to go jogging without a shirt and, for what it's worth, to own a kangaroo.

'Most beautiful town.' The mayor of Palm Beach welcomes visitors to "what must be the most beautiful town in the *world*," and the Beach's visitor's book contains such names as Angie Dickinson, Diahann Caroll, Elizabeth Taylor, Dolly Parton, HRH Prince Charles and Princess Diana, Prince Henry Constantine, and a score of other celebrities — all collected within one year. Burt Reynolds probably wouldn't sign; he was born at Jupiter to the north and now lives in Palm Beach.

Sadly, there is a touch of base metal in the gold bullion. A lifelong townee told me: "Ten years ago I didn't even lock the door. Now I have a burglar alarm, a chain link fence, and two guard dogs."

Shipwrecked. The first recorded European settler on this stretch of coast was Jonathan Dickinson who had no choice in the matter; he was the only survivor of a 1696 shipwreck. The Abaniki tribe of Amerinds harassed him but he managed to escape to St Augustine and tell his story. Today the 11,000-acre (43 sq km) Jonathan Dickinson State Park, just north of Jupiter in Martin County, is unspoiled forest — with 135 campsites.

Wreckers of another kind followed. Pirates, adventurers, and men who deliberately enticed ships onto a lee shore, made themselves almost as good a living as did the early settlers in Key West. By the end of the 19th cent they were holding prayer meetings for specific flotsam, and bemoaning the quality of what the storms sent their way.

In 1873 a small settlement on a long, offshore island was struggling to survive. Five years later the Spanish brigantine *Providencia* ran aground there, shedding its load of coconuts and giving the settlers the excuse to invent the name Palm City. But by 1887 the inhabitants had given up the pretence of city status and renamed their community Palm Beach; it has never again used the title of city and is still just a town.

Henry Flagler. But then came Henry Flagler, taking his Florida East Coast Railroad down to Julia Tuttle's Miami. Flagler liked Palm Beach and in 1894 he freighted down everything that was needed to build his Royal Poinciana Hotel.

Once started, he couldn't stop, and in 1900 he opened The Breakers Hotel, an oceanfront timber building in Renaissance style that soon had the Astors, the Rockefellers, Carnegie and President Harding on its guest list, most of them travelling in their own railroad cars.

West Palm Beach. Right from the start, Flagler decided that Palm Beach would be an exclusive resort. The common workmen, white or black, who built the town and who laid the railway tracks, lived in Flagler's purpose-built industrial suburb which he called West Palm Beach. Soon, black people were allowed into Palm Beach only if they had jobs there — and they had to be out of town by nightfall whether they were domestic staff or the operators of the Beach's only public transport system, the Afromobiles, a variant on the Asiatic rickshaw.

Whitehall. Flagler's *pièce de résistance* in Palm Beach was his own home, built for his second wife Mary Lily. Called simply Whitehall, it faced Lake Worth, the strip of water which separates the very long Palm Beach island from the mainland, with its rear gardens fronting onto the Beach's main thoroughfare, Cocoanut Row (and that's not a spelling mistake). It was completed in 1902 at a cost of $4,000,000 and was super-palatial even for this town in which palaces were common.

Flagler Museum. Flagler slipped on Whitehall's marble floors in 1913, suffering an injury which soon killed him. The house became a hotel in 1925, but in 1959 Flagler's grand-daughter bought the place, demolished the hotel annexe, and restored the family home to its original condition. It's now the Henry Morrison Flagler Museum at 1, Whitehall Way, open Tues-Sat 1000-1700, Sun 1200-1700, for $3.50, and with on-site parking. And as a bonus, Flagler's own railroad car, The Rambler, is on display.

Meanwhile, Ft Lauderdale was little more than the 1838-vintage fort named from Major William Lauderdale, its commander during the Seminole wars, though Julia Tuttle and Henry Flagler were about to start the property boom here as well.

Addison Mizner. The moment created the man. Addison Mizner, an overweight ex-miner and ex-prizefighter arrived in Palm Beach in 1918, talked the heir of the Singer sewing machine company into financing him, and went into business as an overnight architect. His first work was to be a convalescent hospital for the troops, but when the war ended unexpectedly Mizner and Singer converted the place into the mock-Spanish Everglades Club.

Palm Beach loved the styling, and Mizner found himself in fashion. He designed a stream of pseudo-something houses, based on a composite of European medieval architecture, and made frequent trips to Spain to buy furnishings and complete interiors: legend claims that he was on first-name terms with King Alfonso.

Boynton Beach. Mizner's greatest achievement was the 100-room Cloister Inn at Boca Raton which cost him more than $1,200,000. His contacts with Spain prompted him to call the hotel's private approach—road the Camino Real, 'Royal Road.' But Mizner had overspent. He had also bought up the surrounding land and part of Boynton Beach to the north, and he now needed to sell it at a handsome profit. In true American style he invited the big names of the day, including Irving Berlin, to stay at the Cloister, and soon the property rush was on with Mizner making up to $2,000,000 a week.

Then, just as suddenly, fashion changed, and Mizner went broke. In 1928 a Philadelphian millionaire bought the Cloister Inn and turned it into the Boca Raton Club; the first qualification for membership was to have a million dollars in assets. After World War Two an aluminium manufacturer bought it for $22,500,000 and turned it back into a club-hotel. It has now been renovated beyond recognition since Mizner's time but if you want to see his work, take a leisurely stroll along Worth Ave, Palm Beach's fashionable shopping street at the south end of Cocoanut Row.

SEEING THE SIGHTS

Fort Lauderdale. Ft Lauderdale calls itself the yachting capital of the world, the tennis capital of the world — thanks to Chris Evert who was born here — and the Venice of America, but apart from that it doesn't go for the superlatives and you'd probably be wise not to mention the city's other name of Fort Liquordale. It is, however, the most popular beach resort in the state, a result of the founding fathers' decision in 1911 to keep the six miles of golden sands open to the public, and it's the younger generation's winter hideout, particularly the student community and especially at Easter. They keep that Liquordale name alive although it originated during the Prohibition era when prostitutes and rum were brought in from the Bahamas.

Canals and cruisers. The city claims to have 165 miles (265km) of canals, giving everybody who is anybody the chance to moor a boat at the bottom of the garden. Large areas in the city centre and along the Intracoastal Waterway to the north have canals alternating with roads, making Ft Lauderdale a boat—owner's paradise — and they say there are 30,000 small craft in the city.

Intracoastal Waterway. The Intracoastal, by the way, is a navigable channel running from Georgia to Key West, keeping to the natural watercourse that separates the chain of coastal sand-dunes — the 'beaches' at Daytona Beach, Palm Beach and Miami Beach — and the continental peninsula, although occasionally a canal has been necessary. The Intracoastal reaches the open sea at Biscayne Bay then squeezes between Key Largo and the mainland, going under Jewfish Drawbridge. It crosses Florida Bay to Key West, before swinging to the south of the keys and coming back up the Florida Strait, under Seven Mile Bridge, and meeting itself in the bay. It's dredged and buoyed where necessary, and is suitable for small cargo vessels.

Jungle Queen. It's also the ideal watercourse for the *Jungle Queen I* and *II*, boats built as replicas of the Mississippi stern-wheelers, except that they're powered by diesel and lack those beautiful

paddle-wheels. The newer 550-seat *Jungle Queen II* sails from the Jungle Queen docks at Bahia Mar, off SR-A1A, Breeze Blv, ∅462.5596 (Miami, ∅947.6597) for two-hour cruises starting at 1000 and 1400, but the main attraction is both boats' 1900-hr departure four-hour starlight dinner-cruise around the larger waterways, calling in at the *Queens'* own island with its Seminole Indian village for some exotic wildlife and alligator wrestling. By the way, the original Lauderdale fort was between Breeze Blv and the ocean, but nothing remains.

The boats pass along Millionaires' Row where the residents, far from being snobbish despite their palatial homes, flash their house lights on and off in greeting. Some of the guests may not notice as they're already into the eat-all-you-can dinner, and that's followed by a floating vaudeville show for an all-in fare of $6.50 plus tax.

The Spirit. The *Queens* have been in business for 50 years, but *The Spirit* is a newcomer owned by the Diplomat Hotel at 3515 S Ocean Dr, Holywood, ∅458.4999, which offers three-hour dinner cruises with modern-style live entertainment. Departures are at 1900 and the fare is $25.

Port Everglades. Let us not forget that SeaEscape cruisers sail from Port Everglades as well as from Miami and Tampa. The port is also popular with other cruise liners during the winter season, with Britain's own *QE II* among the callers. Port Everglades is an unlikely place to watch manatees, but you might see them and a few tropical fish in the warm fallout waters from a power station. As you enter the port area, bear right and look for a fence with spyholes cut into it.

Ocean World. ⅃ The Ocean World dolphinarium on SE 17th St Cswy, beside the Marriott Hotel, ∅525.6611, is in the highly competitive market of performing dolphins and sea lions, and of hand-fed sharks. I'll let you into a secret: sharks have low metabolism so don't need to eat more than twice a week. When they're fed regularly several times a day the problem is to get them to eat at all, rather than to make sure they don't eat the hand as well. Ocean World also features a tall aquarium allowing you to study the underwater life in comfort. Open daily 1000- 1800, last admission 1615; fee $8.

Flamingo Gardens. Head inland to 3750 Flamingo Rd in Davie for the 60-acre spread of Flamingo Gardens, open daily 0900-1700 for $5; ∅473.0010. A tram, really a Jeep towing open carriages, takes you around the botanical gardens, through the orange groves, and delivers you to 'Gator World to see if you can recognise another clip from the credits of *Miami Vice.* You might be interested in a cluster-fig tree more than 100ft (30m) tall and with a girth of 50ft (15m).

Lesser attractions. Ft Lauderdale city centre is at the intersection of Broward Blv and Andrews Ave, with eastbound streets and northbound avenues given their compass bearings from here. At nearby 231 SW 2nd St stands the **Discovery Center,** ∅462.4116, a child-orientated popular science museum where even the adults can make things work. Open Sep-Jun, Tues-Fri and Sun, 1400-1700, Sat 1200-1700; Jul and Aug, Tues-Sat 1000-1700, Sun 1200-1700, for $2.50.

Beside it is the **King-Cromartie House,** one of the original buildings in Ft Lauderdale and now preserved in that early 20th-cent condition. Open Tues-Fri 1200-1700, restricted hours at weekends, for $2.

And at 219 SW 2nd Ave, near the Discovery Center, is the local **Historical Society Museum,** ✆463.4431, holding what archives the city has, plus a display of Seminole Indian clothing. Entry is free.

A little further away at 333 S Federal Hwy, is Ft Lauderdale's oldest surviving building, the original trading post of 1902. It was built by its owners, Ivy Cromartie and Frank Stranahan, but Frank committed suicide during the Depression leaving Ivy to struggle on alone until her death in 1971. The Historical Society bought it, raised $250,000 to restore it to its original condition, and it's now the **Stranahan House Museum,** open Wed, Fri, Sat 1000-1600, for $3.

East of Ft Lauderdale International Airport the **John U. Lloyd State Recreation Area** offers picnic sites among 245 acres of open woodland, fishing off the Dania Pier, and a near- pristine stretch of beach. Access is along Dania Beach Blv. **Dania,** named from its Danish founders, was a busy tomato growing district in the winter until too much fresh Everglades water was drawn out of the limestone aquifer and sea water intruded. The situation is now reversed, but Dania has become a New Orleans lookalike and gone into the antiques business.

To the south, near the Broward-Dade county boundary, is **Hollywood,** established in 1921 by a party from that other Hollywood in California. When the founders wanted the yacht basins excavated they engaged the best man they could think of — Gen. George Washington Goethals, who had been in command of the Panama Canal project, completed in 1915. Surprisingly, Hollywood has a small Seminole Indian Reservation, bounded by SW 2nd St and the Florida Turnpike.

Broward Boulevard and Broward County, you may like to know, take their name from Napoleon Bonaparte Broward, the state governor early in the century who authorised the cutting of the Miami Canal from Lake Okeechobee and so started the draining of the Everglades.

If you leave Ocean World on US-A1A and cross the Brook Memorial Bridge, you reach the bottom end of a chain of four islands, 45 miles (72km) long but never reaching a mile in width. The islands are separated from the mainland by the Intracoastal Waterway and by Lake Worth (named from a general in the Seminole Wars), while the channels between the isles are narrow; Hillsboro Inlet, Boca Raton Inlet, with its jagged rocks that look like the teeth in the 'rat's mouth', and an insignificant cut further north. But the islands themselves are important as they hold the communities of Lauderdale-by-the Sea, Hillsboro Beach, and Palm Beach itself.

If you want to see one of the strangest street maps in existence, get a copy of the Palm Beach town plan. It's 55 inches long by 3½ inches wide.

The southernmost island also holds the **Hugh Taylor Birch State Park,** a pleasant enclave of 180 acres, mostly growing Australian pine. This pine is a pleasant tree to look at, but it's a terror if it gets out of control. It thrives on disturbed soil and beaches — this park is an ideal home — and is such an effective ground-covering plant that the Floridian native species can't compete with it.

Going north on the mainland, I-95 takes you past the New York Yankees' springtime stadium to **Pompano Beach,** home of harness-racing in the winter and the Texas Rangers in the spring. North-west, at 3600 W Sample Rd, beyond the turnpike, you'll find **Butterfly World** set in three acres of the Tradewinds Park. The butterfly farm shows you the full life cycle of scores of *lepidoptera* from 0900 to 1700 Mon-Sat and 1300-1700 on Sun. Entrance fee is $6.

Palm Beach. Apart from the Flagler Museum already described, the only major thing to look at in Palm Beach is Palm Beach itself. This place oozes elegance at every pore as you'll see on a leisurely drive through the town centre — you'll find it difficult to park your car. If you come in over the Royal Park Bridge (*Royal?* If the USA were a monarchy the king would have his winter palace here!), carry on down Royal Palm Way to Ocean Blv.

No, there's not much beach at Palm Beach; a hurricane swept it away. If you're desperate for sand, go either north or south.

Leave Ocean Blv for Worth Ave, also named from that Seminole War general, and study the elegant boutiques along Mizner's memorial. You're in the market for jewellery, Chanel No 5 or haut couture, or advice on investing your spare $5m? Fine! You just want bread? Too bad!

Turn into Cocoanut Row and drive north to the Flagler Museum. You might be able to park here, or in the grounds of the shingled building opposite, the Chamber of Commerce, allowing you to stroll down Cocoanut Walk and take a look at **The Breakers,** (1 S County Rd, FL 33480, ✆655.6611,) the modern version of that timber hotel Flagler built in 1900. Fire destroyed the original, so what you now stare at in awe is the 1925 version plus its 1989 renovation — and *that* cost a mere $16,000,000!

If you really would like to revel in luxury, start counting: high season rates begin at $250, with dinner an extra $35.

For the **Lion Country Safari** ♿, leave West Palm Beach westbound on Southern Blv, US-98 (SR-80). Fifteen miles (24km) away, in open

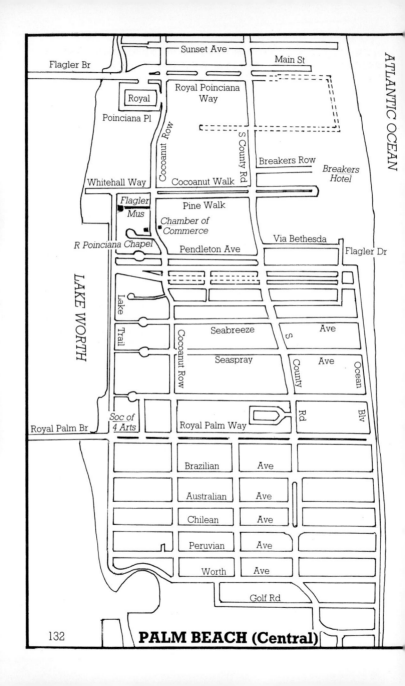

PALM BEACH (Central)

country, you'll find 500 acres (2 sq km) of managed parkland that is a re-creation of the East African bush and plains, where elephant, rhino, giraffe, zebra, several primate species, and lion, roam in limited freedom. The $11 ticket allows you to drive your hardtop car (no convertibles; or you can rent a car on site for $5 an hour) around the safari park and see the 1,000 inhabitants. The ticket allows you to swap the car for a seat on a small boat and an elephant's back for different aspects of the park. Open 0930-1730 daily, last admission 1630.

Palm Beach and its slightly less ostentatious mainland neighbour, West Palm Beach, believe in culture — there's even an Arts Information booth at the airport. You're spoiled for choice of museums and theatres, but culture is the dominant theme everywhere. Try the **Hibel Museum of Art,** billed as 'the only public museum in the western hemisphere dedicated to the art of a living woman — Edna Hibel.' Label me Philistine if you like, but my reaction is: 'Edna Who?' You can call in at 150 Royal Poinciana Plaza, PB, ✆833.6870 Tues-Sat 1000-1700 and find out — free.

The **Ann Norton Sculpture Gardens** at 253 Barcelona Rd, WPB, ✆832.5328, display this late sculptress's work in three acres of tropical greenery and the adjacent house, open Tues-Sat 1400-1600. Or try the **Norton Gallery of Art** at 1451 S Olive Ave, WPB (off US-1), Tu-Fri 1000-1700, ✆832.5194, free entry. The permanent collection features works by Gaugin, Picasso, Renoir, Matisse and Cezanne, with a fresh theme exhibition each season. Open Tues-Sat 1000-1700, donations accepted.

The **Society of the Four Arts** at Four Arts Plaza, PB, ✆655.7226, is open Mon-Sat 1000-1700 (Sun 1400-1700) in winter only. Free entry but a $2.50 donation would be accepted, and the arts involved are painting, sculpture, music and film.

If you're keen on art galleries — or if you're desperate to make your way in the world as an artist — Palm Beach is certainly the place to come; there are 14 other galleries, and the combined population of PB and WPB is only 72,000.

There's a good **Science Museum** at 4801 Dreher Trail N, WPB, ✆832.1988, open Mon—Sat 1000—1700 (Sun 1200—1700) for $3 basic. Permanent displays include an aquarium, a planetarium, and a large public—viewing telescope (come on Friday 1830—2200 to see the night sky), while visiting exhibits have come from the British Museum, Warwick Castle and Egypt.

At Delray Beach, 15 miles (24km) south, the **Morikami Museum of Japanese Culture** at 4000 Morikami Park Rd, ✆499.0631, offers a surprising insight into Oriental culture and horticulture, recalling the Japanese settlers here who developed the pineapple industry. Open Tues—Sun 1000—1700, free, but take your shoes off as you go in.

Theatres? There's the Gilbert & Sullivan Light Opera Society, the Royal Poinciana Playhouse and the Florida Repertory Theatre (they spell it -re, not -er, to show how cultured they are). Then there's the Ballet Florida, the Greater Palm Beach Symphony, and the Palm Beach Orchestra.

And, of course, here one may also indulge in polo and croquet as well as those lesser sports such as golf and tennis. Palm Beach Polo, where Prince Charles played in 1988, has an information line on ✆793.7000. If you wish to arive at the polo pitch in style, hire a white stretch Lincoln Continental limo from Park Cadillac Limousine Service, but if you need to ask the price you certainly can't afford it.

GOLD COAST FACTFILE

Hotels and motels. Gold is the operative word on the Gold Coast. In the Palm Beach area accommodation is expensive, and a 'moderately-priced' restaurant will charge up to $20 per person, but in WPB you'll find some of the ubiquitous fast-food outlets. For motels at a reasonable rate, head west to Lake Okeechobee and look in South Bay or Clewiston (see Chapter 17).

Ft Lauderdale is in the lower end of the Palm Beach price bracket, its hotels including such stars as the 226-room Ft Lauderdale Beach Hilton, which has the toll-free phone number 1.800.HILTONS. There are some excellent restaurants in town, if you're prepared to pay their prices; Historic Bryan Homes, two of the town's oldest houses now converted to this elegant eatery at 301 SW 3rd Ave, ✆523.0177, has plenty of character, but you can pay up to $40 for a meal.

Nightlife. Palm Beach after dark is not much busier than the middle of the Everglades, but there are a few nightspots in the neighbour-hood, notably Wildflower at 551 E Palmetto Park Rd, Boca Raton, ✆391.0000, for snacks, drinks, and non-stop music until 2am.

Ft Lauderdale, on the other hand, could be called forte laughterdale after dark. Its nightspots are bright, brash, and so much in fashion that they're likely to change their decor and style at least once a year. The Candy Store, in the Tradewinds Hotel at 1 N Atlantic Blv, ✆761.1888, started the Miss Wet Tee-shirt Contest and hasn't looked back since. Confettis at 2660 E Commercial Blv, ✆776.4080, is another trendsetter popular with the younger set, but Dejavu at 3299 N Federal Hwy, Pompano Beach, ✆946.7841, is so high-class it should be in Palm Beach.

17: OKEECHOBEE

Sugar country

LAKE OKEECHOBEE IS THE SECOND LARGEST FRESHWATER LAKE completely within the USA. Its average diameter is 45 miles (72km) and it covers 750 sq miles (1,950 sq km), putting it a long way behind number one, Lake Michigan, which has an area of some 22,400 sq miles (58,000 sq km).

Okeechobee is shallow; its greatest known depth is 24ft (7.3m) and its average is around 14ft (4.3m) — and therein lies the cause of one of the USA's greatest natural disasters, if measured in the loss of human life.

Imagine a large frypan with a finger-depth of water in it. Tilt the pan a few degrees and you move almost all the water to one side. Now imagine a bucket of water with the same surface area; tilt it the same angle and you scarcely disturb the surface.

Hurricane. Now picture that frypan to be Lake Okeechobee on 16 September, 1928, at a time before hurricane alerts were perfected and when many households had neither telephone nor radio. There had been reports of a hurricane striking Puerto Rico, but on that Sunday radio reception was particularly bad. By evening, the people of Okeechobee town were anxious about the prematurely-darkening sky and the increasing wind, and they could see that the lake was rising at an unprecedented rate.

Around sunset the hurricane hit Palm Beach with winds gusting to 160mph (250kph), and was heading west, straight to Lake Okeechobee. Because winds revolve clockwise around a Northern Hemisphere depression, the hurricane's leading face was pushing the lake's waters northwards — just as if you were tilting that frypan. By 9pm all of Okeechobee town was flooded and the water was swirling around many houses at first-floor (American second—floor) level, while at Belle Glade on the south shore part of the lake bed was exposed.

Then the eye of the storm passed over the lake and soon the hurricane's trailing edge hit Okeechobee, flushing the floodwaters from the town — and bringing devastation to Belle Glade and Clewiston on the south shore.

Nobody has been able to calculate the death toll of that night as

The 'campervan' has gone up-market; no wonder they call it a 'recreational vehicle.' That's Lake Okeechobee in the backround.

many of the victims were Bahamian labourers brought in for the sugar harvest, but most estimates put it in the region of 2,400.

Herbert Hoover Dike. As a direct result of the 1928 disaster, the federal government built the 40-foot (12m) high Herbert Hoover Dike (dyke) around the lake to prevent any recurrence of flooding, and dug the Hillsboro Canal and the West Palm Beach Canal ostensibly to drain away Okeechobee's surplus waters — the Miami Canal had been dug in 1909, before which the lake had no outlet except its annual spillage to the south which supplied the Shark Valley Slough and the Everglades. In reality the waters were now diverted to the south-east, for mankind's use in the urban area from Miami to Palm Beach, not in the Everglades where nature intended.

As an example of the ecological damage the dyke and canals have done to the Everglades, an account written in April 1886 describes a *sailing* journey through the 'Glades in what is now the dry season.

Drainage system. The tamed lake is now the heart of the south and central Florida drainage and water supply system, receiving the waters of Fisheating Creek, and of the canalised and much enlarged Kissimmee River which drains the higher land as far north as Orlando. The St Lucie Canal brings the Okeechobee Waterway from Stuart on the Atlantic Ocean, while the Caloosahatchee River, now canalised, takes the Okeechobee Waterway from the lake to Ft Myers on the Gulf of Mexico, thus making a short cut for small cargo vessels as well as for private boats. From Ft Myers another branch of the Intracoastal

136

Waterway wanders north past St Petersburg to Tarpon Springs.

Clewiston. Alonzo Clewis, a banker in Tampa, had bought acres of swampland south of the lake, and in 1920 he teamed up with Philadelphians John and Marian Horwitz to build the town of Clewiston, and the Moore Haven & Clewiston Railroad to link with Flagler's East Coast Railroad. Within a year, engineers had come from Memphis to dig Clewiston's canals and lay its streets, and many decided to stay on in the town they'd helped build.

Sugar. Japanese farmers had raised vegetables here since 1915, and migrants from the Caribbean had seen the potential for growing cane sugar in the rich if shallow soils south of the lake, but before the coming of roads and railways there was no way of moving the cane to processing factories or getting the product to market. Now everything had changed. A group of farmers at Canal Point, where the West Palm Beach Canal leaves the lake, founded the Southern Sugar Company and decided to base their operations and processing in Mr Clewis's new town.

More engineers came in to build the sugar mill; some of them stayed on to work it. And after the 1928 hurricane the US Army Corps of Engineers made their base in Clewiston while they built the Hoover Dike. Clewiston was becoming a boom town, and it began to attract musicians, writers and craftsmen.

Then came the Depression. The Southern Sugar Company went bankrupt, struggled on for a year under receivership, and emerged as the United States Sugar Corporation which now runs the industry. When Fidel Castro introduced Marxism to Cuba, the USA put a total ban on trade with this little Communist nation, and Clewiston found itself the 'sweetest town in the States' — and for a while its wealthiest on a per capita basis.

The industry today. Today, sugar cane is the basic crop from Clewiston in the west almost to West Palm Beach's Lion Country Safari in the east, and from Port Mayaca in the north to the Broward County boundary in the south. Around 18,000 people work in the industry, many of them brought in each year from the West Indies for the October-to-March harvest, as most of the cane is still cut by hand-held machetes.

Come to these canefields in winter and you'll see columns of smoke marking the fires that burn off the dead leaves and so make harvesting easier, if dirtier. The burners have to be extremely careful not to set fire to the peaty soil which can smoulder underground for weeks; it's already decomposing at the rate of an inch a year and will be down to bedrock by around 2020.

Machines gather the cut cane and cart it to the refineries by train, either tractors drawing long trains of trailers across the fields or rail wagons on the Seaboard Coast Line and Flagler's Florida East Coast

Line. The railroad is strictly commercial these days and its meanders around the fields make it a slow means of travel.

Molasses. Two major by-products come from the sugar mills. Blackstrap molasses is the base for making fermentation alcohol or is fed to cattle, while the compressed fibres, bagasse, become the fuel for the sugar mills themselves, with any overspill going to the paint and plastics industry or for more cattle fodder. The Belle Glade mill, which can produce 2,000 tons of raw sugar each working day, is claimed to be the world's largest cane-sugar mill — and don't confuse 'mill' with 'refinery,' as the processes are not the same.

Royal Air Force. During the Second World War, Clewiston airport became the 5th British Flying Training School, where American civilians trained British cadets for RAF service. And in recent years, after some devastating frosts in central Florida, citrus growers have moved into the hammock country south-west of Clewiston, where the soil is too thin to carry sugar.

Cabbage palm. The town is also known for its cabbage palms, whose leaves provide the decoration used in Florida's churches on Palm Sunday. The tender green hearts of these palms are served in speciality restaurants — hence the *cabbage* part of the name.

Moore Haven. To the west, Moore Haven has digressed into cattle production and now the longhorned Brahman stock outnumbers the human population. A big cypress tree, estimated to be 450 years old, was a mooring for boats in the days before the lake was tamed, but it's now several miles from open water.

Cypress Knee Museum. US-27 leads on to Palmdale, home of the Cypress Knee Museum run by a self-confessed eccentric. Would any normal person put up a roadsign saying, without the aid of commas, "Lady if he wont stop hit him on head with shoe"? Or twist the language again with this sign: *The cypress knee industry was started by and this museum was built by a selfish reactionary, without any help ever, from any city, county, state, or federal government... No price top, no price bottom, no subsidy, no labor union protection. What you see here can never be duplicated. Souvenirs of a time before civilization covered the United States.*

Tom Gaskins, who signed the notice, began collecting cypress knees in 1934 and now has a large collection of them from 23 states in the Union, which forms his museum. He also sells knees and lets visitors tour his workshop where he cleans and polishes the raw product. Tom's museum and souvenir shop are open daily 0800 to sunset.

So what is a knee? It's a a knobbly, distorted growth from the root of the bald cypress, protruding above the level of the water in time of flood and so presumed to help the tree breathe.

Sebring. US-27 leads north to Sebring, founded by an Ohio man named Sebring who came south to grow avocados. He based the town plan on that of the mythical Heliopolis, with a central park symbolising the sun and with streets radiating from it: it now looks more like a spider's web. During the 1920s property boom Sebring had an official greeter whose duty was to shake hands with every visitor to the town.

State Road 78 skirts the shores of Lake Okeechobee and passes the Brighton Seminole Indian Reservation — but the Seminoles nowadays live in normal houses. *Okeechobee,* by the way, is the Seminole word for 'big water.'

Okeechobee City. At the north of the lake stands Okeechobee City, site of a major battle between the Seminoles and General Zachary Taylor. The Seminoles won the battle, and a monument to their victory stands beside US-98 south of town — but they lost the war and most were shipped out west. Taylor won his next battle, against the Mexican President Santa Ana, then in 1848 he became President of the United States. He died in 1850 in the middle of his term in office.

Wildlife. Despite man's activity in the area, Lake Okeechobee and the surrounding lands are still havens for wildlife. You can see many egrets and great blue herons, lesser numbers of anhingas and migratory sandhill cranes. There are a few wood ibises and bald eagles, and the ardent birdwatcher might spot the rare Everglades kite and the smooth-billed ani, a foot-long black bird now increasing in numbers.

The lake still abounds with fish, particularly the bass, crappie, and shell cracker. If you have plans on catching a few, contact Angler's Marina at 910 Okeechobee Blv, Clewiston, FL 33440, ✆983.2128 or 983.BASS.

VERDICT. The lake and its cane plantations present yet another aspect of this diverse state. Come here if you like solitude, freshwater fishing, or want to see acres of standing sugar. Don't come for the nightlife.

OKEECHOBEE FACTFILE

Accommodation. In Clewiston, try the Angler's Marina (see above); Cane Court Motel, 335 W Sugarland, ✆983.8001; Clewiston Inn, Sugarland & Royal Palm, ✆983.8151; El Patio Motel, 444 W Sugarland Hwy, ✆983.8711; Motel 27, 412 W Sugarland Hwy, ✆983.8810. In South Bay, Okeechobee Inn, at 265 US-27 N, ✆996.6517.

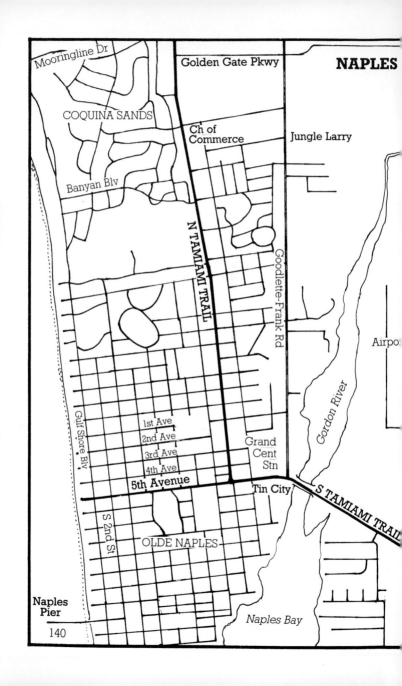

18: NAPLES to FORT MYERS

The Shell Coast

THE FIRST EUROPEAN SETTLEMENT on the North American mainland in recorded history was at Punta Gorda, at the head of Charlotte Harbour, in 1521. Columbus had rediscovered the continent in 1492 (we now know that the Viking Leif Ericson had landed in Labrador centuries earlier), and 29 years after Columbus the Spaniard Ponce de Leon settled here at the 'Fat Headland' in his unending quest for the legendary Fountain of Youth. Six months later a Calusa Indian killed him with a poisoned arrow and the little community faded away. The only reminders of de Leon are the Punta Gorda park which bears his name, and a plaque on the Barron Collier Bridge over the Peace River, telling the story of this first community.

Captiva Island. Years later the Spanish pirate José Gaspar and his ex-slave companion Black Caesar, abandoned their female captives on the offshore islands, supposedly safe from the unwanted attention of the common seamen. According to legend, the isle they chose commemorates that early history in its present name, Captiva. Or was it the more remote North Captiva?

Gasparilla Island. Gaspar had been an admiral in the Spanish navy but had been implicated in a plot to steal the crown jewels. He escaped and became a corsair in the Caribbean, a legend in his own lifetime due to his immaculate dress and his diary which listed, among other barbarous acts, his murder of a woman who refused his advances. Gasparilla Island, the third island north of Captiva, is named from the pirate while the isle's town, Boca Grande, 'big mouth,' is named from the expansive view of Charlotte Harbour. It's now a haven for the super-rich.

Useppa Island. But Gaspar is reputed to have made his base on the tiny Useppa Island, its name a corruption of Josefa, Gaspar's Mexican mistress whom he snatched from a ship bound for Spain. In modern times Useppa was a millionaires' hideaway until it saw service as a training ground for Cubans recruited for the abortive attack on their homeland, the Bay of Pigs fiasco.

Sanibel Island. South of the Captivas, Sanibel Island is named from Saint Isabel, commemorated in Spain on 8 July: could this have been the date the isle was discovered?

Sanibel is now a quiet island renowned for its wildlife and the seashells which are swept onto its beaches with each tide. The Calusa Indians heaped up piles of shells here back in the 8th cent, and modern visitors spend hours patrolling the sands in search of the latest treasure. Treasure? Legend also claims that Gaspar buried his loot in the sands of Sanibel or Captiva, but if that's true the current will have found it long ago.

'Ding' Darling. American cartoonist J.N. 'Ding' Darling had a lifelong interest in conservation, and his persistence resulted in the creation of the **J.N. 'Ding' Darling National Wildlife Refuge** on Sanibel, his favourite island. The 4,800 acres (19 sq km) of the refuge, including most of the north shore mangrove swamps, are home to alligators, sea turtles, manatees, sea otters, the rare white pelicans and the elusive roseate spoonbills. Open daily 0730-1600, admission free; cycles and canoes may be rented at the entrance by Tarpon Bay.

There's also the Sanibel-Captiva Conservation Foundation at 3233 Sanibel-Captiva Rd, ✆472.2329, which controls some 850 acres (3.4 sq km) of swamp. And if you want to see something of local history try the **Island Historical Museum** on Dunlop Rd, ✆472.4648, open free 1000-1400 Thurs and Sat — but remember that the house was moved to Sanibel in 1982; it's typical of south Florida, not of the island.

Pine Island. The largest of the isles, Pine Island, also has a collection of shell heaps left by the Calusa Indians. Pine is noted for the tarpon fish caught in its waters, but the largest catch along this coast was probably the 30-ft devilfish that President Roosevelt took on a line off Captiva Island.

Ft MYERS

When Thomas Alva Edison came to Florida on doctor's orders in 1885, Ft Myers was little more than a village. Edison was a widower and a sick man at the age of 38, told that he would die if he didn't move to a warmer climate and take life easier.

He chose Ft Myers for his winter home — despite medical advice he kept his summer home up north for some years more — and bought 14 acres of virgin forest on the banks of the Calooshatchee River. He designed one of the first prefabricated buildings in the USA, had it made in Maine and shipped down by schooner to Ft Myers, then he came back in 1886 with his new wife Mina Miller — and was here until he died in 1931, aged 84.

Edison Winter Home. ♿ in part. The Edison Winter Home at 2350 McGregor Blv, SR-867 (✆334.3614), is open 0900- 1700 Mon-Sat (Sun 1230-1700) for $4; the last tour starts at 1600. It's a museum to a man who began life as a newsboy on the railway then found he couldn't stop inventing. He improved the telegraph, invented the phonograph, forerunner of the gramophone, the kinetoscope which became the movie camera, and he was granted more than 900 patents.

At the start of his stay in Ft Myers, Edison was working on the electric light bulb. At first he was convinced that fibres from the bamboo would provide the filament for which he was searching; the many bamboos in his garden testify to his experiments. He was wrong there, but the open-air swim pool he built in 1900, one of the first in the state (and fed by an artesian bore 1,100ft (340m) deep), had bamboo reinforcing which has survived to this day.

Later, Edison discovered the carbon fibre for his bulb filament — and some of the bulbs he made at the start of the century are still in use in his home, burning for 12 hours every day. Strangely, his adoptive town wasn't too keen on some of his inventions; he offered to install electric lighting in Ft Myers but the council refused, thinking it would keep the cattle awake at night.

Rubber. After World War One, Edison correctly predicted that a later war would deprive the West of its latex supplies. Financed by Harvey Firestone the tyre maker, and his Ft Myers neighbour Henry Ford, and with Government help, Edison spent years searching for a latex-producing plant that would grow in the USA. Eventually he found it: a hybrid golden rod which grew up to 14ft in a year and contained 12% latex. He didn't live to see the Japanese invade Burma and Malaya in the 1940s and so control the world's rubber supply.

Museum and gardens. Edison collected many weird and unusual plants in his 14-acre gardens, including a banyan which was two inches (6cm) in girth when Firestone gave it to him in 1925. The cluster of aerial roots now measures more than 400ft (125m) in circumference and is probably the largest banyan in the state. The 7,500 sq ft (700 sq m) museum endowed by Edison's son Charles, holds an early Model T Ford, a gift from the car-maker who lived next door, a 1908 Cadillac and an early steam-driven fire engine. And, perhaps the most intriguing exhibit, Edison's laboratory is exactly as he left it in 1931.

Waltzing Waters. Ft Myers's other main attractions are both as distinctive as the Edison home. Waltzing Waters, a few miles south down the Tamiami Trail at 18101 US-41 SE, ☏267.2533, stages a fantastic display of controlled fountains brought to life by multicoloured lasers and background music. The idea came from Germany but this self-styled Rainbow Palace is true American showbiz. Shows are hourly from 0900-2100 daily, for $7 entry, but come after dark for the best performance.

Shell Factory. The Shell Factory across the Caloosahatchee on US-41 N, ☏995.2141, claims the world's largest collection of shells and corals. Open daily 0900-1700; admission free but there's a 75,000 sq ft (7,000 sq m) souvenir shop to tempt you. Beside the factory is **Fantasy**

Isles, ✆997.4204, an amusement park purely for the children. Admission is free, but you pay for each ride. Open 0900-1700 weekends.

Ft Myers. The city of Ft Myers is scarcely a tourist resort although its palm-lined boulevards make it the 'City of Palms.' The city centre has been restored to its original appearance to improve the tourist appeal, but the problem with so many American towns is that recorded history began with great- grandfather. Ft Myers has outclassed its rivals in that field with its **Historical Museum** in the old Atlantic Coastline Railroad depot at 2300 Peck St, ✆332.5955, specialising in Amerind artefacts some of which date from 1,200BC; it also has exhibits from wrecked Spanish galleons and more recent history, and it's open Mon-Fri 0900-1630, 1300-1700 weekends, for $1.

The city has experienced a population explosion in the past 20 years, but across the Edison Bridge the new city of Cape Coral has mushroomed across several miles of countryside. Oil is the latest industry to arrive in this part of Florida, with wells surrounding Cape Coral, extending up the Caloosahatchee and across to Punta Gorda as well as going down towards Immokalee.

Koreshan. South of Ft Myers lies the State Historic Site of Koreshan, home of a bizarre religious sect. In 1894, Dr Cyrus Reed Teed came down from Chicago convinced that the world was inside-out: what we believe to be the atmosphere was Teed's earth; what we called earth was his air. So life was lived on the inside of a giant bubble of air in a mass of rock, with the sun blazing away in the middle.

Teed declared himself to be the Immortal Koresh (whatever that may be) and established the community of Koreshan on the edge of Estero. The town was laid out on grandiose plans as the Immortal Koresh predicted millions of followers would rally to his call and join in his ideal of a life of communal celibacy. Teed died in 1908 and refused to come back to life even though his disciples laid out his body and waited. After several weeks they had to accept the inevitable, yet Teed's cult still lives on and still publishes the Koreshan magazine.

Mound Key. There's another State Historic Site at Mound Key, a mangrove island in Estero Bay; the entire key is believed to have been built by the Calusa Indians who then raised the middle and built a temple; nothing is left of it.

Estero Island. Estero Island, accessible by causeway from Ft Myers and Bonita Springs, is where you'll find Ft Myers Beach — a public strand with plenty of white sands — plus a golf club and a raquet club. Down here they're not so keen on the Shell Coast idea and prefer to call their home the Lee Island Coast. And if you want to try small-boat sailing, here's one of the few places in Florida where you can hire a craft for an hour or a day: try the Happy Sailboat Rental on 1010 Estero Blv.

Everglades Wonder Gardens. Bonita Springs is some way from the Everglades, but that didn't deter the choice of name for the Everglades Wonder Gardens on the corner of W Terry St and the Tamiami Trail, SR-887, ∅992.2591, open daily 0900-1700 (last tour 1600) for $5. This zoo and botanic garden, billed as southwest Florida's oldest attraction, stocks alligators and some of the endangered crocodiles, whitetail deer and Florida panther, as well as the exotica among birds: flamingos, spoonbills, ibis, and a bald eagle rescued from a tar pit. It goes one step further than most zoos by showing the less glamorous, notably the poisonous snakes of the 'Glades.

NAPLES

If you think Ft Myers is elegant, then you should see Naples, Palm Beach's close rival for the title of the smartiest, swankiest, ritziest and priciest city in the state. It's a garden city where even the lawns appear to be trimmed each night.

Yet this opulence is quite recent, even by Florida's standards. In the late 19th cent there was a tiny fishing village here, accessible only by boat or by a track of crushed seashells. Then a group of Kentuckians came looking for a winter hideout, bought 8,700 acres (35 sq km) of mangrove from a Philadelphian banker and began building Naples in the winter of 1885-86.

Naples grew very slowly despite the attentions of Charles Lindbergh, the first man to fly the Atlantic solo, who landed his plane on the main street − Fifth Avenue, of course − on his way to Sanibel Island. By 1950 there were only 1,465 people in the town, and only 6,488 in the entire Collier County. Shortly after that, of course, Florida became the USA's winter holiday resort and retirement home, and by 1987 Naples had added 18,000 people while the county had added 120,000.

Naples is still booming, with some of its Gulf-facing properties now costing $1,000,000, but I'd be reluctant to invest in some of those condos standing less than 50ft from the sea and only three feet above normal high water: what must it be like when a hurricane strikes? What will it be like when the world's oceans rise? The community is one of only three in Florida to have its beach on the mainland instead of on an outlying key, but that means there's even less protection from the elements. (The other two? Venice, south of Sarasota, and Mexico Bay by Panama City in the Panhandle. It's arguable whether Laguna Beach on the Panhandle is island or mainland.)

African Safari Park. There's enough to keep the visitor happy in Naples by day. Go window-shopping, go play golf (there are 20 courses in the area), go greyhound racing, go fishing on the 1,000ft long pier, go on the excellent public beach with its fine white sands −

or go to see Jungle Larry's African Safari Park and Caribbean Gardens on Goodlette-Frank Rd, ✆262.4053, open daily (except Mon, May to Christmas) 0930-1730, with last ticket sales 1600. Jungle Larry's tractor-train will take you on a tour of the 52-acre gardens and drop you off at what I can only describe as a circus, where lions, tigers and leopards jump through hoops: Greenpeace at Key West would not approve.

Naples by night. Naples by night is another matter. There's a good choice of conventional theatres but for $25 you might consider the **Naples Dinner Theatre** at 1025 Piper Blv, ✆597.6031, a high-class restaurant designed like a flattened Roman theatre. When desserts are served at 2015, a stage glides forward and you find you're at a Shakespearean-style theatre-in-the-round.

Or there's Tin City, a corrugated-iron warehouse that's been converted into a smart daytime shopping-centre with some budget-class restaurants for evening fare. Tin City is on US-41 to Miami, beside the bridge over the Gordon River at the south end of town.

Naples offers two cruising experiences that are a little out of the ordinary. **Tiki Tours** operates two catamaran-canoes with Polynesian-style carved prows and cabins with thatched roofs. Each boat can carry up to 48 passengers for a half-day cruise around a few of the Ten Thousand Islands, either gleaning seashells or birdwatching. Tiki Tours is based at the Boat Haven behind Tin City on US-41, but the address is 1271 12th St, ✆262.7577.

You can also find the **Rosie O'Shea** at the Boat Haven — or at 1081 Bald Eagle Drive, Marco Island, where the phone is: ✆394.7531. *Rosie O'Shea's* owners claim she is an authentic Mississippi stern-wheel paddle boat. I'm not so sure about 'authentic;' I'll settle for an excellent diesel-powered reproduction which happens to be 104ft (32m) long, excluding the gangplank she carries at her front end like a bowsprit. This fascinating boat plies between Naples and Marco Island in full daylight or on the more seductive sunset and moonlight dinner cruises, and the owners hope their customers will also dine at O'Shea's Restaurant on Marco Island's Bald Eagle Drive.

Naples has two other distinct attractions. Come here at Thanks-giving and you'll witness some spectacular hot-air ballooning, weather permitting; or on the last Sunday in February and October, when the town marks the hunting season with swamp buggy races. This stunt began in 1949 but in recent years they've added the attraction of electing a Mud Duchess.

Corkscrew Swamp. More serious swampy attractions lie well out of town, such as the 11,000-acre (45 sq km) Corkscrew Swamp, east of Bonita Springs on SR-849. This is a rare chance to look at primeval forest featuring the largest bald cypresses left in the USA, some of which are estimated to be more than 1,000 years old.

Collier-Seminole Park. South of Naples, US-41 cuts through the 6,423-acre (26 sq km) Collier-Seminole Park where you can enjoy a bit of nature-trailing, or canoeing a 13-mile circuit of the Blackwater River. ✆657.3771 for information. From the park SR-92 leads to Marco Island.

MARCO ISLAND

Barron Collier, from whom Collier County is named, bought Marco Island in 1922 to build a deepwater port for the oil industry which he thought would soon be making its appearance in the state. The island had seen its first European inhabitants in the 1880s when it became a small fishing community; by 1883 the **Marco Island Inn** was the one hostelry — and it's still in the hotel business more than a century later; you'll find it at 100 Palm St, ✆394.3131.

There was no oil: it's been discovered much more recently, but by then Marco Island had joined the tourist trade. Blessed with an excellent fine white sandy beach going by the exotic name of Tigertail, two causeways to the mainland, a labyrinth of marinas, and its own airstrip (no longer any scheduled services), Marco Island is an up-market tourist resort in its own right, specialising in condo rentals.

But you can always stay at Marriott's Marco Island Resort if money is no objection. It's at 400 S Collier Blv, FL 33937, ✆394.2511, or 1.800.GET.HERE. This Marriott hotel is a resort in miniature, offering luxury at every turn, from the bedroom to the restaurant and out to the grounds where you'll find tennis and golf among the sports. Low season rates start at $120 and approach the $1,000 mark, per room per day.

VERDICT. The Shell Coast presents yet another aspect of this fascinating state. It's not as classy as Palm Beach, but it's more classy than Ft Lauderdale, and is consistent at this level. The region caters almost exclusively for the American dollar-millionaire class, people who believe they're heading that way, or those who have already been there and have just retired from it. As a consequence, there are no crowds and there's adequate parking space near the beaches — but you should still come early in the day.

Budget accommodation is very scant. From Venice to Naples there is only one motel on US-41, but I can recommend the Trail's End Motel at 309 S Tamiami Trail on US-41 in Naples, near 5th Ave. It has a heated pool, bedside telephones, and costs $33.95 for one double-bed chalet or $2 more for two double beds. ✆262.6336.

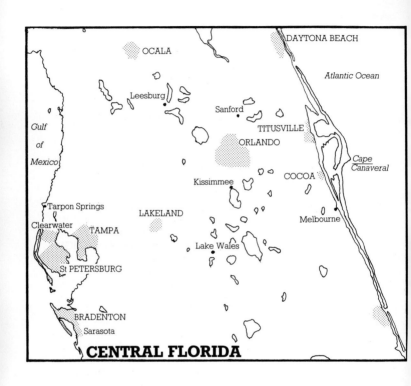

CENTRAL FLORIDA

CENTRAL FLORIDA
Hitting the High Note

19: ORLANDO, KISSIMMEE and WALT DISNEY WORLD

The Mouse that built the 'World'

FIRST, LET'S CLEAR UP THE CONFUSION. *Disneyland* is at Anaheim, Los Angeles. It was opened on 17 July 1955 and covers 160 acres. *Walt Disney World* is on the outskirts of Orlando, Florida, and incorporates the Magic Kingdom, the Epcot Centre, the Disney-MGM Studios, Typhoon Lagoon, the Walt Disney World Shopping Village, the Contemporary Resort, the Polynesian Resort, Disney Inn, Discovery Island with Fort Wilderness, the Caribbean Beach, and the Disney Village Resort. The whole complex covers 27,000 acres (42 sq miles, 109 sq km) which, Disney spokesmen will tell you, is twice the area of New York City. And you can expect 100,000 visitors on a peak day.

The 98-acre (40ha) **Magic Kingdom** opened in October 1971 and includes the self-contained attractions known as Main Street USA, Tomorrowland, Fantasyland, Liberty Square, Frontierland, Adventureland, and the latest addition, Mickey's Birthdayland.

This is unquestionably the world's largest funfair and it's target audience is the young at heart no matter how arthritic the limbs may be.

The **Epcot Center** − the name means *Experimental Prototype Community of Tomorrow* − opened in October 1982 and features the Future World and the World Showcase. Future World is divided into several ideas of what we might expect in the 21st century, with the geodetic sphere of Spaceship Earth at the focal point. The World Showcase offers glimpses of Canada, China, France, Germany, Italy, Japan, Mexico, Morocco, Norway, the United Kingdom, and the American Adventure, all clustered around a small lake.

The target audience here is the person with the inquiring mind, irrespective of age; and you don't have to be a scientific genius to appreciate it.

The latest addition, opened on 1 May 1989, is the Disney-MGM Studios Theme Park south of the Epcot Center; you can see its Earffel Tower landmark (Mickey's ears on a giant water tower) on your way to the Magic Kingdom. If you've ever watched a special effect in the cinema and wondered how it was done, you may find the answer here as you watch and hear stunts, sound effects, animation, and the 'blue screen' explained. And at the end, Catastrophe Canyon awaits you.

Separate attractions. The Magic Kingdom, the Epcot Center, the Disney-MGM Studios and Typhoon Lagoon are all self-contained attractions, with several miles separating the first from the other three. A day ticket at each place is **not valid** for the others; to see them all you must buy separate day tickets (you couldn't do justice to them in a single day) or go for a 4- or 5-day Worldpassport or an Annual Worldpassport (the capital letters are Disney's); the 3-day Worldpassport was phased out when the studios opened.

In principle, the single-day entrance fee covers admission to all attractions on the park of your choice and all on-site transport including the monorail between the Magic Kingdom and the Epcot Center, and the multi-day Worldpassport covers all admissions in all three parks for the time you've bought; beyond that, you pay for everything else separately — food, drinks, souvenirs, stroller hire and refundable deposit on your hired Kodak disc or 35mm camera.

Full details on prices, practical tips, and a behind-the scenes glimpse at Walt Disney World — hereinafter known as WDW for simplicity — are at the end of this basic description of what's on offer.

Disabled. The symbol &. indicates attractions which the WDW management considers accessible to disabled people without leaving their wheelchair; almost all the shops and restaurants are accessible to wheelchairs. Transport around WDW is easiest aboard the ferry boats, but the monorail is a good alternative, provided you don't try to get on or off at the Contemporary Resort by the Magic Kingdom. A limited number of wheelchairs are available for hire at $4 a day, plus refundable deposit, at the entrance to the Magic Kingdom, the Epcot Center and the WDW Shopping Village. The best car park for disabled drivers or passengers is by the Entrance Plaza at the Epcot Center; you can take the monorail from here to the Magic Kingdom if you want.

Access by car. If you're driving to WDW, turn off I-4 at exit 25b for the Magic Kingdom, and exits 26a or 26b for everything else. Exit 25b takes you briefly onto US-192, the Space Coast Parkway, before leading off right to the Magic Kingdom. And the car park fee is $3.

From the Magic Kingdom car park — it's really a collection of parks

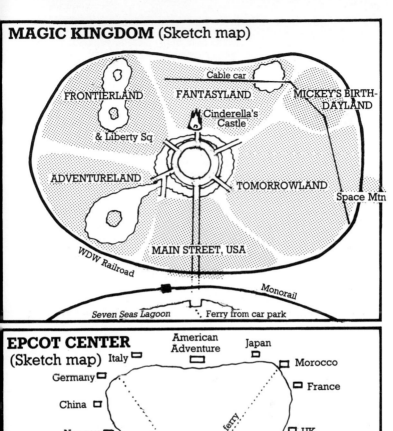

MAGIC KINGDOM (Sketch map)

FRONTIERLAND
& Liberty Sq

ADVENTURELAND

FANTASYLAND

Cinderella's Castle

Cable car

MICKEY'S BIRTH-DAYLAND

TOMORROWLAND

Space Mtn

MAIN STREET, USA

WDW Railroad

Monorail

Seven Seas Lagoon   Ferry from car park

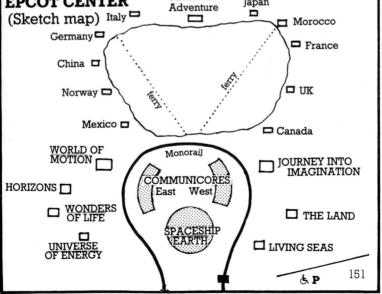

EPCOT CENTER
(Sketch map)

Italy

Germany

China

Norway

Mexico

American Adventure

Japan

Morocco

France

UK

Canada

ferry   ferry

WORLD OF MOTION

HORIZONS

WONDERS OF LIFE

UNIVERSE OF ENERGY

Monorail

COMMUNICORES
East   West

SPACESHIP EARTH

JOURNEY INTO IMAGINATION

THE LAND

LIVING SEAS

&P   151

each one named from a Disney character – a tractor train carries you to the ticket office on the south side of the Seven Seas Lagoon, one of Florida's 30,000 lakes; your destination is on the north shore, accessible either by monorail or by Mississippi-style paddle steamer. Why not go one way and come back the other? The Epcot Center car park is only a short walk from the entrance plaza.

THE MAGIC KINGDOM

MAIN STREET, USA. The principle entrance to the Magic Kingdom leads directly into Main Street, USA, a 19th-cent image of small town East Coast America, with horse-drawn trams operating a continual service around the main square where you first set foot in the Magic Kingdom, and going down Main Street itself, with Cinderella's Castle dominating the middle-distance.

On the right of the square is – or was – the **MGM Studios Preview Center** ⅄ which publicised the forthcoming Disney-MGM Studios Theme Park until it opened on 1 May 1989 south of the Epcot Center.

Beside it on Main Square is **Hospitality House** where you must make your reservation for the Diamond Horseshoe Jamboree in Frontierland (*q.v.*). It's first come, first served, and you can book only for that day's show.

Beyond the square, Main Street leads straight into history as it should have been, with all the warts and pimples removed. On the right the **Main Street Cinema** ⅄ shows a non-stop selection of classic films from the days of the silent screen. Further down on the left, the **Penny Arcade** ⅄ gives an insight into entertainment before William Friese-Green displayed the world's first ciné camera in 1889; Edison, of Ft Myers, patented his version in 1893. By the way, you supply your own pennies and dimes.

Disney characters. Main Street and Birthdayland are the best places to find the Disney characters going walkabout among the crowds or posing for pictures. And if you force your way through the crowds here at 3pm you might see Mickey's All- American Birthday Parade setting out for Cinderella's Castle and Frontierland.

Main Street USA has a generous selection of **shops and restaurants,** including the Harmony Barber Shop for a close encounter with a cut-throat razor, the House of Magic, The Chapeau for hats of all types including those featuring Mickey's ears, the Shadow Box for while-you-wait silhouettes, and Disney Clothiers for cartoon character costumes.

Services. The Sun Bank, on the left of the main square, offers the full range of banking services, and you'll be excused for not realising that behind its antiquated façade it is a genuine bank. Strollers and wheelchairs are available for hire beside the right entrance gate, the Information Center is in the City Hall beside the bank, and the first aid

Try the Chassahowitzka River in Citrus County for leisurely boating.

post is behind the Penny Arcade. Main Street is the best place to post your cards home – but they don't get a special postmark.

WDW Railroad. The WDW Railroad, pulled by a picturesque pseudo-steam locomotive with spark-box on the smoke stack and cattle grille on the front, chugs clockwise in scenic splendour around the entire Magic Kingdom, providing an interesting means of transport. You can stay aboard for an overall view of the Magic Kingdom or you can jump off at any of its three stops: here at Main Street, USA, at Frontierland, or at Mickey's Birthdayland. It doesn't stop at the other three provinces in the Magic Kingdom.

ADVENTURELAND. The Swiss Family Robinson has come back to life in Adventureland. I never could understand how those fictional castaways could meet African lions, Australian kangaroos and Asian tigers on the same island; perhaps you can find the answer in the **Swiss Family Treehouse,** a replica of the Robinson family home, authentically placed on a small island.

The **Jungle Cruise** takes you on an explorer's motor launch along dangerous tropical rivers – but in total comfort and safety, although the hippos and elephants certainly look real enough. If you've been to Key West you can relive some of the buccaneering days with the **Pirates of the Caribbean,** and see some of their treasure chests. Or, more sedately, go on a **Tropical Serenade** & and sing to the flowers.

My feeling is that Adventureland is a bit tame for all but the youngest visitor, which just leaves the **restaurants and shops:** six caterers take you to South Seas, Oriental, and Saharan settings, but their menus are still American-style fast-foods. The souvenir shops take up the adventure theme: the Zanzibar Shell Company stocks shells, Traders of Timbuktu deals in Africana, and the Golden Galleon has Spanish gifts. At Lafitte's Portrait Deck you can have yourself photographed down among the pirates.

FRONTIERLAND and LIBERTY SQUARE. Strangely, Frontierland is where the adventure begins. The **Big Thunder Mountain Railroad** would be nailbiting except that you're using both hands to hold on as the runaway mining train zooms through some spectacular mock-scenery. This is one of several thrills-and-spills attractions which have a special notice-board with a health warning: don't venture aboard if you have spinal or neck problems, or if your head doesn't touch the bottom of the board — that rules out young children.

You can go by raft to **Tom Sawyer Island** and relive those Mark Twain adventures of your childhood. And there's Fort Sam Clemens to explore; maybe the youngsters know that Samuel Langhorne Clemens was Mark Twain's real name? The **Frontierland Shootin' Arcade** ♿ lets you test your trigger finger, and at the **Country Bear Jamboree** ♿ you can join in the singing. But for the **Diamond Horseshoe Jamboree** ♿, a live floor show, you'll need to make a reservation at Hospitality House on Main Street, USA (*q.v.*) as soon as you arrive.

Somewhere in the middle of Frontierland lies **Liberty Square** where the nation's leaders come to life on stage at the **Hall of Presidents** ♿. The **Liberty Square Riverboat** ♿, a stern-wheeler, will cruise you around Tom Sawyer Island, but for something a little more primitive opt for the **Mike Fink Keelboat.** The **Haunted Mansion** is definitely one for the children.

Among the **shops** look for Frontierland Wood Carving and its twin with a near-identical name, the Yankee Trader for something unusual in the kitchen, or find your personalised brolly at the Umbrella Cart. Children might go to Ichabod's Landing for its ghoulish masks. Nine fast-food **restaurants** are waiting to serve you, while the Liberty Tree Tavern offers table service in 1770s style.

FANTASYLAND. Who but Walt Disney would dare to take his cartoon characters on such flights of fantasy! A **Dumbo Roundabout** gets you up in the air beside **Cinderella's Golden Carousel,** a merry-go-round of galloping horses. **Peter Pan** flies over London on his way to Never-Never-Land while the Mad Hatter from *Alice in Wonderland* has his **Mad Tea Party** with animated life-size teacups.

Elsewhere, **Mr Toad's Wild Ride** through Old London relives passages from *The Wind In The Willows* while **Snow White's Adventures** take her to meet the Seven Dwarfs and the Wicked Witch. The children will have a fine time in Fantasyland, but WDW warns that the very young may lose all sense of reality in some of the closed-in attractions where they can no longer relate to the sun and the sky.

There's no such risk with **20,000 Leagues Under the Sea** even though you travel with Jules Verne's Captain Nemo in a submarine that goes through tunnels inside a mountain. **It's a Small World** shows animated dolls in national costumes from many countries, then Kodak's **Magic Journeys** ⅍ exhibit plunges you back into the realms of fantasy with a thrilling display of three-dimensional movies.

While **Cinderella's Castle** is the focal point of Fantasyland, and of the kingdom, its interest is mainly visual. At lunch and dinner times it becomes **King Stefan's Banquet Hall** — make your reservation at the door as early as you can — with the hint that Cinderella herself may join the diners, but at other times the castle serves such mundane roles as a changing room for musicians.

There are seven snack-bars to complement King Stefan's Banquet Hall, with hamburgers, hot dogs, chips and ice cream prominent on the menus. The **shops** show considerable originality within the theme of fantasy; The Mad Hatter sells all kinds of unusual and exotic headgear, Mickey's Christmas Carol stocks Yuletide gifts the year round, and the King's Gallery in Cinderella's Castle has a smart line in European clocks. Why not? Cinders had to be home before her clock struck midnight.

Transport. Main Street's horse trams have a pick-up point outside the castle for that leisurely ride to the WDW Railroad, and just beyond the entrance are the monorail and the ferry boat back to the ticket office. You'll probably notice the overhead cable cars bringing migrants from Tomorrowland and dropping them by the Small World of the singing dolls; from up there you get a good view of most things, including the rails that guide Captain Nemo's submarines, but it's a one-way journey — if you're going from Fantasy to Tomorrow you must travel on foot.

MICKEY'S BIRTHDAYLAND. Tucked into the north-east corner of the Magic Kingdom is its latest and probably its last province, Mickey's Birthdayland. It's also the smallest and for most people the least interesting; I've met several people who find it disappointing. **Mickey's House** is what you'd expect if the cartoon character could really come to life; there's his car, wardrobe and furniture, and out the back is the Birthday Party Tent where Minnie holds her Surprise Birthday Party (Mickey's 60th, first celebrated in 1988 — but don't tell the children!) many times each day.

You shouldn't get too engrossed in birdwatching in the Everglades; on the Anhinga Trail an alligator may come up behind you.

Mickey's Hollywood Theatre gives a backstage glimpse into the life of this superstar and a chance to have yourself photographed with him. And finally there's **Grandma Duck's Farm** borrowed from Duckburg.

TOMORROWLAND. Where Fantasyland brings to life the children's fairground of a more sedate age, Tomorrowland's entertainments — except the **Tomorrowland Theatre** ♿ and the **Carousel of Progress** ♿ — promise a future in which the senses are shocked and nothing seems to stands still. The theatre has Disney characters on stage while the carousel shows how electricity has altered the American way of life in the past century.

Futuristic action begins when **Mission to Mars** ♿ takes you to mission control for a journey to the red planet. **American Journeys** ♿ sounds more sedate, but you have the stunning and thrilling spectacle of wrap-around cinema – the action is in front, behind, and on each side. **If You Could Fly** takes you around the funspots of the Caribbean and the Gulf of Mexico, and **StarJets,** the space rocket in the centre of Tomorrowland, puts you at the controls of your own interplanetary buggy.

And then there are the thrillers, to be avoided if you have spinal or heart problems, or can't touch the warning board with the top of your head. Goodyear's **Grand Prix Raceway,** which you can see from the Skyway to Fantasyland, is a high-speed track but the cars are on individual rails to avoid collisions.

Space Mountain is probably the ultimate in roller-coasters because it's in almost-total darkness and the corners are very sharp; you're thrown left, right, up and down with no warning at all. It's superb for thrills, I'm glad I've done it, but for me once is enough.

In the summer of 1989 **Dreamflight** opened its doors for a history of powered flight from the barnstorming era to modern times, presented by Delta, WDW's official airline.

There are just four fast-food outlets in Tomorrowland, of which the Tomorrowland Terrace is run by Coca-Cola and the Lunching Pad by Sun Giant, specialising in health foods. **Shops** stock futuristic souvenirs including fluorescent clothes and jewellery.

YOUR CITIZEN'S GUIDE TO THE MAGIC KINGDOM

You'll get the free 20-page *Magic Kingdom Guide Book* as you go through immigration control — the 'Ticket Center' — but to get the best out of your stay you should read up all you can the evening before your visit. If you're packing it all into one day, which may be enough for some childless groups despite what WDW proclaims, plan your campaign the previous evening but be flexible for on-the-spot alterations. Make a note to reserve seats for such attractions as the Diamond Horseshoe Jamboree.

If your children have decided you'll be making several forays into the kingdom, get an overall view on the first day and then concentrate on your favourites — but don't waste time in queues.

Plan of campaign. Get there early, at least by 0830. Make a note of your car park's name and your row number. You might be allowed into the kingdom before the official opening hour, if so, try this as a plan of campaign: first to Adventureland on foot for the Pirates of the Caribbean and the Jungle Cruise; cut through to Frontierland for the Big Thunder Mountain and Liberty Square's Hall of Presidents. Remember that everybody else wants to eat at midday so try a midmorning snack and an afternoon top-up instead. And get an early vantage point for Mickey's afternoon parade down Main Street. Leave Tomorrowland until last, and omit Mickey's Birthdayland if time is pressing.

THE EPCOT CENTER: FUTURE WORLD

SPACESHIP EARTH. The 180-ft (55-m) diameter geodetic sphere known as Spaceship Earth is to Epcot what Cinderella's Castle is to the Magic Kingdom. It stands gleaming on its stumpy legs, inviting you to board a carriage for a slow uphill journey through the interior of this amazing globe. Animated exhibits tell the story of mankind's brief adventures on this planet, then show the Solar System in relation to the many galaxies of our universe.

Services. Back on terra firma you'll find the Sun Bank and the stroller rental on the left, and the lost-and-found and package pickup office on the right — you needn't carry your purchases all day; you can collect them here when you leave. Behind Spaceship Earth is the **Earth Station** and the WorldKey Information Service; come here as soon as you can — certainly no later than 0930 — to book a table at one of the Epcot restaurants on the computerised monitor screens. Try to avoid the peak eating times around noon and 6pm.

Beyond the geodesic sphere are the **Communicores** East and West. **East,** on the left, puts human interest into computer science and in Backstage Magic 🔥 gives you a glimpse into how computers help keep WDW moving. The Electronic Forum 🔥 at the other end of Communicore East stages a never-ending opinion poll on a range of subjects, with the results issued to the US media each week.

The oil company Exxon has an Energy Exchange 🔥 exhibit for that awful question of where will tomorrow's energy come from. Two fast-food outlets, a Disney souvenir shop and an American Express stand complete the display.

Communicore **West** has AT&T's FutureCom, for a hands-on glimpse at the communications possibilities of the future, while in Expo Robotics 🔥 a robot will draw your portrait. Next door, another robot will airbrush you a souvenir tee-shirt for a fee.

UNIVERSE OF ENERGY 🔥. Progressing clockwise around the plaza behind Spaceship Earth, you come first to Exxon's spectacular show in the Universe of Energy, demonstrating how the world's oil was created from the decaying body tissues of living organisms millions of years ago. You will travel in solar-powered cars (the solar cells are on the roof) to see dinosaurs fighting in an ancient forest that could have given us today's anthracite.

But what *shall* we do for energy when all the oil wells have run dry? Exxon has several possible answers.

WONDERS OF LIFE. Wonders of Life, which opened in summer 1989, looks at the human body. **Body Wars** explores our immune system in a high-speed race against time, **Cranium Command** shows how the brain works, and **Fitness Fairground** allows you to examine your senses of perception. The sponsor is suitably a life insurance company.

HORIZONS. General Electric is the power behind the Horizons exhibit which plunges you into several options the 21st century might have to offer: voice-controlled robots operating a farm created in the desert, an underwater colony, an orbiting spacecraft where perfect crystals are manufactured in zero gravity, or the city of tomorrow right here on Earth.

WORLD OF MOTION ♿. The human race differs from the rest of creation in many ways, but one of the most important has been mankind's ability to move faster and further than his little legs could carry him. General Motors has borrowed more Audio-Animatronics characters to staff the World of Motion, a humorous look at the evolution of transport, how it has fashioned our history and how it's likely to affect our future.

Under the same roof is the **Transcenter** ♿, for the latest information on the world of motion.

Your clockwise tour takes you to the **Odyssey Complex** on its island site: here is the Odyssey Restaurant and beside it the toilets, the first aid clinic, and facilities for attending to babies' needs and collecting lost children. Cross the main flow of traffic heading south for the World Showcase, and enter the western hemishphere of the Future World.

JOURNEY INTO IMAGINATION. The giant glass pyramid of this building stimulates the imagination even before you step inside your Journey into Imagination, by courtesy of a character called Dreamfinder and with a little help from Kodak, the sponsors. A little creature named Figment then takes you on a journey through the intricacies of the mind, searching for that little spark of genius which can revolutionise the world. Walt Disney had it when he created Mickey Mouse...and look at what it's led to!

Next door is the **Magic Eye Theater** (♿, but beware the special effects and the intense noise), where Michael Jackson stars in Captain EO, a Three Dimensional Musical Motion Picture Space Adventure. On the first floor ('second floor' in American usage), but still accessible to ♿ visitors, **The Image Works** gives you scope to let your imagination run free. Paint a masterpiece! Conduct an orchestra! Become an actor!

The **shop,** you'll not be surprised to learn, sells Kodak cameras and film.

THE LAND ♿. Kraft, the margarine manufacturer, has created one of the most popular of Epcot's attractions in The Land. You're invited to the **Harvest Theater** to watch a film which attempts to strike a balance between mankind's activities and his environment.

And then, below ground level, Bonnie Appetit introduces you to the Kitchen Krackpots, an orchestra of animated cartoon characters whose **Kitchen Kabaret** may make you think this is purely fun time. But **Listen to the Land** then takes you on a short boat trip through several climatic zones to see the problems that agriculture faces. If you want to take the 45-minute guided **Harvest Tour** through glasshouses of experimental crops to see what horticultural wizardry can be done in a controlled environment, you'll need to contact the Guided Tour Waiting Area as soon as you arrive; you'll find it beside the Farmer's Market, one of the two on-site restaurants.

THE LIVING SEAS &. The Epcot Center has its own dolphins, sharks and manatees, and around 80 other marine species, living here in what WDW claims to be the world's largest man-made saltwater aquarium, with a capacity of 5,700,000 US gallons — that's 4,750,000 Imperial gallons or 21,000 cubic metres. Take a lift (Disney's word 'hydrolator' is more apt) down to Sea Base Alpha and learn a little more about the wonders of the sea, from its plankton-based food chain to mankind's involvement in this fascinating but alien environment.

Not surprisingly, the underwater Coral Reef restaurant specialises in fish dishes.

THE EPCOT CENTER: WORLD SHOWCASE

The World Showcase is an assembly of 11 encapsulated nations surrounding a small lake, with more to come. Travelling clockwise, you can visit Mexico, the latest arrival Norway, China, Germany, Italy, the USA represented by the American Adventure, Japan, Morocco, France, the United Kingdom, and Canada.

You can take them in that order or the reverse, on foot — the world will come down to a stroll of 1.2 miles (1.9km) — or catch a veteran double-deck bus, or cross the lagoon by ferry to either Germany or Morocco. Be prepared for quite a bit of walking if you're going to do justice to all the showcase exhibits, and to ease the strain on your arms you can ask for all your purchases to be sent to the Package Pick-up at the Epcot entrance by the monorail station. All the articles on sale throughout the showcase are genuine products of the country concerned, the restaurants use native ingredients where practicable, and most of the staff are from the 10 foreign lands featured. You'll find some interesting variations on English pronunciation.

MEXICO. An ancient Aztec pyramid & in its original condition welcomes you to Mexico, but step inside the pyramid and you'll find yourself in a modern adobe village. Take a boat trip down **El Río del Tiempo** &, the 'River of Time,' through Mexico's history from the Aztec era to the present day. An exhibition of the Art of Mexico & at the entrance shows what the peasant craftsman can accomplish, and there are four **shops** selling Mexican crafts. Two **restaurants** specialise exclusively in native menus.

NORWAY. Cruise on a Viking longboat through the **Maelstrom** in your search for Valhalla, sail through storms in the North Sea, and come down to earth by the 14th-cent Akershus castle in its setting in modern Oslo. The exhibit at the doorway, **1,000 Years of Discovery** &, puts together a millennium of history. Two restaurants and a souvenir shop add to the Scandinavian charm.

CHINA. Visit the Forbidden City in Beijing in the **Wonders of China** &, a spectacular cinema-in-the-round experience that is justifiably one of the most popular features of Epcot. The exhibit, **House of Whispering Willows** &, features Chinese clocks from the 18th cent. Two restaurants serve Chinese dishes, and the Yong Feng Shangdian shop — it means 'Bountiful Harvest' — specialises in Chinese souvenirs.

GERMANY. Germany has no major feature and no exhibition, but you're invited to join in the Oktoberfest at a typical Biergarten. Ten shops sell German specialities from chocolates to glassware: try sorting out their names — Glas und Porzellan, Süssigkeiten (sweets, candies), Weinkeller, Der Teddybär, Volkskunst (folk art), Der Bücherwurm ('the bookworm'), and others.

ITALY. Italy is also devoid of any major feature, but the location is the Piazza San Marco in Venice, with gondolas even though the restaurant is l'Originale Alfredo di Roma. The four shops offer a good line in Venetian glass among their souvenirs.

THE AMERICAN ADVENTURE Benjamin Franklin, the 18th-cent statesman and scientist, joins author Mark Twain, aviation pioneer Frederick Douglass, and woman's rights campaigner Susan B Anthony, in **The American Adventure** &, the story of the United States and its people told in film and with more of those audio animatronics characters: Franklin was the first animated character in Walt Disney World to have the ability to walk.

Facing the main building and with its back to the lagoon, the **America Gardens Theatre** &, puts on live entertainment; under the main roof the static exhibit **We The People** &, explains some of the clauses and amendments in the US Constitution. The **restaurant,** Liberty Inn, is a great place for hot dogs and hamburgers.

JAPAN. The way into Japan is through a traditional Torii gate which leads to a five-storey pagoda and the **Bijutsu-kan Gallery** &, the static exhibit concentrating on Japanese art through the ages. Four restaurants, three of them on the first floor, and two shops help you to capture the Oriental flavour.

MOROCCO. If you haven't seen the real Koutoubia Mosque and its 226-ft (69-m) minaret in Marrakech, then here's an impressive replica.

Morocco has three exhibits around the entrance; the **Gallery of Arts and History** ♿, the **Fès House** for an impressive sample of Moroccan architecture, and the **Moroccan National Tourist Office** ♿ information desk. The Marrakech **Restaurant** at the far end of the display adds authenticity to its atmosphere by having a genuine belly-dancer. Eight **shops** specialise in souvenirs from leather, brass, copper — and the ever-present carpets.

FRANCE. Tour the beautiful French countryside in film at **Impressions de France** ♿, then take your choice from four **restaurants** including the popular Chefs de France. The Boulangerie-Patisserie should give Floridians a taste of real bread!

UNITED KINGDOM. Again, no main feature and no exhibition in the United Kingdom, but you can drink Bass and Guinness (I thought that was Irish?) in the lakeside Rose & Crown pub. The Rose & Crown dining room is among the most popular, and the Pearly Band of singing Cockneys keeps a few people guessing. Seven **shops** give a diversity, with mementos from Scotland and Wales as well as the English regions.

CANADA. Circle-Vision 360 offers another marvel of wrap-around cinema with **O, Canada!** ♿, a film visit to the Calgary Stampede and to the top of the CN Tower in Toronto. The showcase has a single restaurant, and three shops.

Key West still has the Conch Tour Train — but there's no railroad.

YOUR CITIZEN'S GUIDE TO THE EPCOT CENTER

Arrive early, by 0830 at the latest, and make a note of where you park the car. You should have planned your campaign the previous evening, which is why you have details in this book – but look out for the free *Epcot Center Guide Book* – and base your battle tactics on the knowledge that Future Wold is busier in the morning, the World Showcase in the afternoon.

These are the top spots which you should not miss: Canada for its film, China for its film, Journey Into Imagination (but miss Captain EO if you don't like excess noise), The Land (for the boat trip), The Living Seas, Spaceship Earth, and the Universe of Energy. Suggestably, first head for Journey into Imagination or Canada, then play it by ear: take the bus to China or go back to The Land and so to Spaceship Earth. It depends on the crowds.

DISNEY-M.G.M. STUDIOS

Imagine yourself entering a 50ft-deep (15m) gulch in the American southwest. Suddenly the track ahead is blocked by a road tanker taking on a load from an oil-well. The ground moves as an earthquake builds up; electric pylons tremble, showering sparks onto an oil spill. Instantly, a holocaust rages – just as the 'quake strikes. And a storm you weren't aware of chooses that second to manufacture its own cloudburst right overhead. You'll either be roasted, drowned, swept away, or lost in the earthquake.

This is your welcome to **Catastrophe Canyon** &, the major attraction at the Disney-MGM Studios which opened on 1 May 1989. As disaster strikes in this 200ft (60m) cleft you can smell the oil, feel the heat, and experience some of the fear of the real thing – but it's just a cleverly-designed film set to show you one way in which special effects are created for cinema and television.

Studio tour. The backstage adventure begins with a ride in shuttle trailers (&) for a tour of the studios. In the costume department you can see some of the 2,000,000 garments in stock, and watch others being made for forthcoming Disney films as well as for Disney characters in the WDW. You might even see Roger Rabbit.

You progress through technical support, home of 'grip' and 'gaffer' whom you see mentioned in the credits, and suddenly you're on the streets of New York, or anywhere else in the USA. But the impressive buildings are purely façades held in place by steel scaffolding.

Production Stage. The interior scenes are shot at your next destination, the Production Stage, from where you roll on to those special effects departments, Catastrophe Canyon and its companion the Water Effects Tank, in which storms at sea are made to measure. When you've recovered from the excitement you can stroll around the Animation Building where 71 artists create living cartoons.

Superstar Television. Would you like to act in a sequence from *I Love Lucy*? Dress up as a cowboy and ride into the opening credits of *Bonanza*? Read the news 1950s-style in the American current-affairs *Today* show? It's all possible in the Superstar Television studios where visitors are plucked out of the crowds to become instant celebrities. The trouble is, we're all back in the crowds at the end of it.

There's even greater realism when you go on a walking tour of the studios which are producing genuine shows for the Disney Channel on US television.

Blue-screen magic. In another studio two young volunteers take a ride on a giant bee as it bumbles around the garden and, with the wizardry of the blue-screen technique, they can see the result on video and imagine themselves starring in the Disney film *Honey, I Shrunk the Kids.* You've seen television newscasters interviewing a guest who is shown head-and-shoulders on a wall-mounted monitor? In reality the interviewer is talking to a plain blue screen, and the guest's picture is added by backroom technicians.

I feel there's more magic in the Disney-MGM Studios than there is in the Magic Kingdom. Or am I just getting old?

THE LATEST ATTRACTIONS

During the summer of 1989 WDW opened two more attractions. The 50-acre (20-ha) **Typhoon Lagoon** is the fourth of the adventure parks, on a level with the Magic Kingdom, the Epcot Center and the Disney-MGM Studios. It features what Disney claims to be 'the world's largest man-made watershed mountain,' 95-ft (28-m) high and streaming with nine water slides and rapids up to 400 ft (120m) long, as well as a 2½-acre (1 ha) wave-making lagoon. And you can raft along the Upalazy River through a rain forest and a hidden grotto.

Pleasure Island is an evening entertainment centre on the waterfront, with six nightclubs and rows of shops on a six- acre (2.5-ha) island that was the mythical empire of fictional shipbuilder Merriweather Adam Pleasure.

You can dine on one of Mr Pleasure's craft, the pseudo-19th-cent *Empress Lily,* or there's the Adventurer's Club with its Illusions Bar. At Videopolis there's a stainless-steel dance floor, and walls covered in video monitors where you can watch yourself being watched. The XZFR Rockin' RollerDrome is for a strange combination of dining, dancing and roller-skating, the Mannequin Dance Theater has a slowly-revolving floor, and the Comedy Warehouse features an ever-changing bill of stand-up comedians and vaudeville performers.

Pleasure Island marks the Walt Disney Company's admission that it must move with the times, for here is the first place in WDW that you can buy alcohol, and its Neon Armadillo Music Saloon, supposedly set in Mr Pleasure's tropical glasshouse, is WDW's first singles night club.

The 4,516-ft-long Channel Five bridge links Craig Key and Fiesta Key.

PRICES and OPENING TIMES

PRICES. WDW increased its prices on 1 May 1989 to coincide with the opening of the Disney-MGM Studios. **Sales tax, currently at 6%, must be added to all prices.**

One day. A one-day ticket to either the Magic Kingdom or the Epcot Center or the Disney-MGM Studios or Typhoon Lagoon, plus the monorail, costs $23 for a child aged from three to nine; thereafter the adult rate of $29 applies.

Four or five days. The 4-day ticket valid for *all* the four theme parks listed in the previous paragraph, plus unlimited monorail travel between them, costs $77 for a child and $97 for an adult.

The 5-day ticket with the same range and limits, costs $90 for a child and $112 for an adult.

The three-day ticket was withdrawn on 1 May 1989. Tickets are **not available outside the USA.**

TIMES. All theme parks officially **open** at 0900 every day of the year, but in practice the gates are often opened half an hour early, particularly at peak periods. On a few special days the official opening time is 0800.

Closing times vary. The **Magic Kingdom** closes at 1800 most of the year and at 2400 at the busiest times, from late May to mid August, as well as at Christmas and on certain public holidays. Between these extremes, closing times are 2000 and 2100. Main Street Electrical Parade is either at 2100 or 2300, and the firework display is at 2200 unless the park is already closed at that time.

The **Epcot Center** follows the same schedule but its latest closing time is 2300 and its earliest is 2000. The **Disney-MGM Studios** closes at its earliest at 1900 and its latest at 2100.

All closing times, Disney would have you know, are subject to change without notice.

USEFUL PHONE NUMBERS IN WDW

Lost and found, Magic Kingdom, ✆824.4521; Lost and found, Epcot Center, ✆560.6236; Lost children, Magic Kingdom, ✆824.6707; Lost children, Epcot Center, ✆560.7928; hotel reservations, ✆W.DISNEY; emergencies, ✆911.

WALT DISNEY WORLD RESORTS

The Disney empire isn't content with merely offering you the world's most impressive theme parks; it has its own self-contained holiday resorts within WDW and, with Delta Airlines, the WDW official carrier, offers package holidays to WDW from USA and the United Kingdom. Let's look at the resorts, starting with those near the Magic Kingdom. All prices are off-season (high season is mid-June to mid-August), per night per room, (with sales tax to be added) and all apartments have beds for five people except where stated otherwise. For high-season rates, add around 10%.

GRAND FLORIDIAN BEACH RESORT. The Grand Floridian is a 901-room Victorian-style luxury resort on the western shore of the Seven Seas Lagoon, with four rooms for ♿ guests and 202 for non-smokers. The pool is kept at a constant 78°F (20°C), and the services available include valet and babysitting. You can go boating on the lagoon or go to other parts of WDW by monorail, coach and ferry. And in the evening there's a wide choice of restaurants.

Tariff. From $185 to $300 with concierge; suites to $485.

DISNEY INN. The Disney Inn, by the Magnolia and Palm golf courses west of the lagoon, is a luxury mini-resort with 288 rooms in a country-inn atmosphere. Apart from golf, you have tennis, a heated pool, and a games room, and three restaurants to choose from.

Tariff. From $145.

POLYNESIAN VILLAGE RESORT. On the south shore of the Seven Seas Lagoon, the 841-room Polynesian Village Resort is targeted at families with young children. The atmosphere is heavily South Seas, from the Ceremonial House reception office to the 11 long houses which form the resort proper. There are beaches by day and shows by night, with one designed for the children.

Tariff. Rooms start at $155, with suites going to $485.

CONTEMPORARY RESORT. A 15-storey building looking like a giant 'A' from the ends, the Contemporary Resort stands between the Seven Seas Lagoon and Bay Lake — and the monorail runs right through it: wheelchair passengers can *not* use the station.

Look outwards to the Magic Kingdom, or to Bay Lake where you can hire motor or sailing boats, or look inwards in this vast 1,053-room hotel (17 rooms for &) to a 90-foot (28-m) mural and a vast auditorium. Evening entertainment is as contemporary as the resort's name.

Tariff. From $155; suites to $580.

FORT WILDERNESS RESORT. Fort Wilderness is set amid 740 acres (298 ha) of woodland and water south of Bay Lake — and is almost eight times as large as the Magic Kingdom. Here you can hike or bike, fish or swim, relax or play tennis — or even go out and see the rest of WDW. Send the children down to the **River Country** for a day at the 'swimming hole' and the waterslide, then have a campfire sing-song in the evening.

Discovery Island. Set within Fort Wilderness, the 11- acre Discovery Island is a zoo where you can find 90 species of animals and 250 of plants to support them. The world's largest captive population of scarlet ibises lives here, with disabled brown pelicans, bald eagles, sandhill cranes and other birds which have been rescued from a lingering death in the wild. Surprise inhabitants include the brush turkey and the kookaburra from Australia, the Galapagos tortoise, the Madagascan lemur and the Chinese muntjac.

Tariff. The cost of a stay in Fort Wilderness depends on where you sleep. Hire a six-berth caravan for $140, hire a tent for $26 — or bring your own and camp for $4 a night, per person, on one of 829 pitches. Restrooms, water, and cooking areas are available. Discovery Island is not free; it costs $6 for adults, less for children.

CARIBBEAN BEACH RESORT. Between the Epcot Center and the WDW Shopping Village, the 200-acre (0.8 sq km) 2,112-room Caribbean Beach Resort clusters around a 40-acre lake with canoes, sailing boats and paddle boats for hire. The resort is divided into so-called island communities: Aruba, Barbados, Jamaica, Martinique and Trinidad. Coaches take you to the main theme parks.

Tariff. From $65, with maximum sleeping for four.

DISNEY VILLAGE RESORT. You'll find the Disney Village Resort north of Pleasure Island and near the WDW Shopping Center, east of Epcot. You have a choice of accommodation: club suites, with maid and valet service; self-catering vacation villas sleeping four or six; self-catering, three-storey fairway villas sleeping eight; or treehouse villas on stilts, sleeping two.

Your on-site sports are golf, swimming, tennis, jogging, cycling, or toning up in the health club, and coaches run to the main theme parks and the Shopping Center.

Tariff. From $145 to $255, depending upon size.

Reservations. Reservations for any of the WDW resorts can be made from the UK on ✆010.1.407.934.7639; from other countries substitute your own international code for the USA; from within the States, just ✆407.W.DISNEY. Or write to Walt Disney World Company, Central Reservations, PO Box 10,100, Lake Buena Vista, FL 32830. Or go through Utell International; the UK number is ✆01.(081).995.8211.

Package holidays. If you're looking for a holiday based in any of the WDW resorts, you might consider the Delta Airlines package. It won't be the cheapest way of seeing Walt Disney World, but it could be among the most convenient.

The Delta Package could be particularly attractive for people organising large parties concentrating on WDW, especially if there are physically or mentally disabled travellers. Contact your travel agent or, in the UK, ✆01.(071).792.8791.

Preferred Travel in the UK also offers fully-inclusive WDW packages; ✆01.(071).408.0302.

Non-Disney hotels. A cluster of five high-class hotels sends its towers skywards between the Shopping Center and Interstate 4 in this eastern corner of WDW.

Disneyland. And finally . . . well, almost finally . . . a brief, brief mention of Disneyland in California. Did you know that among its major attractions are the old Cunard liner *Queen Mary* and Howard Hughes's wooden aircraft, the Spruce Goose?

BEHIND THE SCENES WITH DISNEY

Walt Disney was a struggling artist when he first sketched his little mouse cartoon character based, so it's claimed, on Walt himself and on a mouse who shared his simple apartment. The character's original name was Mortimer, but Walt thought it didn't sound right, so in 1928 he introduced his offspring to the world as Mickey Mouse.

That early Mickey lacked the sophistication of the 60-plus-year-old sprightly youngster of today, and his squeaky voice was Disney's own. Mickey's first experiment into single-frame animation was the now-classic *Steamboat Willie* which you can see at the Main Street Cinema.

Disney's cartoon characters hit the world at just the right time, and soon Mickey and Minnie, Donald Duck and Goofy, and the scores that followed, were syndicated in newspapers and featured in their own children's comics in many countries. Feature-length cartoons followed, with epics such as *Snow White* and *Dumbo,* though Mickey himself has made only one small film appearance since 1953.

It seemed as though Disney was saving his leading character for better things as the Disney Studios moved into films with real animals, instead of their cartoon counterparts, co-starring with human actors. And now, in the new Disney-MGM Studios, Toontown (cartoon-town) characters and humans appear together on screen. Who framed Roger Rabbit? It could only be Disney.

Walt Disney World. But where was Mickey? He came out of retirement to help publicise Disneyland, called 'Walt's Folly' by some of his more cautious executives. The world's first tentative theme park was such a success that Walt Disney World was inevitable: and where else to site it but in Florida, the USA's most tropical state?

The Disney Company bought up the land around Lake Buena Vista very carefully, using a battery of front companies to avoid sending prices sky-high, as had happened when Flagler and the other entrepreneurs came to town earlier in the century. Soon, the 27,000 acres were ready to become incorporated into the Walt Disney World, with theme parks appearing in succession. And now the empire built on a squeaky-voiced mouse has a Wall Street valuation of $9,000,000,000 and the theme parks bring in 60% of the Walt Disney Company's gross income, which is now around $3,000,000,000.

And at WDW, there are now more than 20,000,000 visitors a year, 750,000 of them from the UK, providing employment for a staff ranging seasonally from 23,000 to 26,500.

Disney University. Every one of those employees must conform to the high standards that the Walt Disney Company expects. They attend a special Disney University which has its main college in Los Angeles, learning the somewhat strict code of conduct that's expected of them. All women staff who meet the public must conform to company guidelines on length of hair and finger nails, on the size and nature of personal jewellery, they must wear a bra, and their make-up must be unobtrusive. Men may not wear moustaches or beards, and their side whiskers must not extend below their ears. On reflection, it's all in keeping with the Disney image of good, clean, homeloving America, and only the bad guys hide behind beards, don't they?

Tailless mouse. But whoever heard of a tailless Mickey Mouse? Since 1985, all the Mickeys around the WDW have been devoid of tails, a decree which was forced upon the Walt Disney Company when a little boy visitor pulled Mickey's tail. That particular Mickey's response was a long way short of the Disney image of good, clean, homeloving America.

Other Disney Worlds. Disney has expanded into Japan with a western-style theme park near Tokyo, and in 1992 Euro Disney World will open near Paris.

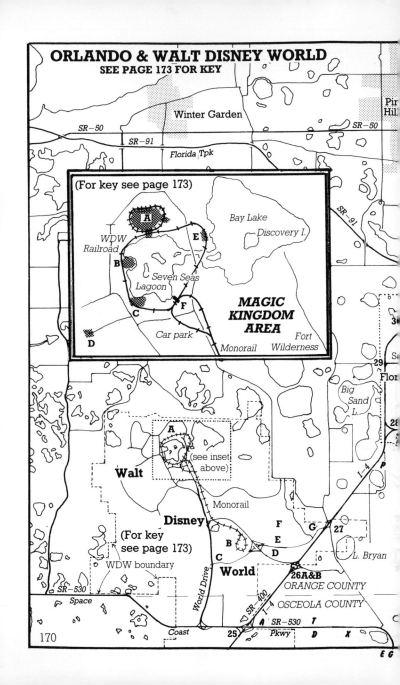

ORLANDO & WALT DISNEY WORLD
SEE PAGE 173 FOR KEY

Winter Garden

SR–50

SR–91

SR–50

Florida Tpk

(For key see page 173)

A

WDW
Railroad

B

Bay Lake

Discovery I.

E

Seven Seas
Lagoon

C

F

D

Car park

Monorail

*MAGIC
KINGDOM
AREA*

Fort
Wilderness

SR–91

29

Flor

Big
Sand
L.

28

A

(see inset
above)

Walt

Monorail

Disney

(For key
see page 173)

WDW boundary

F

E

B

G

27

D

L. Bryan

C

World

26A&B
ORANGE COUNTY
OSCEOLA COUNTY

SR–530

Space

I-4

SR–400

A SR–530

170

Coast

25

Pkwy

Pir
Hil

World Drive

L. Bryan

E G

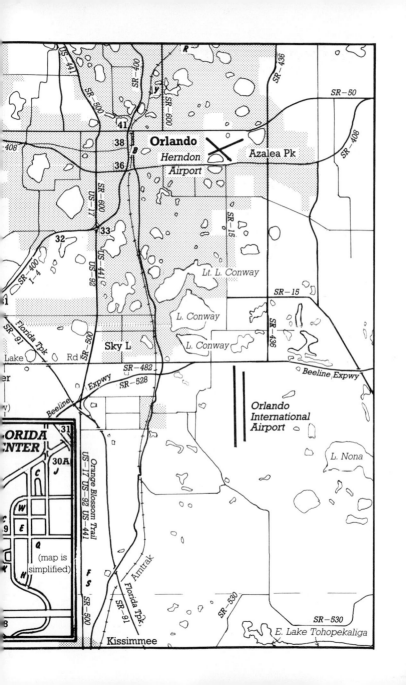

OTHER ADVENTURES AROUND ORLANDO

A few small tourist attractions were in the Orlando area before Walt Disney World arrived, but Mickey's kingdom has certainly stimulated many others to follow, and those originals to expand. This alphabetic list includes **all the tourist attractions of central Florida,** ranging from theme parks and museums to exotic theatre-restaurants. Those shown on the double-page Orlando map have their key letter repeated.

ACTION KARTWAYS

Address: 2120 E. Irlo Bronson Meml Hwy, Kissimmee. **Location:** on US-192, Spacecoast Pkwy E of Kissimmee. ∅846.8585. **Hours:** 1000-2300 daily.

Go-kart and dune buggy rides, mainly for children and teenagers.

ALLIGATORLAND SAFARI ZOO

Location: 4589 Irlo Bronson Meml Hwy, Kissimmee. **Location:** on US-192, midway between Kissimmee and Walt Disney World. ∅396.1012. **Hours:** 0900-sunset, daily.

Not to be confused with Gatorland Zoo on US-17, the Orange Blossom Trail, although the two are similar. The safari zoo has a wider range of animals, starting with Big Boy, an alligator weighing 1500lb (750kg) and going down the scale to hundreds of baby 'gators hatched each year.

The exotic animals include the big cats of Africa and Asia, several primate species, and some of the lesser-known animals including the coati mundi and agouti from South America, with representative birds ranging from tiny finches to ostriches, but I'd like to see fewer bars in evidence.

ARABIAN NIGHTS (A)

Address: 6225 W Irlo Bronson Mem Hwy (Spacecoast Pkwy), Kissimmee, FL 32741. **Location:** at junction of I-4 and US-192, exit 25 from I-4. ∅351.5822 or 1.800.553.6116. **Hours:** 1830-2330, casual dress.
&

In the shadow of the Magic Kingdom, you don't just go out to dine in the evening, neither do you just take in a show. You put the two together at the Arabian Nights dinner-theatre (or, to be fair, at any of its rivals also in this list).

The Arabian Nights, opened in 1988, is spectacular. Its owners, Mark and Galen Miller, describe it as 'the world's most outstanding entertainment showcase for horses and horsemanship,' which is one way of saying it's a 15-act show featuring 60 superb horses who go through their intricate performance in front of around 1,000 guests eating a four-course dinner.

You'll see equine circus acts, horses that dance, chariot races

Miami skyline looking towards Key Biscayne.

borrowed from *Ben Hur,* precision-stepping horses, and the Black Knight on his mysterious black stallion, all in a 90,000 sq ft (8,000 sq m) covered Moroccan-style 'palace.'

BLACK HILLS PASSION PLAY

Address: Passion Play Amphitheatre of Florida, PO Box 17, Lake Wales, FL 33853. **Location:** off US-27A 2 miles south of Lake Wales. ∅676.1495. **Times:** last Sunday in Jan to first Sunday in Apr; 1500, 1800 *or* 1930: check! **Admission:** $6 to $12, according to seat; children ½-price. ♿

German-born Josef Meier has devoted his entire career to the near-continuous direction and production of the Black Hills Passion Play, with a cast of more than 250 professional actors. Meier, who brought the play from Europe, has since 1952 staged it here in central Florida in the winter, and he moves it to his starting-place in the Black Hills of South Dakota for the remainder of the year.

It's a remarkable performance, reflecting Meier's years of study into the background; the costume and architecture, the laws and conditions, in the Holy Land during Christ's last week of life. The permanent outdoor stage is no less impressive, holding the entire set from the Garden of Gethsemane on the left and the Room of the Last Supper at centre stage, to Jerusalem city gate on the right. It's better to come for an evening performance when you can appreciate the subtlety of the lighting. If it rains before the Last Supper scene, you qualify for a refund.

BOARDWALK & BASEBALL

Address: PO Box 800, Orlando, FL 32802. **Location:** at junction of I-4 and US-27; take I-4 exit 23. ∅648.5151. **Hours:** open 0900 daily; closing varies up to 2200. **Admission:** $17 adults. **Lost & found:** ∅424.7113.

The 35 acres of this all-American theme park which are given exclusively to the USA's national sport, may be too American for many European visitors. If you understand baseball then you can practice your game and analyse the result. Otherwise concentrate on the remaining 100 acres, where the boardwalk connects 30 fairground attractions including a big wheel (ferris wheel), the Grand Rapids log flume, and the Florida Hurricane roller coaster, claimed to be the fastest in Florida and a worthy rival to Disney's Space Mountain, without the tight bends.

Everybody, though, enjoys the wild west show with horses and wagons, and the surprise appearance of can-can dancers.

BOK TOWER GARDENS

Address: PO Drawer 3810, Lake Wales, FL 33853. **Location:** north of Lake Wales and difficult to find; from Cypress Gardens take SR-540 east, cross US-27, right onto US-27A and 2nd left. From Lake Wales take US-27A north (Scenic Hwy) for 5 miles; take 1st right after minor crossing of SR-17A. Bok Tower signs are confusing. ✆676.1408. **Hours:** 0800-1730 daily. **Admission:** $2, under 12 free. ♿

In 1923 the Dutch immigrant author-publisher Edward Bok commissioned a landscape gardener to transform the 128 acres (52ha) of Iron Mountain into a place of beauty. Mountain? It's a gentle hill rising to 295 ft (90m) and claimed by many people as the highest point in central Florida.

Bok then decided to built a Dutch-style belltower at this high spot, and in 1929 President Coolidge dedicated the Singing Tower and the Bok sanctuary to the people of the USA.

The tower is 255 feet (77.5m) tall and holds a melodious set of 57 carillon bells — they don't swing as normal church bells do — cast in bronze by John Taylor & Co of Loughborough, England; the smallest weighs 17lb (7½kg) and the largest more than 11 tons. At 3pm each day the carillonneur gives a 45-minute recital of classical music following a programme set in advance, and at half-hour intervals throughout the day, stereophonic recordings of extracts from previous recitals are relayed by loudspeaker.

The grounds surrounding Bok Tower, Mr Bok's original sanctuary, form a restful and quiet escape from the surrounding world, even allowing for the carillon, and Mr Bok is now buried at the base of his Singing Tower.

CHURCH STREET STATION (B)

Address: 124 W Pine St, Orlando. **Location:** south of the city centre east of I-4; take exit 38. ✆849.0901. **Hours:** 1100-0200, daily; entertainments from 1930. **Admission:** $8 in the evening. **Parking:** under I-4, or the Sun Bank garage on South St. ♿

In the late 1980s Orlando decided to rescue its decrepit railroad depot in Church St and the old Orlando Hotel nearby, and make them a tourist attraction. Devotees scoured the country for Victoriana and came up with a selection including 1870-vintage tellers' cages from a Pittsburg bank, 800-pound (350-kg) brass chandeliers from the First National Bank in Boston, fans from a Philadelphia courthouse, bench seats from a railway station in Pensacola, as well as gilt cast-iron tables from a selection of English pubs, and the etched bar-mirrors from the Bull & Brier pub in Glasgow.

The venture became the Church Street Historic District, and by the time everybody had finished, here was a rip-roaring entertainment centre straight out of the 1890s.

The star attraction is **Rosie O'Grady's Good Time Emporium,** ✆422.2434, where the last of the Red Hot Mommas, Dixieland bands, can-can dancers and singing waiters bring the Gay Nineties back to life every night.

But Rosie doesn't have it all. **Lili Marlene's Aviator's Pub** is in the rejuvenated Strand Hotel where almost every floorboard and joist has a chronicled history, such as the French monastery which provided the church-pew seats and a confessional which now serves as a phone kiosk. And the walnut mantelpiece came from the Rothschild's Paris home.

A New Orleans church provided cypress joists holding six half- ton brass chandeliers from St Joseph's Cathedral in Buffalo, which now form the focal point at **Apple Annie's Courtyard,** a pub, restaurant and night show all in one. And **Phineas Phogg's Balloon Works** serves burgers and boogie under a display of miniature hot-air balloons and Peter Pan's airship.

And we mustn't forget the **Cheyenne Saloon and Opera House** which took 2½ years to build, using 250,000 board-feet of oak from an Ohio barn. Lovers of country and western music appreciate the Cheyenne Cloggers dance team, but history buffs admire the guns brought from the Stagecoach Museum in Minnesota, and the stained glass window from the Philadelphia courthouse with its insignia of the Grand Army of the Republic.

Probably the oddest attraction at Church Street Station is **Old Duke,** a 140-ton 0-6-0 steam locomotive built in Baldwin, Ohio, in 1912. It spent its last working years on the Florida Gulf coast and in 1960 was retired to Pensacola, where it featured in a film with John Wayne, William Holden and Henry Fonda. In 1980 it was dismantled and brought to its present site outside the station, and by the time you read this it should have a few antique carriages in tow.

Balloon flights. And don't forget: Phineas Phogg and Rosie O'Grady collaborate in operating three genuine hot-air balloons for early-morning flights over Orlando; ✆422.2434 for information.

CHURCH STREET STATION EXCHANGE

Address: 124 W Pine St, Orlando. **Location:** beside the station. ✆849.0901. **Hours:** 1100-0200 daily. ♿

The CSS Exchange is a complex of 50 shops opened in May 1988 in the same character as the CSS itself.

CITRUS TOWER

Location: US-27, on the north of Clermont. ✆394.8585. **Hours:** 0800-1800 daily. **Admission:** $2.50 ♿.

This solid-looking tower was built in 1956 as a tourist attraction and has felt the benefit of Disney's arrival nearby. A lift (elevator) takes you 200ft (61m) to the deck for a panoramic view of Lake Apopka, the state's largest spring-fed lake, and what was a vast citrus growing region. The sharp frosts of 1985 killed most of the 17,000,000 trees they claim you could see from here, and now the panorama is of open land and young citrus groves, while the frost of February 1989 may have induced other orange growers to think about diversifying. The best time to come is around noon when the sun has cleared the distant mists, but you can never see the sea from here.

The top of the tower is 226ft above ground and 543ft (165m) above sea level, just 7ft short of Bok Tower.

At the base there's a good souvenir shop, a chance to tour a glassblower's workshop, and take a tractor tour around what's left of the citrus groves. There are also the House of Presidents Wax Museum (q.v.) and two motels.

CYPRESS GARDENS

Address: PO Box 1, Cypress Gardens, FL 33880. **Location:** in Cypress Gardens township, by Winter Haven. From Orlando take I-4 to exit 23 (Boardwalk & Baseball) then US- 27 south for 18 miles and west on SR-540. ✆324,2111 or 1.800.351.6606. **Hours:** 0800-sunset, daily. **Admission:** $16.95. ♿

Cypress Gardens is probably central Florida's top spot for beauty, even including Walt Disney World in the reckoning. The gardens have masses of flower beds in full bloom no matter what time of year you call, and the southern belles in their floor- swishing hooped skirts and shoulder-slipping necklines add to nature's bounty. And in the early 1930s this was just a cypress swamp.

Some of the original inhabitants have stayed on and now take part in alligator shows, while goats and macaws feature in the children's petting area and 800 endangered species find sanctuary somewhere in the grounds.

Come in November and you'll be taught how to grow chrysanthemums; come in March and enter the Florida Watermelon Association's seed-spitting contests; come anytime and you might find yourself a guest at a wedding reception.

At **Southern Crossroads** you'll find an antebellum village – that's post-Civil-War – and nearby is the Kodak-sponsored **Island in the Sky,** a revolving circular platform that lifts up to 100 people 150 feet (50m) into the air when the weather is suitable.

The main attraction at Cypress Gardens, though, is the water-skiing, ranging from barefoot skiing and kite flying from skis to the spectacular climax, a pyramid of 10 skiers in three or four tiers.

DeBARY HALL

DeBary town, between I-4 and US-17-92 north of Orlando, takes its name from Baron Friedrich DeBary, a German who brought the first champagne to America. In 1871 he built DeBary Hall, a large mansion whose interconnecting rooms each had a balcony. The hall fell into

Jewfish Drawbridge separates continental USA from Key Largo.

disrepair after its owner's death, like so many in the state, but the Florida Federation of Art saved it in 1967 and restored it in the late 1980s. It's now open open Mon-Fri 0900- 1300, and a free guided tour shows you the furnishings and household tools of a century ago. It's at 210 Sunrise Blv, ✆668.5286.

De LAND MUSEUM

US-17 runs north from DeBary to De Land, where you'll find the De Land Museum, ✆734.4371, an 1892 mansion that's home to collections of dolls and seashells, and fine art from around the world.

De LEON SPRINGS

Ponce de Leon was looking for the Fountain of Youth when he landed on Florida's west coast in 1521. There's no evidence that he ever visited Ponce de Leon Springs in the town of De Leon Springs, five miles north-west of De Land on US-17 — but legend claims this to be the true Fountain of Youth that lured him. The swimming hole is ringed by concrete for safety, and divers and canoeists make this a popular spot.

DON GARLITS'S MUSEUM OF DRAG RACING

Address: 13700 SW 16th Ave, Ocala, FL 32676. **Location:** leave I-75 at exit 67 south of Ocala for SR- 484; it's at the junction. ✆245.8661. **Hours:** 1000-1700 daily except Christmas. **Admission:** $6.

Drag racer Don Garlits, 'Big Daddy' to his American fans, founded the museum in 1976 and opened it on its present 25,000 sq ft (2,300 sq m) site in 1984. Essentially of interest to drag racing enthusiasts, the museum traces the sport from its infancy and holds more than 60 remarkable, and sometimes peculiar, cars.

ELVIS PRESLEY MUSEUMS (C)

Addresses: 5931 American Way and 7200 International Drive. **Locations:** both are in the International Plaza SW of town along I-4; exits 29 or 30A. American Way is a small loop road at the north, near Wet 'n' Wild. ✆345.8860. **Hours:** 0900- 2200 daily. **Admission:** $4, 12 years upwards.

More than 300 of Elvis's souvenirs are at these two locations, including his grand piano from Graceland, his last Cadillac, his Cobra racing car from the film *Spin Out,* a Mercedes 600 limousine, selections from his vast wardrobe, his firearms collection, his bed and saddle, his first guitar ('the guitar that changed the world'), plus photographs and a miscellany of other memorabilia.

FAST TRAX

A new racetrack, with some steeply-banked turns, waiting to be accepted into the sport. Meantime, watch the practise laps, 1000-24000, on International Drive south of Wet 'n' Wild.

FLEA WORLD

Location: 3 miles south of Sanford on US-17-92 north from Orlando, on east of road. ✆645.1792. **Hours:** 0800-1700, Fri-Sun, Labor Day and Memorial Day. **Admission and parking:** free. &

Each weekend around 75,000 people come to Flea World, an amazing market which sells a vast range of goods. More than 1,200 mini-shops cluster on the 104-acre (42ha) site, with everything under cover. Come and buy antiques, 'pre-owned' clothing, bits of cars, food, jewellery, or just junk. Have your hair cut. Consult a lawyer. Pawn your watch. Or come for the free entertainment on stage.

FORT LIBERTY (D)

Address: Scott Blvd, 5260 Hwy 192, Kissimmee, FL 32741. **Location:** a little east of Arabian Nights, exit 25 from I-4. ✆351.5151 or 1.800.521.5152. **Hours:** 1800-2030 daily, but times vary. **Admission:** around $25 for adults.

This dinner-theatre, opened in 1987, must regret that Arabian

Nights opened nearby a year later. Fort Liberty, however, caters for a different class of customer and bases its appeal around the pioneer Fort Liberty, the nearby Indian village, and an early trading post with 26 shops.

Prof Gladstone brings on his travelling medicine show, Dr Hokum saws a baby in half, and other performers get up to similar tricks while you eat your chow from the mess hall and wash it down with unlimited beer (soft drinks for the driver).

Why not drop by from 0700 to 1000 for breakfast, or lunch from 1100 to 1400, for just $2. It all helps the British economy as this venture is owned by a London company.

FUN 'N' WHEELS (E)

Address: 6739 Sand Lake Rd, Orlando, FL 32819. **Location:** at junction of International Dr and Sand Lake Rd, exit 29 from I-4. ✆351.5651. **Also at:** Rt 192, Osceola Sq Mall, Kissimmee. ✆870.2222. **Hours:** 1000- 2400 daily. **Admission:** free; rides cost $2, golf $3.♿ spectators.

These are fun parks for the children, but a lot of fathers join in. Three go-kart tracks, bumper cars, bumper boats, water slides, an amusement arcade, and a big wheel (ferris wheel in the USA) 95ft (28m) high: it's tamer than the Magic Kingdom but it's cheaper.

GATORLAND ZOO (F)

Address: 14501 S Orange Blossom Trail, Orlando, FL 32821. **Location:** 5 miles (8km) north of Kissimmee, next to Tupperware headquarters, on US-17-92-144. ✆857.3848. **Hours:** 0800-1800 winter, - 1700 summer. **Admission:** $5.40 adults. ♿

Five thousand alligators live here, but the count can never be accurate as thousands are hatched each season. Visitors tour the grounds by miniature railway and can watch the awesome sight of alligators, responding to their own names, jump from the water to take food. Covered walkways take you deep into the 'gators' own territory, and if that's not enough you can visit the snake house and try a boa constrictor around your neck. You may already have seen part of Gatorland at the cinema, for the sequence of an alligator feeding frenzy in *Indiana Jones and the Temple of Doom* was filmed here.

Gatorland is also a commercial alligator farm and research centre, rearing what are claimed to be the world's only 'gators fertilised by artificial insemination. You can therefore expect to find alligator skins on sale fashioned into boots, belts and bags at the workshop.

HOUSE OF PRESIDENTS WAX MUSEUM

Location: by Citrus Tower, q.v. **Admission:** $3 adults. ♿

How many presidents preceded George Bush? There are 39 of

them, all life-size, in this building which has a hint of the White House about its architecture.

JUNGLE FALLS (G)

Address; 5285 W. Hwy 192, Kissimmee. **Location:** 2½ miles east of exit 25 on I-4. Ø396.1996. **Hours:** 1100-dusk, daily. **Admission:** free, pay for rides.

A fun park for the youngsters, with a quarter-mile (500m) go- kart track capable of allowing high speeds for these little trucks. Bumper boats and cars, video games and kiddie karts.

KING HENRY'S FEAST (H)

Address: 8984 International Dr, Orlando, FL 32819. **Location:** South of Sand Lake Rd, take either exit 28 or 29 from I-4. Ø351.5151. **Hours:** 1930-2215 ¦daily; ¦show ˙starts 2000. **Admission:** around $25, less if not drinking the unlimited alcohol. ♿

It's Henry VIII if you wondered, with several of his wives, dining in regal style while they — and you — are entertained by court jesters, jousting knights in jangling armour, magicians, singers and dancers, and a musician or two. The setting is near authentic, as a British company was engaged to built this $3,500,000 moated castle, using materials from Britain. His Majesty gives American children an insight into European history, and manages to involve some of them in the nightly court dramas.

The five-course meal has something of the early 16th-cent but there's more than a hint of modern America in the menu.

A barred owl, one of the exotic species of the Everglades.

MALIBU GRAND PRIX (J)

Address: 5863 American Way, Orlando. **Location:** between exits 30A and 30B on I-4. ✆351.4132. ᚦ

Show your driving licence if you'd like to try your hand behind the wheel of a full-sized racing car, but not on a full-size track — or watch the youngsters battle it out in go-karts. Mini golf, baseball practice and slot machines complete the amusements.

MARDI GRAS AT MERCADO (K)

Address: 8445 International Dr, Orlando. **Location:** the Mercado Festival Center; take exit 29 from I-4. ✆351.5151. **Hours:** 1930-2200 daily. **Admission:** $22.95 adults. ᚦ

The New Orleans and Caribbean influence comes through at Mardi Gras (Shrove Tuesday), beginning with a mint julep and strengthening throughout the four-course creole meal. The lights dim, the entertainment begins, and a 22-piece New Orleans jazz band leads you into a spectacle of song and dance from the major carnivals around the world, but particularly in the Mississippi Delta and the Carib isles. The setting was by those same Britons who created King Henry's Feast.

MEDIEVAL TIMES (L)

Location: Spacecoast Pkwy (Hwy 192) to Kissimmee, just off our map. ✆239.0214 or 1.800.432.0768. **Hours:** Sun-Fri, 1900, Sat 1800 & 2030. **Admission:** $23 13 yrs and older.

As near an authentic medieval banquet in what is obviously a mock 11th-cent castle. The tempo is fast as knights on horseback joust, duel, and sometimes battle with swords for a lady's honour. The four-course banquet has a medieval touch and as the target audience is the family, there's no strong liquor.

MULBERRY PHOSPHATE MUSEUM

This strangely-named museum is in Mulberry (population 3,000) on SR-60 west of Bartow. The museum itself is on SR-37 one block south of the town-centre crossroads, open 1000-1630 Tues-Sat, and holds an extraordinary collection of fossils found during the excavations for phosphates.

MYSTERY FUN HOUSE (M)

Address: 5767 Major Blv, Orlando. **Location:** in the triangle made by the Florida Turnpike, I-4 and SR-435. ✆351.3357. **Hours:** 1000-2300, daily. **Admission:** $6 adults.

Optical illusions abound here, in the topsy-turvy room, in the hall of distorting mirrors and in the glass-walled maze which might just have the odd mirror. Climb a crazy ladder, walk the magic floor, travel the twisting tunnel — or go for something nearly normal and play the 18-hole mystery mini-golf. Don't confuse the chamber of horrors with the recent Florida sports hall of fame where there are mementos from the state's top sportsmen.

The **Mystery Fun House Trolley** is an old-style tram that trundles around the tourist trail, calling at major attractions, hotels, shopping malls — and, of course, the Mystery Fun House.

OLD TOWN (N)

Address: 5770 Spacecoast Pkwy, Kissimmee. **Location:** US-192 a mile east of exit 25 on I-4. ✆396.4888. **Hours:** 1000-2200 daily. **Admission:** free. &

Old Town is what its name implies: a shopping centre built in turn-of-the century architecture. The streets are made of bricks, the local transport is a surrey — that's a horse-drawn carriage with open sides, and a flat roof with a 'fringe on top.' But if you come by car there's plenty of parking space.

There's entertainment too. At the entrance to the town's single street stands Big Eli, a big wheel (ferris wheel) built in 1928 but totally restored; it now takes 32 people on a round trip to 56 feet above ground. Opposite is the launch-pad for tethered flights in a hot air balloon every evening, weather permitting, and at the far end of Old Town Boulevard is the 1910-vintage carousel (merry-go-round), once again in spanking order and selling sedate 75¢ rides.

ORANGE COUNTY HISTORICAL MUSEUM (Y)

Location: Mills Ave, off Orlando Ave. ✆898.8320. &

It's difficult to find much history in Orlando, but the museum manages to bring together furniture, Amerind tools, a reconstructed smithy from 1880, and a newspaper printing works with hot-metal type. Nearby you'll find an oak tree believed to be 350 years old which is now a designated national historic site.

Nearby are the Loch Haven Arts Center in Loch Haven Park, the Orlando Museum of Art, and the Young Science Center.

PLACES OF LEARNING (P)

Address: 6825 Academic Dr, Orlando. **Location:** south-west of Sea World, off I-4. ✆345.1038. **Hours:** 0900-1800, longer in school holidays. **Admission:** free. &

Here's probably the largest map of the USA, covering an acre (5,000 sq m), with flags of all the 50 states. The Parents' Store has one of the largest children's bookshops in the 50 states.

REPTILE WORLD

Address: 4727 E Spacecoast Pkwy, St Cloud. **Location:** 3 miles east of St Cloud on US-192-441. ✆892.6905. **Hours:** 0900-1730; closed Mon, Thanksgiving and Christmas. **Admission:** $3.25. ♿

Snakes, alligators, crocodiles, lizards; if it's reptilian, it's here. The Reptile World Serpentarium started in 1972 purely for the production of snake venom for the manufacture of serum, but if you're running any exotic business in central Florida you soon realise it's worth opening your doors to the public.

From 1976, therefore, visitors have been able to see in complete safety the milking of venom at 1100, 1400 and 1700 from mambas, cobras, rattlesnakes, vipers and others.

RISE AND FLOAT BALLOON TOURS

Address: PO Box 620755, Orlando. Location: opposite Wet 'n' Wild, q.v. ✆352.8191. **Hours:** sunrise and sunset.

Come fly with me! Free flying in a hot air balloon, subject to weather, with a champagne breakfast or supper to follow.

RIVERSHIP ROMANCE

Address; 433 N Palmetto Dr, Sanford, FL 32771. **Location:** Monroe Harbor Marina. ✆321.5091 or 1.800.423.7401.

Come aboard the 110-ft (34m) triple-decker for a cruise on the St Johns River. Departures at 1100 for the luncheon cruise (prices to $34), at 1930 for the dinner-dance cruise ($36), or for $200 go on the Sun-Mon two-day cruise.

SEA WORLD (Q)

Address: 7007 Sea World Dr, Orlando, FL 32821. **Location:** near the junction of I-4 and the Beeline Expwy, SR-528. Exit 28 from I-4. ✆351.0021. **Hours:** 0900-1900 daily, later in summer and holidays. **Admission:** $16.50 adults, week-long pass around $21.50. Sky Tower and radio- controlled boats extra. **Lost & found:** ✆351.3600 ext 493. ♿

Sea World of Florida is the leading theme park outside of Walt Disney World, and to do the place justice you should spend at least five hours here. The park is divided into sections for convenience; the first one you enter is **Beneath the Sea,** centred on the Tropical Reef, a 160,000 US gallon (130,000 Imperial gallons, 600 cu m) aquarium of tropical fish. Several smaller tanks show much smaller marine creatures.

Other entertainment in this section is a diversion from the main theme: Fantasy Theatre, and its magical-mystical show in the evenings; the Polynesian revue at Hawaiian Rhythms, and the Sea World band at the Beach Stage.

You're back on theme with the Dolphin Feeding Pool where you're invited to stroke and pat these beautiful mammals. And the theme continues with the 2,000 marine creatures in the Tide Pool.

Left, north-east, leads to **Ocean Friends** and the Whale and Dolphin Show where marine mammals from around the world put on their joint performance. Cap'n Kid's World, nearby, is a play area for the youngsters. The new Penguin Encounter holds 200 birds of various sub-species, and in the seal and stingray feeding pools you have an insight into these creatures' private lives.

Back to Beneath the Sea, and south-east into **Sea Lions and Sharks** for, first, the Sea Lion and Otter Stadium for some neat performances, and then to Sharks, where you travel through a tunnel of very thick acrylic plastic and admire sharks swimming around you in their 600,000 US gallon (500,000 Imp gall, 2,250 cu m) home. This is understandably a popular thrill and you may have to wait a while. Sea World researches into the care and breeding of several species of ocean mammals, and the Sea World Theatre offers visitors an insight into training techniques, but not enough to persuade Greenpeace in Key West, and other environmentalists, that intelligent marine mammals shouldn't be performing tricks for mankind; however, the performance drew 320,000 British visitors in 1988.

Sky Tower rises 400ft (120m) from the shore of the main lake, where a boardwalk crosses it to **Shamu Stadium.** Shamu the killer whale is not only Sea World's biggest attraction − in two senses, since she weighs more than two tons − she is also the park's trade mark. And she is female; Sea World's television commercials show her giving birth underwater to Baby Shamu in November 1988.

Back in that main lake, the **Atlantis Theatre** team puts on a precision water-ski show which rivals the human pyramid display at Cypress Gardens . . . but that's not surprising, as you'll soon see.

Sea World's professionalism is of the top order, and if you plan to take in only one performing animal act in Florida, this is the one. There are other Sea Worlds in California, Ohio and Texas, and the company also runs Cypress Gardens and Boardwalk & Baseball.

SHELL MUSEUM (R)

Address and location: Rollins College, Holt St, Winter Park, Orlando, on the top edge of our map. ✆646.2364. **Hours:** 1000-1200, 1300-1600 Mon-Fri. **Admission:** $1 adults.

The Beal-Maltbie Shell Museum, part of Rollins College, has a display of more than 2,000,000 sea shells from around the world, including some that are extremely rare.

The nearby **Walk of Fame** at the college, has 800 inscribed stones and slabs brought from the birthplaces and the homes of the famous.

SILVER SPRINGS

Location: on SR-40, east of Ocala. ✆236.2121. **Hours:** 0900-1730 daily. **Admission:** $12 adults.

Silver Springs is a peaceful recreational area around the springs that feed the Silver River. It's been a beauty spot for many years, but now you can tour the crystal-clear waters in a glass-bottomed boat and see east African and North American wildlife, visit the reptile house and the deer park — and for a complete change, take a look at the classic car collection.

Nearby, and under the same management, is **Wild Waters,** opened in 1978 as a water-based theme park for children. It's open late March to mid September, 1000-2000, for $8 adults, $3 children. ✆236.2043.

SKI HOLIDAYS

Address: PO Box 22007, Lake Buena Vista, FL 32830. **Location:** leave I-4 at exit 27 on SR-5535 south; 500 ft (150m) from junction turn onto private dirt road. Not marked on our map. ✆239.4444.

This is the place to come to learn how to waterski, whether you're a beginner or wanting to take on the experts. On the 350- acre Lake Bryan you can rent a boat and driver, and as many pairs of skis as your party needs, for $50 an hour. Jet ski rentals begin at $30 an hour, and you can also try your hand at parascending.

STARS HALL OF FAME

Address: 6825 Starway Dr, Orlando. **Location:** on county road near Sea World. ✆351.2628. **Hours:** winter, 1000-2030; summer 0900-2200 daily. ♿

A waxworks museum specialising in show-business personalities from the early silent films to the latest TV stars, it would benefit from some of Disney's animatronics. An unusual feature is for selected visitors to have the chance of acting a sequence from a TV series and have a video of their performance sent to 20th Century Fox. Occasionally one of the tapes produces an invitation to act in a real TV show.

TUPPERWARE HEADQUARTERS (S)

Location: on US-17-92-441, the Orange Blossom Trail beteen Orlando and Kissimmee, beside Gatorland Zoo. ✆847.311. **Hours:** 0900-1600, Mon-Fri. **Admission:** free. ♿

Tupperware International Headquarters has a small museum showing the history of storage containers from 4,000BC to the present. You'll also see a film explaining how Tupperware makes its own plastic containers, and see a display of the finished products.

UNIVERSAL STUDIOS

Late in 1989 at 1000 Universal Studios Plaza, Orlando (✆363.8200), the 444-acre studios was due to open to the public as an answer to the Disney-MGM Studios. Leave I-4 at exit 30B north, and take SR-435.

WARBIRD AIR MUSEUM

Address; 231 N Airport Rd, Kissimmee, FL 32741. **Location:** Airport Rd is on the south of US-192, west of airport entrance. ✆933.1942. **Hours:** Mon-Fri 0800-2000, Sat 0900-2000, Sun 0900-1800. **Admission:** $5; younger than 12 or older than 60, $4. ♿

The phone number is a good clue: this is a museum of American World War Two military aircraft. A museum with a major difference, however, as you'll be able to see mechanics working on the restoration of several of these beautiful planes, and when they've done a pilot will make a test flight, or just take the machine up out of pure nostalgia.

If you remember the war you'll remember the Flying Fortress, the Mitchell, Mustang, Typhoon, and many others. If not, come and learn something of history. There's also a working Tiger Moth here.

WATER MANIA (T)

Address: 6073 W Spacecoast Pkwy (W Irlo Bronson Meml Hwy), Kissimmee. **Location:** on US-192 past Arabian Nights; exit 25 from I-4. ✆396.2626 or 1.800.527.3092. **Hours:** summer, 0900-2100, spring & autumn 1000-1700, closed Dec thru Feb. ♿ spectators.

Water Mania undispudedly had Florida's largest wave-making machine until Walt Disney World created Typhoon Lagoon; now I wouldn't like to comment. There's certainly plenty of scope for getting wet here — try the Mad Skipper, with twin toboggan flumes, go one better with three spiralling chutes in the Looney Flume, tackle the Double Berserker, or stake everything on the Screamer which has a 72-ft (22-m) near-vertical drop to get you moving. Or you can relax on the beach; there's a three-acre wooded picnic area, too.

WET 'N' WILD (W)

Address: 6200 International Dr, Orlando, FL 32819. **Location:** exit 30A from I-4; see inset map. ✆351.3200. **Hours:** daily, summer 0900-2100, spring & autumn 1000- 1800, closed late Nov to early Feb. **Admission:** $13 aged 13 up. **Lost & found:** ✆351.1800 ext 242. ♿ spectators.

The name says it all. This is central Florida's answer to anybody who wants to jump in at the deep end — or come down a water slide that starts 50 feet up. Whitewater slide, corkscrew flume, water roller coaster, bumper boats, speedboats: they're all here. Just bring your swimming gear.

XANADU (X)
Location: on US-192 east of exit 25 on I-4; or come down SR-535 from exit 27. ✆396.1992. **Hours:** 1000-2200 daily. **Admission:** $4.75 adults.

After a drug-induced sleep, Samuel Taylor Coleridge woke and began writing a mystic poem that his brain had composed:

> In Xanadu did Kubla Khan
> A stately pleasure dome decree,
> Where Alph, the sacred river, ran
> Through caverns measureless to man
> Down to a sunless sea . . .

Florida's Xanadu is equally mystic but lacks any link with the past. It's billed as the Home of the Future, a 15-room house (for want of a better word) where computers control the environment and respond to the human voice, where a robot does the drudgery, where the bathroom has a built-in waterfall and where the art gallery is electronic. All the rooms are circular and from outside Xanadu looks something like an animated ice-cream melting in the hot sun. It's weird, but fun.

YOUNG SCIENCE CENTRE (Y)
Location: Mills Ave, off Orlando Ave. ✆896.7151. **Hours:** Mon-Thur 0900-1700, Fri 0900-2100, Sat 1200-2100, Sun 1200-1700. **Admission:** $2 to $6.

Not really about young science; it's the science centre named from John Young, but it still attracts youngsters with its Science Arcade of working models and practical experiments relating to pure science as well as to the living sciences. There are the John Young Planetarium and an observatory, and nearby are the Loch Haven Arts Center, the Orlando Museum of Art, and the Orange County Historical Museum.

OFFBEAT IN ORLANDO AND KISSIMMEE

By now you will have realised that Florida, in particular that part of the state surrounding Walt Disney World, is like nowhere else on this planet; the nearest you're likely to come to it is in California.

You won't therefore be surprised to find a few really offbeat attractions. For example, go to Lake Wales, follow the signs to **Spook Hill** at North Ave and 5th St. Park your car at the spot marked on the road, release the brake, and you'll gradually roll *uphill*. Legend claims it's the work of an Indian protecting his tribe, but science has the truth: it's an optical illusion.

For a holiday with a difference try the **Cypress Cove Nudist Resort** on SR-531, at 4425 Pleasant Hill Rd, 10 miles (16km) south of

Kissimmee, between Reedy Creek Swamp and Brown Lake; ℄933.5870. It has 80 campsites, a pool, playground, tennis courts, canoe rental, a shop and even a *laundry*. Admission is $19 per couple.

If clothes, particularly uniforms, appeal, call in on Friday no later than 0930 at the **US Naval Training Center** via General Reese Rd, off SR-50 opposite Hendon Airport in east Orlando, and you'll be a guest at the weekly passout parade of Naval recruits. And it's free.

Shortly after spiritualism — contact with the spirits of the dead — began in the USA in the 19th cent, George Colby and his three ghostly guides established the town of **Cassadaga** and gave a small chunk of its ground to build a spiritualist church. Cassadaga is still the home of spiritualism, with many mediums advertising their services; it's a tiny village now, though marked on the state maps, and you'll find it if you drive from Orlando city centre 27 miles north on I-4 and turn off right just before Lake Helen.

In Kissimmee which, by the way, is pronounced Kiss*simm*ee, you might take a look at the Osceola County **Courthouse** in Emmett St. Built in 1889, it's the oldest in Florida still in use as a court of law, and it's now a National Historic Site. And Osceola is pronounced Ossee*oh*la.

If you still fancy an unusual experience and you're here in high summer, then go ice skating. The **Orlando Ice Skating Palace** is at 3123 W Colonial Dr, ℄299.5440, open Wed-Sun 1930-2230, and in the afternoons on Wed, Sat and Sun.

Oranges are the main agricultural product of Orange County and the surrounding district, despite the occasional ravages of frost in places such as Clermont and Frostproof, but if you go to **Zellwood,** north-west of Orlando on US-441, between Christmas and Easter, you'll find yourself in the Garden of Florida where much of eastern USA's tender winter salads and vegetables are grown. Once again, the industry has seen the tourist potential and for $9 you can take a guided tour of thousands of acres of farmland. ℄966.2517 for details.

ORLANDO-KISSIMMEE FACTFILE

Exits from I-4. Reading south to north, these are the exits from Interstate Highway 4, and what they lead to:

23. To US-27 north and south; at junction, Boardwalk & Baseball; south to Cypress Gardens, Bok Tower, Lake Wales, Black Hills Passion Play.

24. To SR-532 east, only; leads to US-17-92 and to Kissimmee.

25A. East onto US-192, also known as the Spacecoast Pkwy and Irlo Bronson Meml Hwy, leading to Arabian Nights, Action Kartways, Water Mania, Old Town, Fort Liberty, Xanadu, Alligatorland Safari Zoo, Medieval Times, Jungle Falls, Warbird Air Museum. Via Kissimmee to Gatorland Zoo and Tupperware; via Kissimmee and St Cloud to Reptile World.

25B. West onto US-192 to Magic Kingdom.

26A and 26B. Also known as the Epcot-Disney Connector; west on SR-536 to Walt Disney World and eventually the Magic Kingdom. Proposed eastward extension to connect with Beeline Expwy.

27. Onto SR-535. East to Ski Holidays almost on junction; road meets US-192 by Xanadu. West to Hotel Plaza Blv in Walt Disney World.

28. East only to SR-528, Beeline Expwy (toll). Places of Learning, Sea World, Orlando Airport, Kennedy Space Center.

29. East to Sand Lake Rd, SR-482, and Florida Center for Wet 'n' Wild, Fun 'n' Wheels. See Florida Center inset in Orlando map. West exit is county road.

30A. South-east to Republic Drive and Florida Center; see inset map.

30B. To SR-435; south to Florida Center; see inset map. North to Universal Studios, Rise & Float Balloon Tours, Mystery Fun House, and Pine Hills district of Orlando.

31. To Florida Turnpike.

32. To 33rd St.

33A. To US-441; north to Apopka, south to Kissimmee.

36. To East-West Expwy (toll). West to Citrus Tower, Don Garlits's Drag Museum. East to Kennedy Space Center.

38. To Church Street Station.

40. Robinson St, to central Orlando.

41. Amelia Ave, Colonial Dr (US-50) and central Orlando.

43. To Loch Haven Park and museums.

It can get cold in the Keys; that's 41° Fahrenheit!

ORLANDO FACTFILE

PUBLIC TRANSPORT. Orlando has a conventional city bus service for the locals but most public transport is based on the one idea of moving the tourist between airport, hotel, and attraction. If you haven't rented a car your options are limited to tourist-style coaches; taxis are far too expensive for general travel, but if money is no problem there's **Yellow Cabs** on ✆422.4455 in Orlando and ✆846.2222 in Kissimmee.

The **Greyhound Bus** station in Orlando is on Amelia Ave, south-west of exit 41 from I-4.

Guests at the smart hotels in Lake Buena Vista have access to free **shuttle buses** every 15 minutes to Walt Disney World – but you've already paid for them in your hotel reservation. **Rabbit Bus** (✆291.2424) operates the round trip from Florida Center (International Drive) to Kissimmee and along US- 192 to WDW for $5; **Gray Line** (✆422.0744) charges $6 per adult and includes downtown Orlando in its schedule – and both will carry you further afield at a price, for example $20 to the Kennedy Space Center.

Don't ignore the **Mystery Fun House** (q.v.) trolley tours around the most popular route, and the **Sightseeing Trolley Tour of Orlando** which has a service from Church St Station to International Drive and Lake Buena Vista.

There are many firms in the contract-coach business, most of them tied to the larger hotels, to tour operators, or available only for larger parties. This list mentions the few which may be of service to the individual carless tourist:

Airport Limousine Service: 324 W Gore St, Orlando. ✆423.5566, with desk at the airport. Airport-hotels-attractions.

All Points Travel: 1809 Edgewater Dr, Orlando, FL 32804. ✆422.6442 or 1.800.255.7662. ♿ Caters for individual traveller.

American Express Destination Services: 5401 Kirkman Rd, Suite 700, Orlando, FL 32819. ✆351.4545 or 1.800.327.1365. Also arranges transfers, tickets, tour escorts.

Demare Travel & Tours: 517 S Chickasaw Dr, Orlando. ✆277.7799 or 1.800.433.8315. ♿ Airport-hotels-attractions, plus individuals to dinner-theatres, etc.

Sunset Limousines of Central Florida: 526 Hunter Circle, Kissimmee. ✆933.0003. Limos and taxis; charters and tours.

Sailing yachts for hire or charter, with crew, from Clearwater Beach.

ACCOMMODATION. Accommodation in the Orlando area concentrates at the top end of the market, with very little scope at the budget end. Even so, there are more than 130,000 beds available and a basic guide of the hotels would be much longer than this chapter.

Condominiums. Around 20 to 30 condominium rentals are on the market at rates *starting at* around $400 a week, which is reasonable when a party of up to 10 is sharing. If you're in this market, contact the **Orlando Convention & Visitors' Bureau** at PO Box 36, Southall, Mddx, UB2 5JN or at 7208 Sand Lake Rd, Orlando, FL 32819, ✆363.5800, and ask for its official visitor guide.

Camping. Camping is a possibility if your budget is tight, but remember the mosquitos. Apart from Fort Wilderness in WDW, campgrounds are at **Fort Summit,** PO Box 22182 Lake Buena Vista, on US-27 by exit 23 from I-4. ✆424.1880 or 1.800.4244999. You have 300 pitches with lots of facilities, including ♿.

North of Orlando is **Katie's Wekiva River Landing;** leave I-4 for SR-46 westbound and travel 5 miles. ✆322.4470 or 1.800.628.1482. You can hire a canoe at Katie's. **Yogi Bear** has two Jellystone Park campsites, with heavy emphasis on juvenile fun. One is on US-192 *west* of WDW, ✆239.4148 or 1.800.327.7115 with 703 sites; the other is on SR-482 *west* of exit 29 from I-4, near Wet 'n' Wild, with 500 sites.

The **American Adventure** with 680 sites (✆396.6101) and **Outdoor Resorts of America** with 980 (✆422.7461) are near the first Jellystone Park campsite; **Holiday Village Campground** with 450 sites (✆396.4595) is near Arabian Nights on US-192, and near Xanadu on this same highway you'll find **KOA** (Kampgrounds of America) with 374 sites (✆396.2400), **Kissimmee Campground** with a mere 52 sites (✆396.6851) and **Orange Grove Campground** with 192 sites (✆396.6655). There are several others, including the nudist camp.

There's a **youth hostel** at 227 Eola Dr (✆843.8888); from I-4 exit 41 go south to Robinson St, then turn east. Membership of the IYHA is advisable.

RESTAURANTS. I've already listed the theatre- restaurants; apart from them there are hundreds of eateries, ranging from those with a floor show which is not quite up to the theatre-restaurant standard, to the fast-food outlets. You can pay a small fortune for a dinner, but the majority of places not tied to hotels charge less than $10. A few — a very few — are listed here, more for their novelty than for their cuisine.

At 5100 Adanson St, Orlando, (off I-4) is **Bathtub Ginny's,** also known as J. J. Whispers, a modestly-priced 1920s-style restaurant with live music and a hint of Las Vegas. In Lake Buena Vista, **Empress Lilly's** looks like a triple-deck Mississippi riverboat that's run aground.

There are classy restaurants on each deck with décor to match the Disney image.

Back at the budget end, try **TGI Friday** ('Thank God It's Friday'?) at 6424 Carrier Dr off International Dr, (✆345.8822), open every day and usually with some impromptu entertainment from the waiters.

For serious sampling of Orlando's culinary fare, get the Orlando-Orange County Convention & Visitor's Bureau guide already mentioned, and take your pick of menus from America, China, France, Italy, Japan, Mexico, Polynesia, Spain, Thailand, Vietnam and even the United Kingdom.

VISITOR CENTER and MERCADO.

The main Visitor Center for Orlando and Orange County is at the Mercado Festival Center at 8445 International Drive, in the Florida Center; exit 29 from I-4. ✆363.5871. If you call at any other Chamber of Commerce in the Orlando area you're likely to be redirected here; hours are 0800-2000 daily.

While you're at the center, take a look at the Mercado Festival Center. It's a $20,000,000 showpiece shopping mall with plenty of budget restaurants and food shops, and usually with some lively street entertainment.

A TOUCH OF HISTORY

It's so easy to forget that Orlando was here long before Mickey Mouse came along. In 1857 the new town, known in those early days as Jernigan, became the seat of the equally-new Orange County as the citrus industry grew. It was one of the first places in the state to become popular with the retired, and it soon changed its name to that of the main character in *As You Like It*.

VERDICT. Central Florida holds the world's largest concentration of theme parks and fairgrounds. If you have a dread of being in crowds or you desperately want to be alone on your holidays, give the Orlando area a miss. Otherwise, even if you're not a lover of theme parks, it's a once-in-a-lifetime experience to see what other people call fun, and it's certainly a pity to come to Florida and not spend a day or two at Walt Disney World.

On the other hand, theme park and amusement ground devotees will have here a preview of what their particular Heaven may be like. A fortnight's holiday in central Florida will give you enough time to absorb Walt Disney World and most of the other attractions in considerable detail, but if you plan to see everything possible, including the Kennedy Space Center, allow yourself three weeks and a lot of money, and be prepared to emerge shell-shocked and battle-scarred. Or do it in at least two stages; half this year and the remainder next.

20: OCALA

Equine estates

OCALA IS THE CENTRE OF FLORIDA'S HORSEBREEDING INDUS-
TRY and is becoming a serious rival to Kentucky as it has the
advantage of a much milder winter climate. Around 150 stud farms are
scattered amid the pinewoods on the gently-rolling limestone hills in
mid-state, and you can forget you're only an hour's drive from Walt
Disney World. The town – stress the 'O,' not the first 'A' – has a
population of about 40,000 most of whom are deeply involved in
breeding thoroughbred racehorses, rivalling the blue-grass estates of
Kentucky; several breeders have moved south to take advantage of
Florida's warmer climate.

Some of the stud farms are open to visitors; if you don't see a sign at
the end of the drive, contact the Ocala – Marion County Chamber of
Commerce on ✆(904).629.8051 for the latest information, or try Grosse
Pointe Stud Farm at 8998 W Fort King St, Ocala, ✆237.3348.

Osceola. In 1835 the Seminole chief Osceola (ossi-*oh*-la) received
bad news as his tribe were in camp where Ocala now stands. The
Indian agent told him that the palefaces had decided to move the
Seminoles *en masse* to the other side of the Mississippi. Osceola
refused to move, so the agent stopped the sale of guns.

Indignant Osceola planned to ambush the paleface chief, Major
Francis Dade, and killed him with 100 of his troops near Bushnell
(down I-75 towards Tampa) on Christmas Eve, 1835, so starting the
second Seminole War. Dade, of course, is remembered in the name
of the county holding Miami, but Osceola is also honoured; Kissimmee
is the seat of Osceola County.

Osceola National Forest. East of Ocala, and beyond Silver Springs
(see Chap 19), the Osceola National Forest encloses 366,000 acres
(1,615 sq km) of sand pine forest, probably the world's largest stand of
this particular conifer. SR-19 runs north-to-south through the forest but
there is a grid of county roads and tracks to allow you to get right
away from the human race.

But if you like a little company, 300 campsites are licenced in the
forest in at least 15 isolated locations; ✆685.2048 for information on
those in the north, and 669.3522 for those in the south.

Springs. The forest has several natural springs welling up from the limestone aquifer much like the commercialised Silver Springs. Florida has more springs than any other part of the world of similar size, mainly because the rainfall is high, the elevation low, and the limestone so porous, allowing water to bubble to the surface almost anywhere. Of the state's 66 recognised springs, 27 are of the first magnitude, yielding at least 64,000,000 US gallons (53,000,000 Imperial gallons, 240,000 cu m) per day; Silver Springs, one of the biggest, produces 530,000,000 US gallons (2,600,000 cu m) daily, and three lesser springs are in the forest.

North of SR-40 which bisects the area horizontally, **Juniper Springs** is organised as a mini-resort but nearby **Fern Hammock Springs** is as nature intended, plus a boardwalk. **Salt Springs,** which isn't saline, is on the south shore of Lake Kerr, beside SR-314.

VERDICT. The Ocala area offers an interlude of solitude and wilderness, surprisingly close to the crowds around Orlando. Camp here for a couple of days and you could imagine yourself in the backwoods a century ago, until you hear the noise of a car engine filtering through the trees.

This must be the tropics! A schooner at her berth in Miami's Bayside.

21: CAPE CANAVERAL AND THE ATLANTIC

Out of this world

SPACE TECHNOLOGY AND WILDLIFE CONSERVATION exist side by side on Cape Canaveral. Bald eagles nest within sight of the shuttle launch pad, and alligators live completely wild in the creeks surrounding the Kennedy Space Center (KSC).

We'll have to separate the two for the sake of clarity, but let's get one point clear: Cape Canaveral is a headland on the coast; the Cape Canaveral Air Force Base behind it is involved in space exploration; but if you want to go on a conducted tour of it all (you're not allowed to wander around alone), follow signs to the John F Kennedy Space Center and Spaceport USA.

Spaceport USA. Most maps of the state mark 'Spaceport USA' on SR-405, Nasa Parkway West, standing in the middle of the southern part of Merritt Island; access from Orlando is along SR- 50 or, to the south, SR-528, the Beeline Expwy; you can also reach Spaceport from the south, from Merritt Island town and Cocoa, along SR-3.

Spaceport is open 0900-1830 (-1900 in summer) daily, except launch days: if you want to be here for a shuttle launch, write to NASA Visitors Services, John F Kennedy Space Center Headquarters, FL 32899, or ✆452.2121. Allow plenty of time and expect disappointment, as few passes are issued.

Spaceport itself has ♿ restrooms, but wheelchair visitors cannot use the double-deck coaches and there are stairs to negotiate around KSC. If a disabled person wants to go on from here, he or she must make advance arrangements for a guide to travel in the visitor's own car; call the number in the previous paragraph, ext 260, and arrange a date.

As soon as you arrive, go to one of the eight kiosks and buy your tour ticket for either or both of the tours: **RED** tour goes around KSC, Launch Complex 39, the Shuttle launch site, the Apollo moon mission control centre, and to the museum holding Skylab and the Apollo-Soyuz link-up. **BLUE** tour goes to Cape Canaveral Air Force Base (AFB), the Mercury and Gemini launch pads, and to launch sites past and present. Red is the more popular.

Your ticket ($4 for adults and $1.75 for children younger than 12, per tour) gives you a boarding time for each two-hour tour, but *seats are not reserved;* coaches leave continuously from 0945 until 1630 but join the queue early.

If you have time to spare, look at Spaceport USA itself: the **Galaxy Center** is an impressive museum of space technology, including a chunk of moon rock; it's open 0900-1845, free. The **Galaxy Theater** screens films about space exploration; go in at five minutes past the hour from 1005 to 1605 for a 30-minute film, or go in at 40 minutes past from 0940 to 1640 for a 15-minute film. And it's free. You pay $2.75 (children to 12, $1.75) for the 37-minute film shown 10 times daily in the **Imax Theater,** but the screen is more than 40 feet high and the experience is next to reality. Both theatres are in the Galaxy Center. Postcards dropped in the mailboxes here will receive a special KSC cancellation.

The **Rocket Garden** has some unusual plants: a selection of early space rockets and a prototype of one of the first soft- landing unmanned lunar modules.

Tours. Red Tour takes you north to the **Vehicle Assembly Building,** the VAB, inside which the space shuttles are prepared for their missions. The VAB is yet another superlative: it's 525 feet (159m) tall, covers eight acres (3.2ha), and has 129,482,000 cubic feet of space inside it — that's 3,700,000 cubic metres, and the Empire State Building has a total volume of only 1,000,000 cu m. The VAB's doors are 156 feet tall, weight 800 tons, and take 45 minutes to open — and, no, you're not allowed inside.

In the same complex is a **Saturn 5 rocket,** of the type used on the early moon missions. When fuelled up, it weighed 2,812 tons and stood 363 ft (110m) tall. It's now on its side, giving you chance to see the four exhaust flumes, each large enough to stand in. Red Tour goes on down the crawlerway to the shuttle launch pads.

Blue Tour takes you to Cape Canaveral AFB and on to a selection of the launch pads around the headland which include those for Polaris and Poseidon weapons testing, and the Mercury, Apollo, Gemini and Titan space probes. You'll also see the base's space museum.

Both tours show you around Spaceport museums for a look at an actual space capsule; look at the heat stains on its re-entry shield — and a glimpse of a prototype lunar landing module. And then into mission control, the actual control centre used on Saturn 5 launches. Everything is set for countdown but is held at T minus 3 minutes 25 seconds until you're all inside; once the doors close, countdown resumes and you're in for an experience of a lifetime as the rocket is launched no more than 100 ft in front of you. It may be only on film, but it's realistic — and so is the noise.

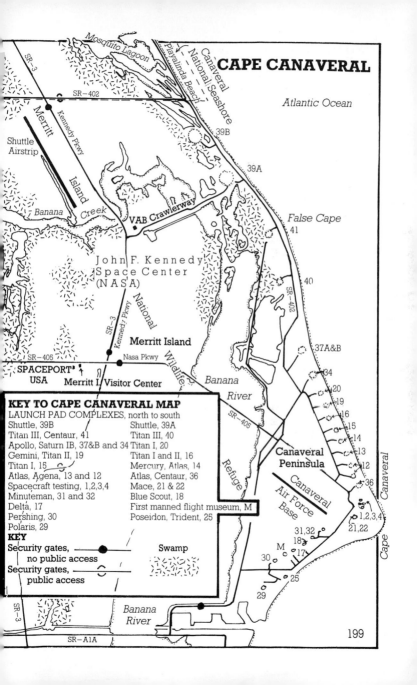

CAPE CANAVERAL

Mosquito Lagoon

SR–3

SR–402

Atlantic Ocean

Canaveral National Seashore

Playalinda Beach

Merritt

Kennedy Pkwy

Shuttle Airstrip

Banana Creek

39B

39A

VAB Crawlerway

False Cape

41

John F. Kennedy Space Center (NASA)

Kennedy Pkwy

40

SR–402

SR–405

Merritt Island

SR–3

Nasa Pkwy

37A&B

SPACEPORT USA

Merritt I. Visitor Center

National Wildlife

34

20

19

16

15

14

13

12

36

Banana River

SR–405

KEY TO CAPE CANAVERAL MAP

LAUNCH PAD COMPLEXES, north to south

Shuttle, 39B   Shuttle, 39A
Titan III, Centaur, 41   Titan III, 40
Apollo, Saturn IB, 37&B and 34 Titan I, 20
Gemini, Titan II, 19   Titan I and II, 16
Titan I, 15   Mercury, Atlas, 14
Atlas, Agena, 13 and 12   Atlas, Centaur, 36
Spacecraft testing, 1,2,3,4   Mace, 21 & 22
Minuteman, 31 and 32   Blue Scout, 18
Delta, 17   First manned flight museum, M
Pershing, 30   Poseidon, Trident, 25
Polaris, 29

KEY

Security gates, ——●——
   no public access   Swamp

Security gates, ——⌒——
   public access

Canaveral Peninsula

Canaveral Air Force Base

Refuge

Cape Canaveral

31,32

18

M

17

21,22

1,2,3,4

36

30

25

29

SR–3

Banana River

SR–A1A

The tours, which have been available since 1966, are operated by TW Recreational Services, a concessionaire; contact it at Spaceport USA, Kennedy Space Center, FL 32899, ∅452.2121, for any information other than that directly relating to the KSC operations.

The Shuttle: why here? The US Government chose Canaveral because it was the closest to the equator for any suitable launch pad on continental territory. At the geographic poles the earth is rotating on the spot, but here the rotation means that Canaveral is moving east at 915 miles an hour (1,473 kph) relative to the sun. This boost allows a shuttle and its cargo to weigh 29.5 tonnes at launch into an easterly orbit, while the same launch from the slightly more northerly Vandenberg AFB in California into a polar orbit — losing the rotational bonus — would limit the shuttle to 18 tonnes. And if there's an accident, as when Challenger exploded on 28 January, 1986, the wreckage falls into the sea.

Space spinoffs. Each shuttle costs around $1,000,000,000 to build, but space research has developed many materials which have other uses here on earth. By-products of research have given us tiny insulin pumps for diabetics, improved dental braces, new flame-resistant materials, anti-corrosion paint, water recycling systems (already in use at Epcot Center), and the non-stick lining for fry pans.

Background. The National Aeronautics and Space Administration, NASA, was established in 1958 shortly before the first rocket was launched from Cape Canaveral AFB. The first sub-orbital manned flight was in 1961, and this Spaceport location was built in 1964 to hold mission control for the Apollo launches. The KSC now occupies 140,000 acres (218 sq miles, 624 sq km), employs 2,000 staff directly and another 11,000 through contractors. But back in 1963 the US Fish and Wildlife Service established the Merritt Island National Wildlife Refuge on the KSC lands as a sanctuary for winter migrant birds, then in 1975 the Canaveral National Seashore made a sanctuary from the KSC northern boundary almost to New Smyrna Beach.

MERRITT ISLAND NATIONAL WILDLIFE REFUGE

Around 300 species of bird have been recorded on Merritt Island, including gulls, terns, herons, egrets, ibises, pelicans, and bald eagles. The refuge is also a permanent home to raccoons, armadillos, bobcats, deer, otters, manatees, and more than 4,000 alligators; other reptiles include the pine, king and eastern indigo snakes, the Atlantic salt marsh snake and the diamond-back rattlesnake, as well as loggerhead and green turtles, which lay their eggs in the beaches.

During the winter up to 70,000 duck of 20 sub-species, and more than 100,000 coots, either stay here or call in on their way to southern Florida.

Human visitors. Access is strictly limited due to KSC security; you can drive along SR-405 between Titusville and Spaceport, and south on US-3, but you'll still see plenty of birds and a few alligators. Otherwise come in on SR-402 from north Titusville to the Visitor Center and see the 67,000 acres of the **Canaveral National Seashore** (CNS).

There's a road to Playalinda ('beautiful beach') Beach north from KSC but at the *south* of the CNS; there's also a road to Apollo Beach in the *north* of the CNS, with access through New Smyrna Beach and passing another Visitor Center. You can walk the 13 miles (21km) that separate these roads, but it's hard going and at high tide you'll be struggling through sand dunes.

If you come to CNS in high summer watch the weather, as violent thunderstorms build rapidly over the cape and lightning strikes are a hazard. Mosquito Lagoon is another hazard; unless there's an onshore breeze you'll understand exactly why the lagoon has this name.

Turtle Mound. At the north end of Apollo Beach, Turtle Mound is a 600-year-old 50-ft Amerind heap of sea shells now preserved as a historic site. The mound is the highest point along the seashore and gives a good view across Mosquito Lagoon: it also proves that while this coastline may look vulnerable to the ocean's currents, it hasn't changed much in several centuries.

Sugar mill ruins. On the western edge of New Smyrna Beach (the part on the mainland), a few walls mark the ruins of a sugar mill and plantation burned by Seminole Indians in 1935.

Contacts. Canaveral National Seashore, PO Box 6447; Merritt Island National Wildlife Refuge, PO Box 6504; both at Titusville, FL 32782.

Home for manatees. And south of KSC is the Banana River Aquatic Preserve claiming the waters of the Banana River down to its narrow junction with the Indian River. This is a favoured overwintering place for the manatee.

VERDICT. Cape Canaveral is yet another part of Florida that is unique, not only in the USA but in the world. The KSC tours provide an excellent insight into space technology, but disabled people need to plan their visit well in advance.

The wildlife is not as noticeable as in the Everglades, but if you're concentrating your stay in central Florida, this is the best place to see alligators in their natural habitat.

CANAVERAL FACTFILE. Surprisingly, KSC's crowds are tiny compared with those at Walt Disney World. This means there's no great proliferation of **hotels, motels** and nightlife. I stayed several nights at the Garden Court Motel south of Rockledge, five minutes' walk from the Indian River, but there are other motels along US-1. The Rodeway Inn at 3655 Cheney Hwy, Titusville, is just three miles from the Space Center and is not too expensive at $30 upward. **Nightlife** is music while you dine at restaurants from Titusville to Melbourne.

THE ATLANTIC COAST: DAYTONA BEACH

Daytona Beach owes its origins to railway builder Henry Flagler, but it owes its reputation as the home of motor racing to a group of early car makers. William Vanderbilt, Louis Chevrolet, Alexander Winston and Ransom Olds stayed at the Ormond Hotel, built in the 1880s in the little town of Ormond Beach which had been founded in 1873. Henry Ford, who didn't like the hotel bill, slept in one of his cars.

Olds and Winston decided to race their respective vehicles on the 23 miles of beach that faced the ocean on the barrier islands across the Halifax River, stretching from today's Ormond-by-the-Sea to the Ponce de Leon Inlet. Authorities disagree on the winner's speed, some claiming 27mph while others say it was 57mph (91kph).

The event stimulated interest around the motor-conscious world, and by 1904 the Winter Speed Carnival had begun at Daytona Beach. Three years later a Stanley Steamer car — it had a steam-driven engine just like a railway locomotive, and needed an hour to get started — covered the course at . . . well, some authorities claim 127 mph (204kph)!

Malcolm Campbell. British racing driver Malcolm Campbell came to the Beach in 1928 with his Bluebird, powered by a Rolls Royce aero engine, and covered the measured distance at 206.96 mph (333.06kph). He improved his speed in successive years, reaching his fastest, 276mph (444kph), in 1935.

The Depression had hit the Beach, and the Hitler war kept motor racing out of the news, but in 1950 Daytona held its first race meeting for old cars, and the sport of stock car racing was born. It was soon obvious that the increased population of the area made beach racing dangerous, and the last meet was in 1958. The next year NASCAR, the National Stock Car Auto Racing organisation, moved to the new Daytona International Speedway Stadium on Volusia Ave, near the airport.

Beach motoring. But the beach was not closed to motoring. You can still take a leisurely drive along the low-tide 500-ft-wide sands at a maximum speed of 10mph, though parking on the dunes is inadvisable. Daytona Beach offers another unique sight: cars queueing to get off the sands while the incoming tide washes around their wheels.

Daytona? For the record, there is no such place as Daytona although most of Daytona Beach's 55,000 inhabitants live on the mainland in the districts of South Daytona, Port Orange and Holly Hill.

On the island to the south of town is Daytona Beach Shores, while to the north Ormond Beach spreads across both island and mainland.

The Casements. John D Rockefeller spent several winters as a resident at the Ormond Hotel until — according to legend — he realised he was being overcharged. He wasn't pleased, so in 1918 he moved out to his purpose-built house, The Casements, almost opposite at 25 Riverside Dr. This was an elegant three-storey villa with clean-cut architecture, plenty of windows of the casement variety, and an enormous atrium (central court). Rockefeller's latest declared ambition was to reach his 100th birthday, but he died here in 1937, a little more than two years short of his target, and the house gradually fell into decay.

The city council saved it and it's now operated by the Ormond Beach Cultural and Civic Affairs Department as a multi-museum, currently displaying Hungarian folklore, Italian ceramics and Historic Boy Scout displays as well as more transient exhibits. It's open Mon-Fri 1000-1500, Sat 1000-1200, for guided tours. No fee, but donations are welcome. ✆673.4701. ♿ ground floor.

OTHER POINTS OF INTEREST

North of Ormond Beach, the ruins of the **Addison Blockhouse** stand in marshes beside the Tomoka River. The blockhouse saw limited action in the Second Seminole War but is now almost inaccessible. The Tomoka River joins the Halifax River — the long saltwater inlet separating the barrier beaches and the mainland — by the 1,000-acre **Tomoka State Park,** site of a Timucuan Indian village which in the 18th-cent became a plantation for indigo, sugar cane and rice. The park has plenty of raccoons and opossums and is open 0800 to sunset.

More plantation ruins lie in the regenerated forest at **Bulow,** 11 miles north of Ormond Beach along I-95. Major Charles Bulow used slave labour to clear 2,200 of his 4,675 acres, bought in 1821. For a few years he grew sugar, cotton, indigo and rice, but he fell victim to the Seminole Wars. Entry is free at any time.

Relics from Amerind settlements, from early European plantations, and from offshore wrecks, are on display at the **Halifax Historical Museum** in the Merchants Bank at 252 South Beach St, Daytona Beach; it's on the mainland facing the Halifax River. Tues-Sat 1000-1600, free, ✆225.6976.

When you're passing Daytona Speedway Stadium eastbound on Volusia Ave, I-92, turn right onto S Seneca Blv for the **Museum of Arts and Sciences** at 1040 Museum Blv, ✆255.0285; it's also accessible SR-5A, S Nova Rd. The history starts in the Pleistocene era a million years ago with the fossil of a giant sloth, regarded as the best example of this creature yet found. The art specialises in sculpture, some of it considered to be among the best in the USA, and the science features a living nature trail in the grounds. Open Tues-Fri, 0900-1600, Sat 1200-1700, for $2. The museum's **Planetarium** opens Wed 1500, Fri 1900, Sat and Sun 1300 and 1500 for set programmes; $2.

The old police and fire station at 160 E Granada Blv, Ormond Beach — that's on the island — was converted in 1977 into the **Birthplace of Speed Museum.** Opening hours have varied but you should be lucky any weekday afternoon; admission $1. The museum holds photos and exhibits from that first beach race to the last in 1958, and a Stanley Steamer car, but is it the one that raced in 1906? And did it reach 127mph? Sort out the evidence and make up your own mind.

Down near the tip of the beach stands the 175-ft (53-m) **Ponce de Leon Inlet Lighthouse,** completed in 1887 and now offering the best vantage points for miles around to anybody capable of climbing to the top. It's open 1000-1900; ✆761.1821 to check.

Dixie Queen. Daytona Beach has another touch of nostalgia in the *Dixie Queen,* a replica triple-deck Mississippi stern-wheel paddleboat which cruises the Halifax River from its base at 841 Ballough Rd (by SR-430, Seabreeze Bridge, the most northerly in Daytona). ✆255.1997 for reservations and the latest sailings. Your options range from an evening dance-party for $9 and a 2½-hr Sunday brunch cruise for $18.95, to the 6½-hr voyage up the Intracoastal Waterway to St Augustine, for $59.

DAYTONA BEACH FACTFILE and VERDICT

Daytona Beach is a magnet for anybody interested in motor racing, be it the origins of the sport or its modern Daytona variation, the stock car race. Other people will find little of interest here; true, the beach is fine, firm, and silvery — but do you really want to share it with cars? Ormond Beach is a pleasant dormitory and retirement town of 22,000 people, its only feature being the million-year-old giant sloth.

If you come for the racing, be prepared to pay at least $40 a room in the cheapest motel; it costs at least $30 a night to park your own RV by the race track. There's no great proliferation of **hotels and motels,** and out-of-state visitors take everything available as far north as St Augustine. I hear the cheapest room in town is at the Youth Hostel at 140 S Atlantic Ave (SR-A1A, near Broadway Bridge), Daytona Beach, ✆258.6937; $10 for IYHF members, $13 for non-members.

Students add to the vitality at Easter and in high summer, but nightlife is always rather subdued, the emphasis being on concerts, symphonies and ballet: if that's for you the best place to see it is at the 2,560-seat **Peabody Auditorium** at 600 Auditorium Blv, near the Main St Bridge. ✆252.0821 for the latest programme.

22: TAMPA AND THE GULF

The Sunshine Coast

PANFILO DE NARVAEZ AND HIS FOUR GALLEONS were blown into this large west-coast bay during a storm in 1527. The Spaniard met some of the local Apalachee Indians and realised they had gold ornaments. Gold! Few Spanish *conquistadores* were pure explorers; if they weren't saving heathen souls they were lusting for gold. But de Narvaez's bullion was a false lure, as the local Indians had found it in an earlier galleon wreck on this coast.

De Narvaez named his landfall Bahía Boca Ciega, 'Bay of the Blind Woman's Mouth' (it's between St Petersburg Beach and the mainland) and he probably called the wooded peninsula behind it, Pinedas, from its pine-woods; today it's the southern end of tiny Pinellas County. And then he withdrew, but not before the Apalachee had murdered most of his sailors.

Origin of names. Twelve years later Hernando de Soto came south overland with several hundred troops, and managed to make peace with the Apalachee; the first maps of the area, drawn in 1625, are said to carry the word *Tampa*, marking the Apalachee village.

The first Europeans arrived in the Tampa area in 1823 and kept within the shelter of their Fort Brook for, although the Apalachee had gone their Seminole successors, a breakaway from the Creek Indians were just as troublesome. 'Seminole' is a corruption of *cimarrón*, Spanish for 'runaway,' 'maroon.'

In 1876 John Williams of Detroit established the town of Pinellas on that wooded peninsula, then urged the wealthy Russian exile Pyotr Alexeivitch Dementyef (he preferred to call himself Peter Demens) to build a spur railway from Flagler's East Coast Railroad at Sanford, to Tarpon Springs and on to Pinellas, in order to carry oranges to the colder north: Henry Flagler wasn't going to have all the trade. When the Orange Belt Railroad reached its destination Williams let Demens choose a new name for the town, and the Russian opted for St Petersburg, honouring his birthplace. Pinellas eventually became the name of the county.

Growth was still slow, as it was throughout Florida, despite the land auctions. St Pete — which is how the locals choose to call their city —

had its own auction in 1911. The year before, the *St Petersburg Evening Independent* began promoting the climate by giving away its entire edition on the day after a totally sunless day: it never gave away many editions.

Old folks. By the mid-20s, St Pete had only 50,000 people, most of them retired; the city put out 5,000 green- painted bench seats for the elderly as another promotion, but the few remaining are now orange. Nonetheless, the city is still popular with senior citizens and some hotels won't cater for anybody younger than 70.

Industry. Tampa, however, has, been industrial since 1884 when Henry Plant brought in the narrow-gauge South Florida Railroad and developed the port; it now ranks eighth for size in the USA and handles vast amounts of phosphates — have you seen the ugly face of Florida, the vast open-cast and strip mines by Bartow? Plant, however, rivalled Flagler in the hotel-building boom, creating in 1891 the Moroccan-styled Tampa Bay Hotel with elegant domes and minarets. Flagler was invited to its opening but cabled the sarcastic reply: "Where's Tampa?"

Ybor City. Two years later, fire destroyed the cigar-rolling industry in Key West so Vincente Martínez Ybor rebuilt his business here in Tampa, bringing in labour from Spanish-held Cuba (Spain had sold most of the territory to the USA in 1819 in the 'Florida Purchase,' though bits by New Orleans and Pensacola changed hands in 1810 and 1813).

Art deco in Miami Beach.

Immigrant poet José Martí urged the tobacco workers to fight for Cuban independence, and Tampa became the US main base in the Spanish-American War of 1898. Teddy Roosevelt, America's President from 1901 to '09, embarked his Rough Riders cavalry outfit in Tampa after practising drill at Plant's Tampa Bay Hotel. The war resulted in independence for Cuba, while the USA bought the Philippines, Guam and Puerto Rico.

And Ybor City? It became the cigar-rolling capital of the world and is now the main downtown tourist attraction in Tampa, its slightly seedy old buildings full of character. Ybor, pronounced *Eebo,* is just east of our Tampa map, bounded west and east by Nebraska Ave (near I-275) and 22nd St (SR-585); its north and south bounds are Columbus Dr and E Broadway. In the centre at Ybor Square is the original brick-built cigar factory and a 1902 annexe now holding the Rough Riders Restaurant where Roosevelt's rehearsals are re-created. The **Ybor City State Museum** at 1818 Ninth Ave (✆247.6323 open 0900-1700, $1), relives the tobacco-rolling past and still rolls a few today – but come for the February and October Latin–American Ybor City fiesta.

Tampa Bay Hotel. Part of Henry Plant's fantastic Tampa Bay Hotel is now the University of Tampa's offices, with the original exterior preserved, but on the ground floor is the **Henry B Plant Museum** ♿, ✆253.8861, open Tues-Sat 1000-1600, free, and holding a selection of the tableware and furniture from the original hotel. Some is good, some ghastly. And in the grounds stands the oak tree where Hernando de Soto is said to have met the Indian chief.

Municipal Pier. St Petersburg ignored many of these commercial happenings, but a Philadelphian printer, F A Davis, brought electricity to the city then in 1889 built the 3,000-ft city-centre 'electric' pier – it's still one of the city's landmarks and is a good spot for fishing. H W Fuller laid an electric tramway to Boca Ciega Bay then joined Davis in the Favourite Line shipping company. But in 1914 Tony Jannus made history with the world's first scheduled airline route by flying–boat – across the bay to Tampa.

Clearwater. Henry Plant bought out Pyotr Dementyef's Orange Belt Railroad after a sharp frost killed the orange trees, and began developing Clearwater, starting with the Belleview Hotel which was the largest timber–frame building of its time standing on a 625-acre (252-ha) site. It's now the Belleview-Biltmore, at 25 Belleview Blv, ✆442.6171, and as Plant's armed guard has gone you can wander in to stand in awe at the splendour. Stay the night and it'll cost you from $90 high season.

The Holiday Isles. The string of barrier islands starts with Honeymoon Island in the north and finishes with St Petersburg Beach in the south, but other keys form stepping-stones across Tampa Bay and on down to Venice. **Honeymoon Island** has its own causeway access and beyond the built-up part the 2½-sq-mile Recreational Area is open 0800 to sunset; out of state visitors pay $2 for car and driver and $1 for each passenger. The beach is fine and sandy.

The next key down, **Caladesi Island,** was formed when a hurricane cut it from its neighbour, and so it missed the developers' bulldozers. It's now a 1,400-acre state park (q.v.) acessible only by ferry from Dunedin Municipal Marina; ✆443.5903 for information.

From Clearwater Beach Island to St Petersburg Beach there is continuous development on both sides of the SR-699, which has its share of traffic jams. The districts range from smart to tatty, but the dominant fact is the extreme shortage of parking space which thus controls your access to the beach. Unless you're staying in a hotel or motel here, come early or you'll never get in.

When you've parked you find your way to the sands through gaps in the ribbon development, but watch out for private gaps to private beaches. The result is worth the effort; the sand is fine, white, and usually quite wide. It's an excellent beach for children – but beware the risk of sunburn.

Island oddities. The Don CeSar Hotel, built at St Petersburg Beach in 1928, is noted across the USA for its pink and white icing-sugar architecture. It was destined for demolition in 1969 but restored at a cost of $7,000,000, and it's now a protected historic place. Address? 3400 Gulf Blv, ✆360.1881.

When a property developer can't sell his stock he must use a little trickery. "Pirate treasure is buried in these sands!" It wasn't, but the low-cost area is still known as Treasure Island. And Madeira Beach took its name from the Portuguese for 'wood,' recalling the pines that grew here.

Passe-a-Grille is a corruption of a French name which came from the grilling of fish on the beach; the keys continue south in a zigzag to Cabbage Key which is a mélange of marinas, and the beautiful **Mullet Key** in Fort De Soto County Park. Access to here is along SR-679, Pinellas Bayway, a toll road.

Fort De Soto. This 884-acre (3.5 sq km) W-shaped island has miles of white sandy beach, with changing rooms available; there are several hundred picnic tables set up, scores of barbecue pits, a vast launching ramp, and plenty of camping sites. The fort still has its cannon from the days of the Spanish-American War.

Sunshine Skyway. From St Pete, I-275 heads south across Tampa Bay via the Sunshine Skyway, Florida's longest suspension bridge set in a causeway 15 miles (24km) long: toll is 50¢. The bridge was built in 1954 with a span of 864ft (263m), but in May 1980 a cargo ship rammed one of the piers and brought down half the carriageway and all the cars on it.

Reflecting on life by the Tamiami Canal.

SIGHTSEEING IN TAMPA and St PETERSBURG

ADVENTURE ISLAND

Address and location: as for Busch Gardens, which is nearby. ℰ988.5171. **Hours:** vary. 0900-2000 in high summer, otherwise 1000-1700. Open mid-Apr to mid Sep then intermittent to end Oct. **Admission:** $12; $6.50 after 1500hrs.

A water-based fun park offering slides, flumes, waterfalls, and more leisurely tubing. The Gulf Scream is a 40-ft thriller.

BUSCH GARDENS

Address: PO Box 9158, (3000 Busch Blv) Tampa, FL 33674. **Location:** take exit 54 from I-75 (Fowler Ave) or exit 33 from I-275 for SR-580, Busch Blv. ℰ977.6606 or 1.800.323.7328. **Hours:** 0900-1930 daily. **Admission:** $21, but $15 from 1630hrs. **Parking:** come early for small park on 40th St (McKinley Dr), later for larger park, later still park in backstreets.

Subtitled 'The Dark Continent,' Busch Gardens is an adventure park on an African theme, and the main attraction on this coast. Enter via Morocco, with snake charmers and belly dancers, then explore the Serengeti where more than 500 east African animals live. Raft down the Congo River Rapids and take the Stanley Falls water flume. Visit the Nairobi Field Station where sick animals are nursed. Then for something more exciting try the Scorpion double-loop roller-coaster before relaxing aboard the African Queen.

Some of the rides close when it rains — which may be early afternoon in summer — but there's no refund on the ticket. The park covers 300 acres (1.2 sq km) and internal transport is by old-style pseudo-steam train or modern suspended monorail. The Anheuser-Busch brewery financed the gardens, and you can have a few free samples as a memento; but why not go on to the **Schlitz Brewery** at 1111 N 30th St, ✆971.7075, where you have a free tour of the works Mon-Fri 1000-1500 followed by another free sample.

GREAT EXPECTATIONS

This 'hands-on' museum at 1120 4th St S, in St Pete's Bayside, ✆821.8885, is really a scientific playground where you play with lasers, computers and lights, and blow square bubbles. It's easy! Open 100-1700 Mon-Sat.

LONDON WAX MUSEUM

Address: 5505 Gulf Blv, St Pete's Beach; on SR-699. ✆360.6985. **Hours:** 0900-2000 daily (1200-2000 Sun). **Admission:** $2. &

Completely rebuilt on new premises behind the original, doubling the number of exhibits to 100. The upgraded museum has introduced animation to its dummies, who include figures from royalty, show business, fiction, and the Chamber of Horrors.

LOWRY PARK ZOO

At 7525 N Blv by Sligh Ave in north Tampa, ✆935.8552, the zoo is open daily 1000-1800 for $7. See wildlife in relative freedom from elevated walkways or spyholes. Several endangered species are in this zoo, whose policy is to simulate natural environments and so encourage breeding.

SALVADOR DALI MUSEUM

Address: 100 Third St S, St Pete; Bayfront area. ✆823.3767. **Hours:** Tues-Sat 1000-1700, Sun 1300-1700. &

Clocks that drape across branches, bizarre sculpture, and saucy clothes: the essence of Dali is here, though the Spanish painter never visited the place. A plastics manufacturer offered his Dali collection to any city that would build a museum for it, and St Petersburg accepted.

SUNKEN GARDENS

At 1825 4th St (US-92), five acres of city-centre gardens, with a walk-through aviary of 500 birds, flamingo and alligator pools, and 50,000 plants bedded out each year. Gift shops, adequate parking, & open 0900-1700 daily — for $5.25. ✆896.3186.

TIKI GARDENS

Location: 196th Ave and Gulf Blv (SR-699) on Indian Shores. ✆595.2567. **Hours:** 1000-1800. **Admission:** $2.

Polynesia's stone gods are re-created in 12 acres of seafront mystique, with a hint of pagan customs. Look for Trader Frank's Restaurant.

CONVENTIONAL MUSEUMS

The region has several museums that don't fit the Salvador Dali image. The **Museum of Fine Arts** at 255 Beach Dr NE, ✆896.2667, has American, European and Oriental paintings and sculpture; open 1000-1700 except Mon, free. **St Petersburg Historical Museum** at 335 2nd Ave, ✆894.1052, has a weird offering including a mummy 3,000 years old, a log canoe 400 years old, and a sugar bowl used by Tom Thumb. Same hours as above, but a $2 admission.

Perhaps **Heritage Park** isn't conventional either. It's at 11909 125th St N, Walsingham Rd, SR-688 to Indian Rocks Beach, ✆462.3474, where ten ancient buildings have been relocated, including the House of the Seven Gables (1888), a honeymoon cottage 14ft square, and the Coachman-McMullen Loghouse of 1852, which is *very* old for the USA; more than 50 children were born in it. The park is open 1000-1600 (closed Mon), and is free.

CRUISING – WITH A DIFFERENCE

There are numerous ways to get afloat in the St Petersburg and Holiday Isles area. The already-mentioned **SeaEscape** ♿ offers one-day cruises from the Cruise Port to Nowhere (that's what the ticket says); ✆1.800.327.7400.

The *Belle of St Petersburg,* a replica stern-wheel paddleboat, takes you around Tampa Bay for 2-hr lunch tours or 7-hr day voyages, with several options between. Prices start at $9 for adults, including the lunch. ✆823.1665 or 823.8171, or call at 401 2nd Ave NE.

Clearwater Beach marina has several charter vessels and group-tour operators, with **Captain Memo's Pirate Cruise** among the most colourful. Memo – Bill Wozencraft – and his female crew operate the 57-ft (17-m) *Sea Hogge* ♿, built in 1976 for sponge diving but now converted to a pirate galleon. A 2-hour cruise costs $23; ✆446.2587. For $17.50 you can pack in 2½ hours' sailing on a 38-ft yacht, or $22.50 buys 2½hrs on the 65-ft windjammer *Tradewinds,* sailing from the same marina. ✆581.4662.

Among the drive-yourself offers is **Beach Motor Boat Rentals,** ✆446.5503, also at Clearwater. Rates range from a 16-ft powerboat costing $75 for half a day, to a 115-hp boat at $210 all day. And if you stay at some of the larger motel efficiencies or the tourist hotels, you'll be in touch with many more options.

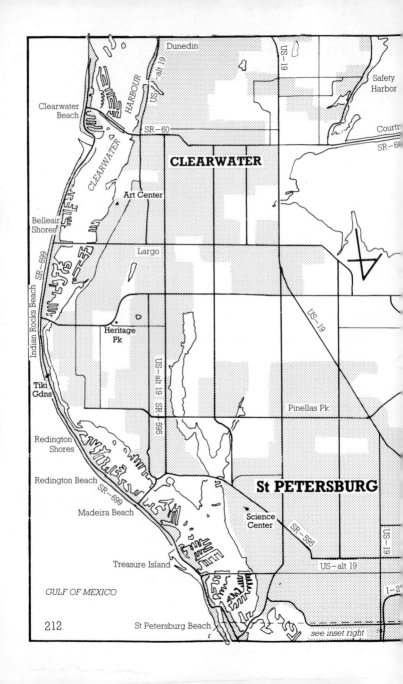

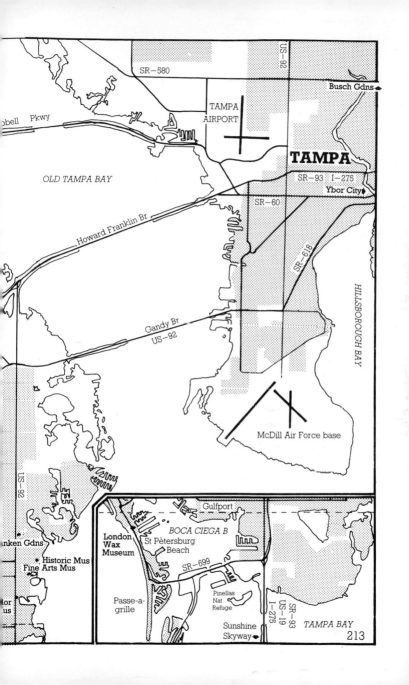

OLD TAMPA BAY

SR-580

US-92

TAMPA
AIRPORT

Busch Gdns

TAMPA

SR-93 I-275

Ybor City

SR-60

SR-618

Howard Franklin Br

Gandy Br
US-92

HILLSBOROUGH BAY

McDill Air Force base

Gulfport

BOCA CIEGA B

London
Wax
Museum

St Petersburg
Beach

SR-699

Historic Mus
Fine Arts Mus

Pinellas
Nat
Refuge

Passe-a-
grille

SR-93
US-19
I-275

TAMPA BAY

Sunshine
Skyway

213

obell Pkwy

US-92

nken Gdns

lor
us

TAMPA – St PETERSBURG CALENDAR

This selection comes from the scores of events in the official entertainments calendar of the area: **February,** Josée Gasparilla Pirate Fiesta on the bay and in Tampa; **March and April,** Festival of the States, with parades, concerts and fireworks in St Pete; **June,** Pirate Days festival on Treasure Island; **December,** illuminated boat parades in the Holiday Isles.

TAMPA – St PETERSBURG FACTFILE

If you're touring the district you'll have great difficulty in finding reasonably-priced one-night accommodation in the Holiday Isles. There are plenty of motels – 85 in Madeira Beach alone – but they're in the efficiency business and almost all are interested only in longer lets, and for that you'll need to make reservations several weeks in advance; contact the relevant Chamber of Commerce.

A possible exception is the Beach-House Motel at 12100 Gulf Blv, Treasure Island, St Petersburg, FL 33706, ✆360.1153, with waterfront on the Gulf of Mexico and the sheltered inland water. High season (Feb and Mar) rates per night are $40 per room dropping to $24 from mid June to mid Aug, with stages between. You might catch a midsummer vacancy but otherwise book as far ahead as possible.

The conventional **motels** at conventional prices are on Hillsboro Ave, Tampa, with the fast-food restaurants, but there's no other action here: for **nightlife** you'll need to go to the smarter hotels on the isles, such as the Holiday Inn at St Pete's Beach for rooftop dancing or Tiki Gardens for South Seas entertainment.

Or for classier entertainment try the Bayfront Center which has had a $19,000,000 facelift and now has seating for 10,250 people. To draw those crowds it stages big-name artists from all branches of show business.

SOUTH TO SARASOTA

Sarasota calls itself the Cultural Capital of Florida, which is no mean claim in a state which already has Palm Beach and Naples. Sarasota is equally smart, its public lawns of Bermuda grass neatly manicured and its statues looking as if they have just stepped from the bath.

The city owes its origins to Mrs Potter Palmer, a pillar of Chicago society who built her winter home here in 1910; she also bought the land around a nearby lake and presented it to the state, the beginnings of Lake Myakka State Park.

John Ringling. But it was circus owner John Ringling who took the city into the public eye, beginning in 1911 when he moved here to build not only his own winter palace but also a haven for the Ringling Brothers Circus. Following Ringling's example, artists, writers and society people began moving to Sarasota, and they are still coming.

Venice. The Ringling Brothers and Barnum and Bailey Circus soon moved a little way down the coast to Venice, planned as the retirement home of the Brotherhood of Railroad Engineers and built on a sheltered harbour, but with its new occupants soon to become the centre of America's circus industry. It's the place to come in midwinter if you want to have a preview of the coming season's circus attractions; the address is 1410 Ringling Dr S, the admission around $10, and ✆484.9511 for times. This is the only city in the world to have a college for clowns, where some 5,000 applicants a year compete for 60 job vacancies.

Venice also claims another unusual attraction in the vast number of fossilised shark-teeth that are found on its beaches, with a lesser number of other fossils, brought up from the sea bed by storms.

Ringling Museums. But back in Sarasota the Ringlings were hard at work building the Venetian-Gothic style **Ca'd'Zan,** Venetian for 'House of John,' a palace for John and Mabel standing in 68 acres and costing $2,000,000, including the solid-gold taps. John spent another fortune on art, including $150,000 for a Rubens collection, and Mabel filled the 30 rooms with the world's finest furniture including an organ with 4,000 pipes. And when John died in 1936 he gave everything to the State of Florida, which broke the estate into a manageable collection of museums.

Ca'd'Zan, the Ringling Mansion at 5401 Bayshore Dr, ✆355.5101, is open to the public daily 1000-1500 for $4.50, which includes the

Coming into berth at the quay at Plantation Key.

Museum of Art and the Circus Museum. The estate is on the west of the Tamiami Trail in north Sarasota, immediately south of the Sarasota-Bradenton Airport; & and plenty of on-site parking space.

The Museum of Art, housed in a mock-15th-cent Italian villa, is full of sculpture and masonry plundered from all over Italy, and dominated by a copy of Michaelangelo's David; not even Ringling could aquire the original. The Museum of the Circus holds a vast array from the great days of the big top.

The **Asolo Theater** was built in 1798 in Asolo, Italy, and dismantled stone by stone in 1939 to make way for a cinema. After the war Florida bought it and shipped it over, rebuilding it here in 1950. It's open 0900-2200 daily, ∅355.5137, and has the twin reputation of being one of the most architecturally interesting theatres in the USA, and the place to come for excellent entertainment where a modern drama on tour from Broadway may give way to a Shakespearean comedy the following week. The curtain rises at 2015 nightly.

Bellm's Cars. Cross the main road from the Ringling Museums and you find yourself at Bellm's Cars and Music of Yesterday at 5500 N Tamiami Trail, ∅355.6228, &, open Mon- Sat 0830-1800 and from 0930 on Sun, for $5. The museum holds more than 200 classic and antique cars, including John Ringling's Rolls-Royce and a Stanley Steamer of 1902 (see 'Daytona Beach'), and 2,000 music-making machines such as nickelodeons, musical boxes, phonographs (early gramophones, now replaced by record players), and a 30-ft organ. The collection is claimed to be the world's largest of its type.

Walter Bellm bought the original display of 25 cars in 1965 and has scoured the world for the later exhibits.

Lionel Trains. At 8184 N Tamiami Trail, a mile north of the Ringling Museums and opposite Bradenton Airport, stands a replica railroad depot of the late 19th cent, home of the Lionel Train and Seashell Museum, ∅355.8184, &, open daily 0900- 1700; the train museum costs $2.50 but the shell collection is free.

Lionel Trains in the USA are what Dinky Toys are in Britain, and here you can indulge in model railways to your heart's content with a working railway system — or climb aboard a real 1903 trolley-car.

Jungle Gardens. A mile south of the Ringling Museums is Jungle Gardens at 3701 Bayshore Rd, just off US-41, ∅355.5305, open daily 0900-1700 for $5. In 15 acres of landscaped gardens you'll find snakes, alligators, monkeys, leopards, a small amusement park, and performing parrots.

Selby Botanical Gardens. The Tamiami Trail runs through the centre of Sarasota, with the Visitor Centre at the north and the Selby Botanical Gardens at the south. The 10-acre garden, named from a prominent resident of the 1920s, features orchids and air plants, and has a botanical museum. ∅366.5730, open daily 1000-1700 for $4.

Leave Sarasota by John Ringling Blv on the causeway to **Bird Key,** for some of the smartest homes in the district. The road leads on to **Lido Key,** crossing St Armand's Circle, an artificial island with an elegant shopping centre. Lido has plenty of holiday accommodation for longer-stay visitors with moderately-large wallets, and its beach is excellent; at the north of the key by the radio towers you'll find the **Mote Marine Science Aquarium,** ✆388.2451, open Tues-Sun 1000-1700 for $5.

SR-789 leads north to 10-mile-long **Longboat Key,** much of which is intentionally undeveloped, with the condos and the hotels, as well as a good shopping district, concentrated at the northern tip. The road takes you north again to **Anna Maria Island** and Bradenton Beach, a conglomerate of bottom-of-the-market properties. If you don't mind the heavy traffic you might find some cheap accommodation here.

The other barrier island off Sarasota is **Siesta Key,** accessible by causeway from the southern part of the city. It's a polyglot place, with relatively cheap motels in the crowded north, to pricier efficiencies in the open south along Midnight Pass Rd. Sands range from the crowded Siesta Beach to the near-empty Turtle Beach in the south.

Bradenton. North of Sarasota and accessible along the Tamiami Trail or from Anna Maria Island, Bradenton has a place in history as the spot where Hernando de Soto landed with 600 *conquistadores* in 1539. They gradually moved north, discovering the Mississippi River in 1541, into whose waters de Soto's body was dropped in 1542.

Bradenton, which takes its name from the Dr Joseph Braden who started a plantation here in 1850, publicises its history with the summer-only costume shows at the **De Soto National Memorial,** across Tampa Bay from the Ft Desoto County Park in St Pete. Ponce de Leon had beached his ship around here in 1513 to scrape the weed from its bottom, losing one of his men in an Indian attack — the first white soldier to die on the North American continent.

South Florida Museum. In downtown Bradenton stands the South Florida Museum and Bishop Planetarium, at 201 10th St W (Business US-41), ✆746.4131 or 746.STAR, open daily except Mon. Times vary, and $2 fee admits to museum or planetarium, $3 admits to both, with laser show extra.

The museum traces Florida's history from prehistory to present, with a replica said to be of de Soto's 16th-cent Spanish home, while the 200-seat planetarium talks of comets, quasars, and UFOs. Come at 2100 on alternate weekends (check in advance) for a glance through the 12½-inch reflecting telescope. And as we're near the Manatee River, don't be surprised to see the planetarium's own manatee, born in captivity back in 1948.

Cross the Manatee River to Ellenton for the **Gamble Plantation** on US-301, ✆722.1017, open daily 0900-1700 for $1. This restored mansion of the 1840s — the oldest building on Florida's west coast — was the home of Major Robert Gamble but is now a Confederate museum with contemporary furniture. The Confederate Secretary of State Judah Benjamin hid here before escaping to England. If you head back for the Sunshine Skyway but turn left on Terra Cela Island you should find the **Madira Bickel Mound,** 170 ft (52m) long by 20 ft (6m) high, a pile of sand, shells and other debris left by the earlier Indians.

Other places of interest are the Manatee Village Historical Park at 6th Ave E and 15th St E, Bradenton, holding the area's oldest church, an original cracker home, and the Manatee County Court. Open Mon-Fri 0900-1500, free.

Spanish Point, at 500 Tamiami Trail in Osprey, north of Venice, ✆966.5214, has another Indian midden with early European homes nearby; open 0900-1600 Tues-Sat for $2. Nearby is the Oscar Scherer State Park with 462 acres of pine and palmetto, while east of Venice on US-41 is the town of Warm Mineral Springs; no prizes for guessing the origin of the name. The springs produce 10,000,000 gallons of water a day at a constant 87°F (30°C). Open daily 0900-1700 for $6.

South of Warm Mineral Springs is North Port, on US-41, where the American Police Hall of Fame has a black museum of murder weapons and the occasional electric chair, while north-east at Arcadia, on US-17, you'll find Florida's last cowboy town, where the bi-annual state rodeo is still the main attraction.

They used to race cars on Daytona Beach. Now they get traffic jams.

VERDICT

Sarasota is bypassed by the I-75 and therefore by most tourists, but the Ringling Museums make a diversion worthwhile and from there it's just a stroll to Bellm's unusual museum. This is a pleasant city but its only other noteworthy attraction is the Asolo State Theater.

SARASOTA FACTFILE

In this, the cultural capital of Florida, nightlife centres on theatres, with the Asolo setting the standard though followed closely by the Van Wezel Performing Arts Hall near the Visitor Center, the Sarasota Opera and others.

The Golden Apple Dinner Theater at 25 N Pineapple Ave, ✆366.5454, offers Broadway productions while you dine, nightly except Mon, from $20. For dinner cruises on Sarasota Bay, ✆366,9255 for a reservation on *Marina Jack II,* a replica stern-wheel paddleboat sailing from Marina Plaza, Island Park, in the downtown area. If you're wondering, the original Marina Jack is a conventional restaurant.

Try the keys or the Tamiami Trail for a wider range of restaurants such as Captain Curt's Crab & Oyster Bar on Siesta Key, Pirate's Cove at 7700 S Tamiami for 'traditional English fish and chips,' but for the bizarre Walt's Raw Oyster Bar you must go to 560 N Washington Blv. This is where Vernon Bass swallowed 684 raw oysters in 20 minutes in 1976 to win the world title.

The area is not well endowed with moderately-priced motels. You might find a one-night room on Anna Maria Island, but if you've come prepared you have a choice of several small campsites in and around Venice. The larger sites by Sarasota are RV specialists.

The **Visitor Center** is at 655 N Tamiami Trail in downtown Sarasota, ✆957.8177.

NORTH TO THE SUWANNEE RIVER

North of Clearwater, Florida's Gulf of Mexico coastline is virgin mangrove swamp until you reach Apalachee Bay, south of Tallahassee, showing yet another aspect of this remarkable state. On the northern fringe of Clearwater, **Dunedin**'s name recalls the two Scotsmen who opened a store here in the 1880s. The town celebrates its Gallic origins in the Heather and Thistle Holiday late in March, and with the skirl of the bagpipes played by kilted pipers on the first Sunday each month; and the local church is called a kirk.

Tarpon Springs marks the northern end of the Intracoastal Waterway but is much better known for its sponge fishery operated by Greeks who moved from Key West in 1905. They were nearly driven from business by a disease which hit the sponges in 1940, and by the invention of plastic foam in later decades, but they did what all good Floridians do and opened their industry to the tourists.

The Spongeorama exhibit (∅942.3771) on Dodecanese Blv is a little bit of Greece showing the story of sponge-gathering, with the occasional hint of drama; the museum is free but the film show costs $1. From this same area you can cruise on a sponger's boat (∅937.9887 for information) every half-hour down the Anclote River to the sea. Or come to the Sponge Exchange early on Tuesday or Friday to see a sponge auction. After the Scottish kirk at Dunedin don't be surprised to find the St Nicholas Greek Orthodox Cathedral, a miniature of Istanbul's St Sophia.

Tarpon Springs was founded by Philadelphian businessman Hamilton Disston who bought 4,000,000 acres of coastal swamp in 1880 and named his creation from the tarpon fish in the river; too bad they're really mullet! The city's most illustrious resident was the Duke of Sutherland, a cousin of Queen Victoria, who lived here with his lady friend.

Just south of town is the **Chimp Farm,** ∅937.8683, a retirement home for abandoned primates, including gorillas and orang-utans, and a bear; open daily 1000 to dusk.

Way inland on US-301 is **Zephyrhills,** whose zephyrs have made the town noted for its parachuting. The Crystal Springs here are privately-run for swimming, diving and picnicking.

Weeki Wachee. Back on the coast, US-19 cruises north to Weeki Wachee, the self-styled 'city of live mermaids' where you can watch young women in flipper suits swimming with the fish. The tourist attraction, open daily 0900-1800 for $10.95, ∅596.2067, &, offers its unique underwater show plus a boat trip to the pelican orphanage and a display of birds of prey, but the springs themselves are worthy of note as they yield more than 100,000 US gallons (380 cu m) of water a minute at 74°F (23°C). The nearby Buccaneer Bay water-theme park with its river flume, is open late March to Mid-September; details as above.

Fourteen miles (22km) north, turn left onto SR-480 for the uncommercialised yet first-magnitude Chassahowitzka Springs, but another five miles brings you to Weeki Wachee's rival, Homosassa Springs, whose name recalls the local Amerind word for 'place of the pepper trees.'

Homosassa Springs. Built around another first- magnitude gusher, the Homosassa Springs attraction is aimed at the nature-lover with the unique feature of freshwater and marine life living together. In the 72°F (22°C) 6,000,000 gallon (230 cu m) surge, visitors can walk in an underwater corridor through the Spring of Ten Thousand Fish and see, in addition, hippopotamus, otter, alligator, and manatee. The manatee programmes begin at 1130, 1330 and 1530, with other animal shows an hour earlier, plus a 1630 show. Open 0900, last admission 1600; fee $6.95; ∅628.2311.

Take US-490 (not US-490A) for the **Yulee Sugar Mill State Historic Site,** where the ruins of an 1850s mill have been partly restored; ✆795.3815 for information.

Yuli, a grand vizier of Morocco, bought as wife a London-born Jewish girl whose ship had been captured by Barbary pirates. A son, born in the harem, emigrated to the Virgin Islands and made a fortune before moving to Florida. His son, named David Levy in honour of the Jewish grandmother, became a Florida senator before changing his name to Yulee, and building this mill which supplied the Confederate Army with sugar. A decade later Yulee built a railway between Cedar Key and Fernandina (near Jacksonville), and little remains of that, either.

The most important Amerind relics in Florida are at **Crystal River,** and are now incorporated in the State Archaeological Site, two miles west of US-19-98; Indians were on this site from 200BC to 1400AD and left remains of temples. Since 1903 450 burial mounds have been excavated, and recently two standing stones have been linked with possible solar observations. The small museum, ✆795.3817, is open daily. The Crystal River Springs, not to be confused with Crystal Springs at Zephyrhills, have at least 30 sources and are first-magnitude. Scuba diving is ideal here, and in winter you'll meet manatees.

Suncoast Blv, US-19, runs north through miles of near virgin forest and swamp, relieved only at Gulf Hammock by a Patterson & McInnis steam locomotive standing at the roadside, a relic of Yulee's cross-state railroad. At Otter Creek crossroads SR-24 offers a choice: right, through more virgin woodland towards Bronson, is Blue Spring, the source of the Waccasassa River. Left, through swamp and forest, lies **Cedar Key,** a real 'boondocks' (back of beyond) town.

Cedar Key thrived as long as it had its railroad and its cedars, but 15 pencil-manufacturers soon cut down all the timber — and then there was no 'point' in staying. Some diehards made brushes from palmetto leaves, but plastic substitutes killed that trade and so Cedar Key now relies on fishing, and the tourists who come to see a dying town that just won't die. The crumbling timber-frame warehouses and shops, the rotting pier and boatyards, would make an ideal film set, but right on the waterfront Cedar Key is beginning to rebuild. There's no beach, but there are enough motels and restaurants to encourage an overnight stay. If it's any inducement, the people elected the Island Hotel manager as mayor because of her cooking!

S'wannee River. Stephen Collins Foster, who was born in Pittsburg, Pennsylvania in 1826, featured the "S'wannee River" in his song *Old Folks At Home* because it sounded right, though he had to drop a letter to get the metre (rhythm) correct. The tune became accepted as one of the greatest of the negro spirituals — but Foster,

Stephen Foster put the line "Way down upon the S'wannee River" in his song "Old Folks at Home," without ever seeing the Suwannee. Here it is at Fanning Springs.

who died in 1864, never saw the river he immortalised.

You recall the tune?

> *Way down upon de Swannee Ribber,*
> *Far, far away,*
> *Dere's where my heart is [re]turning eber,*
> *Dere's where the old folks stay.*
> *All up and down the whole creation*
> *Sadly I roam,*
> *Still longing for de old plantation,*
> *And for de old folks at home.*

Chorus:

> *All de world am sad and dreary*
> *Eberywhere I roam.*
> *Oh, darkies, how my heart grows weary,*
> *Far from de old folks at home . . .*

The Suwannee River rises in the north of Georgia's Okefenokee Swamp and enters the Gulf of Mexico north of Cedar Key; if it were not for Foster the stream would be unknown.

NORTH FLORIDA
Historic Highlights

23: JACKSONVILLE TO THE SUWANNEE

The Historic North

St AUGUSTINE IS THE OLDEST TOWN IN THE UNITED STATES
and has North America's oldest European-style building, not counting
any that have been torn from their European foundations and shipped
over. The town has lived under the flags of Spain, Britain (the first
Union flag, without the cross of St Patrick), the Confederates, and the
United States.

But Amelia Island, to the north of Jacksonville, has known *nine* flags:
those of France, Spain, England, Britain (first Union), two versions of
the Republic of Florida, an assembly of pirates, Mexico, and the
United States.

Jacksonville, named from South Carolina's Andrew Jackson who
was president from 1829 to 1837, claims to be America's largest city in
area because its boundaries almost match those of Duval County —
but most of that area is still open land.

Up here in the north of Florida we are far from the snowbird scene;
this is tourist territory only in the summer when it has to compete with
everywhere else in the USA except, perhaps, southern Florida. As a
result there are few man-made attractions, and little to entice the
transatlantic tourist who must return to Orlando or Miami airport. Even
the history, though impressive for Americans, is relatively modern by
European standards.

The Spaniard Ponce de Léon, who had sailed with Columbus in
1492, led his own expedition from Europe and landed in Florida in
1513, supposedly searching for the *Fuente de Juventud,* the Fountain
of Youth, but the Indians repelled him and he went back to his former
base at Puerto Rico.

St Augustine. Two years later on 8 September,which was then San

Agustin's Day in Spain, General Pedro Menéndez de Avilez landed to establish the first European colony on the continent, 108 years before the English settlement at Jamestown. Naturally, the town became San Agustin — St Augustine in English.

Avilez's presence was more for protecting Spain's homeward trade routes from piracy than with expanding its territory, and pirates attacked the little town twice before Avilez managed to build the Castillo de San Marco, which cost a small fortune in gold and 15 years of hard labour.

Jean Ribault. Huguenots arrived at Amelia Island in 1562, flying the French flag, and their leader Jean Ribault went on south to establish Fort Caroline near where Marineland stands today. Avilez sacked the little colony in 1565, killing 245 Frenchmen and thereby giving the area, and the coastal creek up to San Agustin the name Matanza, Spanish for 'massacre.' In 1586 Sir Francis Drake plundered San Agustin and became the first Englishman to see Florida.

Ft Matanzas. The Spanish took control of Amelia Island, giving it its second flag; they built an outpost here in 1686, and in 1740 they built Ft Matanzas near the scene of the massacre; it's a small coquina ('cockleshell') fortress that's now a national monument (open daily

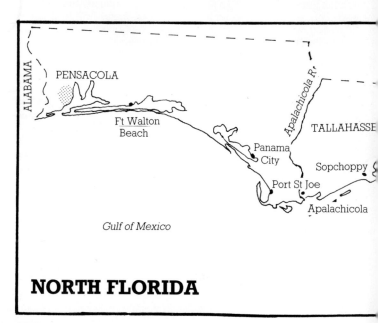

NORTH FLORIDA

free, ⌀471.0116, access by free ferry operating 0900-1630).

English attack. James Moore, governor of South Carolina, attacked the island in 1702, and when James Oglethorpe from Georgia came back 30 years later he found the isle almost empty; it was he who gave it the name Amelia Island, from George II's sister, and he planted the English cross of St George in its soil, the third flag.

On the far side of the Atlantic, England was haggling with Spain over the return of Gibraltar, seized in 1704, and in 1720 George I offered The Rock in exchange for Florida, but Felipe V declined.

The Spanish seized Amelia Island again briefly but the English — now the British, hence a fourth flag — took Amelia once more in 1763. And this time the British took St Augustine as well, ending a 198-year Spanish occupation. 1763 was also the year when France ceded the Louisana Territory (New Orleans to the Canadian border) to Britain.

Fort Clinch. Twenty years later the Boston Tea Party led to the American War of Independence and the creation of the United States, stretching from Maine to Georgia — its nearest point just half a mile from Amelia Island across the Cumberland Sound. The British, holding on in what was still Spanish Florida, built a fort to protect themselves from the still-hostile United States; during the Civil War it

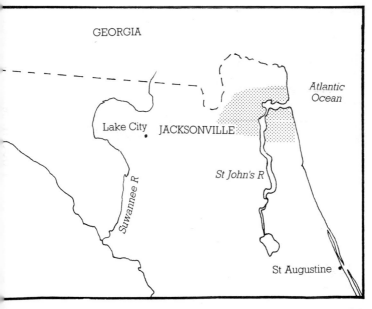

became Fort Clinch and is now a state park (park open 0800 to dusk, fort 0900-1700, entry to each $1) where time has stood still since 1864 and park rangers dress as Union soldiers.

Louisiana Purchase. But back in 1783 the British outpost on Amelia Island surrendered to Spain, followed by St Augustine. Spain handed Amelia Island to one Domingo Fernandez, from whom the town of Fernandina Beach is named. Fernandez saw the Louisiana Territory restored to France in 1800, then on 1 May 1803 the United States almost trebled its size by buying the territory, for £3,000,000. When the USA abolished slavery in 1808, Fernandez allowed the slave traders access through Amelia Island, which was already the base for a number of pirates including the legendary Captain Kidd. We don't know if Fernandez, the pirates, or the slavers ran up a flag, but this was the fifth effective sovereignty of the island.

Republic of Florida. James Madison (president 1809-1817) fearing Britain would seize Florida to quell the slave trade — Britain had abolished slavery in 1807 — sent 200 troops in to Amelia Island in 1812 with orders to declare their own 'Republic of Florida' and hoist their own flag, the island's sixth.

Spain and Britain protested, and the troops withdrew, but ten years later Sir Gregor MacGregor seized Amelia and flew his Green Cross of Florida over Fort San Carlos in Fernandina. This seventh flag flew for a mere few months before the Spanish ousted Sir Gregor, but almost on their heels came Pennsylvanian Jared Irwin and Frenchborn Louis Aury, both leading bands of pirates.

Aury seized Amelia, and as he had been governor of Mexican-held Texas, he raised the Mexican banner, the isle's eighth flag; he made Irwin his adjutant-general.

Finally, James Monroe (president 1817-1825) seized the island and planted the flag of the United States in its soil. By 1819 the USA had bought Florida and Spanish claims to the Oregon Territory, for $5,000,000; Florida became a territory in 1822 and achieved statehood in 1845.

KEY TO St AUGUSTINE MAP (main map and inset)

1 Believe It Or Not Museum
2 Castillo de San Marcos
3 Cathedral
4 City Gate
5 Flagler College
6 Fountain of Youth
7 Lightner Museum
8 Oldest House
9 Oldest Store Museum
10 Old Jail
11 Spanish Quarter
12 Tours departure points
13 Wax Museum
14 Zorayda Castle
P Parking space

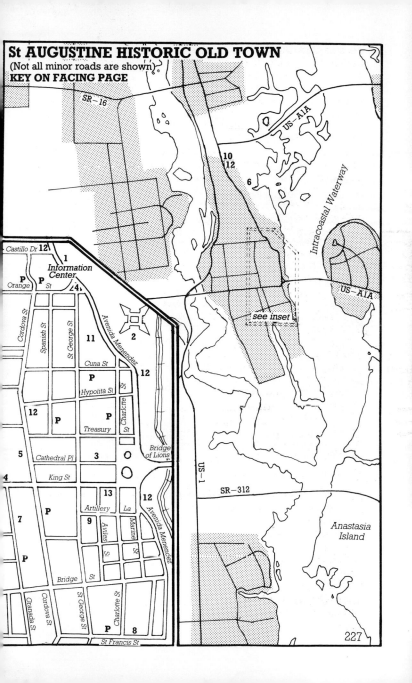

St AUGUSTINE HISTORIC OLD TOWN

(Not all minor roads are shown)
KEY ON FACING PAGE

SR–16

US–A1A

10
12

6

Intracoastal Waterway

US–A1A

Castillo Dr 12 | 1

Information
Center

P | P | St | 24
Orange

see inset

Cordova St

Spanish St

St George St

Avenida Menendez

11 | 2

Cuna St

P | 12

Hypolita St

Charlotte St

12 | P | P

Treasury

Bridge
of Lions

5 | Cathedral Pl | 3

King St

4

US–1

SR–312

13 | 12

Artillery | La

9 | Aviles St | Marine St

7 | P

Anastasia
Island

P

Bridge | St

Cordova St

St George St

Charlotte St

Granada St

P | 8

St Francis St

227

St AUGUSTINE

North America's oldest European-built town is small, with a population of 15,000, but the historic area is even smaller, reaching half a mile from Castillo Dr in the north to St Francis St in the south, and fronting Matanzas Bay.

Oldest House. The United States' oldest European-built house (there are far older Amerind dwellings) is at 14 St Francis St, ✆824.2872, open daily 0900-1700 for $3; free parking on site. The original building of around 1650, a palm-thatch roof on a wooden frame, was burned in 1702. Its replacement was a single-storey coquina stone structure, home to artilleryman Tomás Gonzales y Hernández. Gerónimo Alvarez bought it in 1790, and it stayed in his family until 1882, acquiring a timber-frame upper storey. The St Augustine Historical Society bought the Gonzalez-Alvarez House in 1918 and converted it into a museum, preserving the lifestyles of its Spanish, British and American occupants, while outside the Confederate flag flies beside the stars and stripes, the first British Union flag and two versions of the Spanish flag.

Oldest Store. Charlotte St leads you north to Artillery St for the Oldest Store Museum, open 0900-1700 Mon-Sat, 1200-1700 Sun, for $3, where you can see a vast array of 19th-cent artefacts such as apple peelers, lace-up corsets, butter churns and cracker barrels, recalling a typical general store.

Potter's Wax Museum. North again, at 17 King St, ✆829.9056, is Potter's Wax Museum, open daily 0900-2000 in summer, -1700 winter, for $3.95. Billed as the largest waxworks in the USA, Potter's has introduced some animation and opened its workshop to the public.

West along King St stands **Zorayda Castle,** a scaled- down version of one wing of the Alhambra at Granada, Spain, open daily from 0900 for $3. On the opposite side of King St is **Flagler College,** occupying what was the elegant Ponce de Leon Hotel, built by railroad magnate Henry Flagler in 1885-88.

At the corner of Cordova St and King St is the **Lightner Museum,** which has nothing in common with St Augustine but has a good display, including one of Napoleon's desks. Open daily 0900-1700 for $3. Otto Lightner was the founder of *Hobbies magazine* who took over another Flagler hotel to create this museum in 1948. Go north along Cordova to Cuna St, then follow St George's St into the **Spanish Quarter,** San Agustin Antiguo, where, for $5 you can tour a tiny section of the old city restored from its 18th-cent Spanish occupation and including the Oldest Schoolhouse (visitors get a diploma) and the Museum of Yesterday's Toys. You'll see people dressed in costume of the time; open daily 0900-1700.

Castillo de San Marcos. Fort Alley leads to Avenida Menendez and the showpiece of St Augustine, the Castillo de San Marcos, open daily 0830-1715 for $1, where ancient guns are fired several times a day. The castle has frequently been a prison, its most notable inmate being Osceola the Seminole Indian chief.

The **Visitor Center** on Avenida Menenzez (open daily 0830-1730) is near the reconstructed **City Gate,** behind which the **Zero Milestone** marks the start of the Old Spanish Trail which ran to Pensacola but which now ends in San Diego, California.

Ave Menendez, SR-5A, becomes San Marco Ave by a Spanish-style hotel now holding **Ripley's Believe It Or Not Museum,** ✆824.1606, open daily from 0900 for $4.95. Next right is Myrtle Ave which leads to the **Fountain of Youth Discovery Park** at 155, ✆829.3168, marking the site where Ponce de Leon set foot in North America. Apart from the fountain there's a planetarium and a museum; open daily 0900-16.45 for $3.

You cannot fail to see the 208-ft (63-m) tall stainless steel cross of the shrine of **Our Lady of La Leche** (Our Lady of the Milk) marking the point (more or less) where Christianity arrived in North America; open daily 0700 to dusk, donations accepted.

Dufferin St takes you back to San Marco Ave by the **Old Jail,** now a museum of weapons used in crime, open daily 0800-1700 for $3.25, but I feel the dummy escaping convicts on the roof look out of place. At front is a large mock cannon used in the film *The Pride And The Passion.*

Town Tours. The forecourt of the Old Jail is the starting-point for St Augustine Sightseeing Trains, an hour-long tour costing $3.25, a two-hour trip at $9.70 or five hours for $19.60. The rival Historical Tours also start from here at 30-minute intervals. Colee's Carriage Tours start from the bayfront south of San Marcos Castle with horse carriage rides rom $7; the Horseless Pedal Carriage operates from the Hypolita St — Cordova St junction; pedal yourself for $10 an hour for the carriage. Or go to the waterfront south of Bridge of Lions (the Spanish-style bridge carrying SR-A1A to Anastasia Island) for the *Victory II* Scenic Cruise; 75 minutes for $6.

St Augustine Alligator Farm, founded in 1893, is at the entry to Anastasia Island and has a heron and egret rookery on the site as well as a display of other birds and mammals. Wildlife shows hourly 1000-1700; open daily, ✆829.6545.

Fifteen miles south in Flagler County is **Marineland,** a city with a population of 20 as well as one of the original marine theme parks. This Marineland, open daily 0900-1700, started in 1938 and now has a splendid 3D cinema in the Aquarius Theater as well as the usual dolphin displays. Open daily from 0900; ✆471.1111.

St AUGUSTINE FACTFILE AND VERDICT

The oldest town in North America has much to interest American visitors, but Europeans, who have much more history at home, may find less here than they expect. Serious historians would find the archives of great interest.

The town is a summer tourist resort for Americans who stay at St Augustine Beach on Anastasia Island; the area is rich in condo rentals and efficiencies, and reservations are required in summer. Vilano Beach and Ponte Vedra Beach, to the north, have narrow sand, few amenities, and the chalets and poor-grade motels are squeezed between road and ocean. The beach, north and south, has several camping sites.

JACKSONVILLE

Jacksonville, named from President Andrew Jackson, is a summer beach resort for Americans, but they're really staying at Jacksonville Beach which has a good fishing pier and some fine white sand. The city proper has little to attract European visitors, though you might appreciate the **Anheuser-Busch Brewery** at 111 Busch Drive, offering a tour of the premises with free sampling. The floodlit Friendship Fountain in St John's Riverside Park is an after-dark spectacle, and the city Zoo is claimed to be among the USA's finest.

Harriet Beecher Stowe, author of *Uncle Tom's Cabin,* lived on the St John's River frontage at Mandarin, south of the city, and became a tourist sight in her own right when steamboat companies paid her to sit on the lawn and wave.

Nowadays the **Mayport Naval Station** at the mouth of the river is perhaps the best attraction — and it's free. Call at the security building on the right of the entry road, show your driving licence and hire car key, and you'll receive a pass. From there on nobody will show you the way but if you ask often enough you'll join a party touring one of the United States's warships, usually a minesweeper. Photography is not allowed, but there's nobody to stop you as security is deplorably bad.

GAINESVILLE

The university city of Gainesville has one of the USA's top museums, the Florida State Museum on the corner of SR-24 and US-441, opposite the University of Florida. The University's Art Gallery is downtown on University Ave, SR-40.

Gainesville's most unusual attraction is the **Devil's Millhopper,** a natural sinkhole 120 feet deep and 500 ft wide, lying north-west of town. Steps lead down to the bottom, lost amid lush vegetation.

SR-20 leads north-west to **Ichetucknee Springs,** the source of the River Ichetucknee, a tributary of the Suwannee. Around 215,000,000 US gallons (178,000,000 Imperial gallons) of water a day surge here in a collection of springs, so popular with tubers (people who drift on inner-tubes) and snorkellers that entry is restricted to 3,000 people a day.

24: THE PANHANDLE

Tallahassee to Pensacola

POLITICALLY THE PANHANDLE is part of Florida, but in all other senses it belongs more to the cotton-pickin' bale-totin' image of the southern states. It's closer to New Orleans than to the Keys, it's a summer vacation spot for Americans, its people have the southern drawl of neighbouring Georgia and Alabama — "y'all welcome, d'ya he-ar?" — and it doesn't have any of the theme parks or other major attractions for which Florida is now so well known in Europe. For those reasons, this chapter offers a limited look at this long strip of land which runs into two time zones and contains the state capital, Tallahassee.

Tallahassee . The Spanish built a trail of missions along this stretch of country in the mid-17th cent, but a century later a troop of English and Seminoles destroyed them. One mission that was rebuilt took the name of 'abandoned village' — Tallahassee in the Indian language.

The city is small by 'capital' standards: 150,000, and it became the state capital by default. St Augustine was the seat of the first state government, followed by Pensacola which has a history almost as impressive. The debate raged over which of the ancient towns should rule the state until a compromise decision settled the issue: Tallahassee, midway between the rivals, would be capital.

Today Tallahassee is quiet, interested only in finance and education — it's a major banking centre and university city — and preserving its history.

The 22-storey $38,000,000 **Capitol Building** and the recently-restored Old Capitol are open to the public 0830-1630 on weekdays and 1100-1600 at weekends; as Florida was the first of the states to demand open government, you're free to look in at democracy at work.

Museums include the Museum of Florida History at 500 S Bronough, with much of Spanish interest, and the Black Archives Center features the involvement of the African slave. The Junior Museum at Museum Dr is an open-air farm kept in 1880s style, and **Lake Jackson Mounds Archaeological Site** on Crowder Rd north of town, where Hernando de Soto camped in 1539, saw its first human inhabitants 3,500 years

Motorist's view of Seven-mile Bridge on the Overseas Highway.

ago. And Florida Caverns, on Caverns Rd, are limestone caves with stalactites displayed in coloured lighting.

South of Tallahassee is **Wakulla Springs** at the head of the Wakulla River. At 200 ft (60m) this is claimed to be the world's deepest spring; it's also prolific with a daily flow of up to 1,245,000 US gallons (1,033,000 Imperial gallons) of clear water. The site is popular with picnickers, snorkellers and alligators, but in separate areas.

East of Wakulla Springs are the first-magnitude Natural Bridge and St Marks springs, almost unspoiled. Natural Bridge Springs is the setting for the only Civil War battle fought in Florida — 6 March 1865 — but the bridge is a misnomer: the river goes underground for just a few yards.

On Apalachee Bay (watch the spelling) is San Marcos de Apalache, a state museum and nature trail near the small town of St Marks where there are ruins of a 17th-cent Spanish fort. The museum recalls the career of William Bowles, born in Maryland but enlisted in the Royal Navy. After being thrown from the service he married an Indian, led an uprising against the Spanish, and called himself the King of Florida. He was back in favour in Britain — but was actually in a prison in Madrid. He escaped, was recaptured, and starved himself to death in a Havana prison.

The **Apalachicola National Forest** stretches for 556,500 acres (2,251 sq km) from Tallahassee to the Apalachicola River. At the river's mouth is Apalachicola town, whose name means 'friendly people' and whose beautiful houses recall the days of the cotton boom. The town's John Gorrie State Museum honours the man who invented air conditioning and ice-making equipment for, although Dr Gorrie was pursuing a cure for malaria, his inventions allowed the mass colonisation of the Florida Peninsula in more recent times.

Two causeways lead from town to St George Island, 18 miles long and with some splendid isolated beaches. Or US-98 leads west to **Port St Joe,** on the site of St Joseph, capital of the Territory of Florida and where the state's Constitution Convention was held in 1838; a local museum has the full story, including St Joseph's destruction by yellow fever and hurricane in 1841 and '44.

Here is the start of **Miracle Strip,** a series of beaches made of tiny white rounded grains of silica which squeak as you walk on them. The beaches are forever changing, and the coastline itself alters during each storm. Miracle Strip runs to the Alabama state line, and its resorts are popular in summer with Alabamans.

Panama City, originally known as St Andrews, is a glittering seaside resort built to attract children. At Panama City Beach, several miles west on the 'Redneck Riviera,' are Miracle Strip and Shipwreck Island, the Panhandle's only amusement parks, operating May-September. The Snake-A-Torium and the Gulf World Aquarium could be overspills from the Orlando attractions.

Continue along the coast through Seaside, a town of beautiful timber-frame houses, to **Fort Walton Beach,** home of the Gulfarium and its performing penguins and porpoises, as well as the Indian Temple Mound Museum which holds human artefacts from the area going back 10,000 years.

Fort Walton owes its existence to **Eglin Air Force Base** which, at 700 sq miles (1,800 sq km), is the world's largest military base. The weapons which destroyed Hitler's V1 (Vergeltungswaffe 1 or 'doodle-bug') launchers were developed here, and General Jimmy Doolittle's squadron used Eglin to train for its attack on Japan. In high summer there are guided coach tours of the base which has one big airfield near Valparaiso and around 15 smaller fields scattered in the backwoods, seeming to merge with the 10 naval air bases around Pensacola.

Visit the Air Force Armaments Museum at Valparaiso for a view of military aircraft from the earliest days to the present, or see the Historical Museum for more conventional exhibits.

There's a fascinating mini-Gibraltar called Peñiscola on Spain's east coast. Spain's early colonists gave the name to a town in Florida but the British corrupted it to **Pensacola,** unique in the United States for having changed hands 13 times and living under the flags of France, the Confederates, the USA, Britain and Spain — and on one occasion under Spanish and British flags at the same time. The Spanish built the fort, the British laid out the streets, and the Americans built the first naval base in 1825.

The Naval Air Station west of town is open to the public, and the Naval Aviation Museum rivals the Air Force Armaments Museum in Valparaiso — but has a Skylab as well. When the aircraft carrier *Lexington* is in port it's probably the most unusual tourist attraction in Florida — and it's free.

Pensacola's Spanish origin is recorded in its street names: Alcaniz, Cervantes, Saragossa, Tarragona — and Sevile Square, now a preservation area.

And when you've seen it all, Interstate 10 takes you back to Tallahassee, allowing a call at **Marianna** to take in the first magnitude Blue Springs and its underwater caverns, and the Florida Caverns State Park holding limestone caves discovered as recently as 1937. By now you'll agree that Florida is a state with vast tourist potential and Walt Disney World is only a tiny part of it.

You must be joking!

234

AMERICAN — ENGLISH VOCABULARY

Aerie. Eyrie; eagle's nest. Often used in business names.

Apartment. A flat; living accommodation. A 'flat' in the USA is a punctured tyre (tire).

Bahama bed. Also 'Hollywood bed.' Single bed with no headboard.

Bathroom. Bathroom, whether or not there is a bath or just a shower. Also a euphemism for 'toilet.' Property adverts offering '2½ bathrooms' mean 2 bathrooms (or shower rooms) plus separate toilet. See 'restroom.'

Blush. Rosé, when talking of wine.

Condo. Short for condominium, a block of flats in which residents own their apartments. The owners form a management corporation to settle points of common interest and to approve outsiders wishing to buy their way in. Some condo managements rent special apartments on a hotel basis to provide extra income, hence the 'condo resort.'

Cookie. Biscuit. Chocolate chip cookies are popular.

Cracker. Person born in Florida or Georgia. Contested origin; either from the early settlers who cracked their corn (maize) to make 'grits' or from cowherds who cracked their whips. Old-style homes are 'cracker houses.'

Date. Americans write the date as *month, day, year.*

Deli. Short for delicatessen. Shop specialising in salads, hams, sandwiches; usually take-away but now also for eating on premises, thus some Florida delis are becoming snack bars. The word has a different meaning in northern states.

Diaper. Nappy; disposable or washable cloth around baby's bottom.

Dimmed lights. Dipped headlights on car; not main beam.

Drape. Curtain.

Drugstore. Originally only for patent medicines, but now sells virtually anything including motor spares, magazines and diapers, and often processes film on the premises.

Duplex. A property occupied by two families, each with separate entrance. May be divided horizontally or vertically; the latter is the British 'semi-detached' property. By extension, 'triplex' and '4-plex.'

Efficiency. Noun; a motel bungalow equipped with cooker and sink. The European version is a self-catering chalet.

Fawcet. Tap.

Fender. On a car the front wing (mudguard), not the bumper.

First floor. Ground floor. The Europeans' first floor (*premier étage, Erster Stock*) is the Americans' second.

Florida room. Main living room of a home, not kept smart for visitors.

Gas. Short for gasoline, petrol. Hence 'gas station.'

Glider. Verandah chair hanging from chains, common in the Keys.

Hammock. In the Everglades, a slight rise in the limestone bedrock allowing hardwoods to flourish.

Hood. The bonnet, or engine cover, of a car.

Jai alai. Ball game similar to the Basque pelota. Pronounce 'j' as 'h'.

235

John. Spelled with a small 'j.' Toilet; either the lavatory compartment or the toilet installation.

Key. Or cay. Island.

Mailbox. US Mail street collection box; also the box into which the mailman delivers the mail.

Median. The central reservation on a dual carriageway (divided highway).

Pari-mutuel. Betting shop which by Florida law must be at the sporting event on which the bets are being placed.

Pavement. The hard surface of the road; *not* the pedestrian path (sidewalk) beside it.

Plaza. Usually used as 'shopping plaza,' shops built around three sides of a square car park; also known as 'mall.' 'Toll plaza' is a paying-point on a toll road.

Preserve. Jam.

Realtor. Real estate agent; person who sells property. Pronounced 'real-t'r' and not 're-allt'r.'

Restroom. Public toilet. 'Toilet' in America means the lavatory pan (bowl) and is not polite. Rest rooms usually have washbasins.

R.V. Recreational vehicle, predominantly a bus or van converted or purpose-built as a travelling home; formerly known as a camper. Not to be confused with a 'mobile home' which is a large caravan or prefabricated bungalow permanently sited but which can be towed away.

Sidewalk. Pavement; pedestrian path beside roadway.

Slough. In the Everglades, the slow-flowing 'river' seeping through the swamp. Pronounced 'slew.'

Sneakers. Training shoes.

Sod. Turf; lawns are usually bought as 'sods.'

Stroller. Folding push chair for a child.

Thru. Usually means 'to, inclusive,' i.e. 'May thru July' means May to July, both months included. Thru also means through, as in drive-thru bank, where the customer need not leave his car.

Trunk. The boot, or luggage compartment, of a car.

Washcloth. Cloth used for washing the face, not the dishes.

INDEX

238